Queen of the Professions

Queen of the Professions

The Rise and Decline of Medical Prestige and Power in America

Charles E. McClelland

ROWMAN & LITTLEFIELD
Lanham • Boulder • New York • London

Published by Rowman & Littlefield
A wholly owned subsidiary of The Rowman & Littlefield Publishing Group, Inc.
4501 Forbes Boulevard, Suite 200, Lanham, Maryland 20706
www.rowman.com

16 Carlisle Street, London W1D 3BT, United Kingdom

British Library Cataloguing in Publication Information Available

Library of Congress Cataloging-in-Publication Data

McClelland, Charles E.
Queen of the professions : the rise and decline of medical prestige and power in America / Charles E. McClelland.
pages cm
Summary: "Only in the latter part of the nineteenth century did medicine achieve the full eight characteristics of a modern profession. And yet, so quickly, it has seen one--autonomy--erode significantly and is beginning to experience the crumbling of another: monopoly of the market of services. Can social prestige and economic rewards be far behind?"--Provided by publisher.
Includes bibliographical references and index.
ISBN 978-1-4422-2630-2 (cloth : alkaline paper) -- ISBN 978-1-4422-2631-9 (electronic)
1. Medicine--United States--History. 2. Physicians--United States--History. 3. Medical ethics--United States--History. 4. Medical economics--United States--History. 5. Prestige--History. 6. Power (Social sciences)--History. 7. Autonomy--History. 8. Monopolies--History. I. Title.
R152.M35 2014
610.973--dc23
2014021708

∞™ The paper used in this publication meets the minimum requirements of American National Standard for Information Sciences Permanence of Paper for Printed Library Materials, ANSI/NISO Z39.48-1992.

Printed in the United States of America

Dedicated to the memory of

Prudarilla Rebecca Metcalf McClelland (1847-1924), who brought medical care to the Texas frontier.

Contents

Acknowledgments and Preface

This book originated from a series of public lectures given at the University of Texas (UT) in 2011. I was then an invited visiting scholar at the Institute for Medical Humanities (IMH) at UT's first and oldest medical center, its "Medical Branch" in Galveston. As an experienced specialist in the history of such organized knowledge bases as universities and learned professions, I was intrigued to be able to shift the focus of my research from the traditional and almost hidebound concentration on now-famous medical schools in Europe and on the American East and (to some extent) West coasts and to concentrate on how medical education, research, and therapeutic efficacy had really begun as a national and even regional movement around 1900. I owe to the kindness and encouragement of all my colleagues there—professors as well as graduate students, other visiting scholars from around the world, librarians and curators of collections—the origins and (with so many useful suggestions for improvement) development of a public lecture series that became this book. Just as IMH is but one of a handful of pioneering programs in biomedical ethics and medical humanities in the world, its emphasis on interdisciplinarity not only tolerated but encouraged venturing beyond the narrow confines of one or two disciplines. Its many tasks include not only spreading humanistic and ethical approaches to the education of medical professionals, but also to the outside lay world.

In a similar vein, this book aspires to provoke thought and reflection about how physicians and nurses have become and now become "professionals," as well as to explain to an often uncomprehending public the demanding parameters and hurdles of professional service and integrity in the face—literally—of life-and-death decisions. The location of the IMH amid a busy and prestigious yet not gigantic medical school—one of the first in America to rise to the challenge of putting medicine on an ascending arc of scientific research and application—provided an especially stimulating and broadening experience when compared with working as a historian on a huge and far-flung "megauniversity" campus (as I had recently done for several years in Berlin).

Therefore this book takes Texas, and its then major port and one of its largest cities, Galveston, as a frequent reference point to contrast with the national scramble to redo medical care—one that barely reached renowned institutions like Harvard and Yale much earlier. It also refers often to European comparisons, not only because American medical professionalization once owed so much to European traditions in its evolution, but also because American ideas of professionalization developed in a special "American" context. Indeed, the conceptual framework of learned professions, including medicine, evolved over the past century or so largely within a relatively ahistorical discourse about Anglo-American experience. Classical social science treatments of such professions shared the often-unstated assumption that the British or North American experience was universal and any that deviated from it were therefore not professional at all. This work therefore aims at setting new standards of comparative history, clearly at odds with ideologies proclaiming American "exceptionalism" as a reason to ignore the rest of the world. Unlike some learned professions, medicine—especially evident in Texas—depends on strong international and intercultural exchange and a cosmopolitan approach. The "professionalism" of American and some European medical systems today brings ambitious and idealistic students from all over the world to learn. That has always been the best sign of how well any highly qualified and expert occupation is doing. But ignorance of how the American medical profession rose—and how it may decline—may be dispelled a little by this book.

The concept of professionalization runs like a red thread through this book. Although the notion is explained thoroughly, it should be understood by the reader that the central point of being a medical professional has not always been saving lives, healing illness, or being responsible for the health of patients. That is a relatively new concept, and although our contemporary culture accepts that as a goal, we must also understand that there are competing systems of "professional activity" that may curb or defeat the noblest goals of medicine. No matter how well meaning, other professionals (such as law school graduates and the tiny number of them who become dominant members of legislatures) can also distort, limit, and pervert the urge to heal.

Uniquely next to the traditional, university-based *learned* professions (theology, law, and the diffuse disciplines of what Americans call "arts and sciences"), medicine was traditionally the least respected discipline at universities until the late nineteenth century. Yet the older "queen sciences" remain to some extent even today palpably embedded in their national cultures. The difficulties involved in American and European experts in theology, law, and the humanities speaking in an international vocabulary reflect this. The natural sciences are truly international, and dialogue in medicine has followed to become so, also. Yet, for example, European lawyers trained in the traditions of Roman law find American laws about many things bizarre. Theologians face problems about what is allowed as a part of their discipline or mere epiphenomena of American "born-again" social psychology, between the extremes of charismatic mega churches in the United States and more traditional explication of religious authority in Europe. And even in the humanistic disciplines, American interpretations (or misinterpretations based on the inability to read texts correctly in their original languages) produce massive distortions in such fields as philosophy, literature theory, and even the social sciences. On both sides of the Atlantic, a problem of "reception" (interpreting and reacting to the original stimulus with an informed sense of its local origin in time and place) persists and becomes perhaps ever larger. American exceptionalism can then be invoked to denigrate all comparative experience of other countries, as happens repeatedly in discussions about medical care.

Yet the future of medical care in the United States is not only of central interest to Americans, but to the entire developed and developing world. The evolution of "professional" care for the ill has a long history, and it will go on having one.

The central definition of "health care professional"—as laid out in this book—has always had one essential element: personal interaction between the ill person and the caregiver. The danger looming in the twenty-first century will be that this will be lost; machines may increasingly influence decisions formerly made by humans. Many medical schools have had to encourage their students and residents to look at the monitor above the patient's bed rather than talk to the patient—a major mistake, as one of the great pioneers of modern medical teaching, Sir William Osler, insisted. Fortunately, his works are still assigned and read in some medical schools. But as spiraling techno-overload and overwork absorb ever more time as health care professionals are "socialized," attention to Osler and, indeed, to the individual patient may appear to be luxuries like the humanities in college curricula or the arts in schools. I was privileged to be embraced also by one of the few centers devoted to keeping Osler's influence vivid, the John P. McGovern Academy of Oslerian Medicine at the University of Texas Medical Branch. Under its aegis I was also privileged during my year as a visiting scholar and for years thereafter as an adjunct faculty member to be involved in designing a new medical history museum for the University of Texas Medical Branch to be located in its historic architectural masterpiece, the Ashbel Smith Building.

Space is lacking here to give thanks to each and every person who helped me with this project, but a few went far out of their way and deserve mention.

Dr. Howard Brody, chairperson of IMH, and Dr. William Winslade, head of the Visiting Scholars Program, were crucial to encouraging my project, and Dr. Brody was kind enough to serve as a reader of the final draft. Donna Vickers, the utterly capable, cheerful, and helpful administrative coordinator of IMH, made working on a campus still recovering from the devastation of Hurricane Ike (2008) pleasant and easy. UTMB's Moody Medical Library, particularly reference librarian Janet Burk, made obtaining complex and often rare interdisciplinary materials smooth and rapid. Friends and colleagues such as the medievalist professor, Edward M. Peters (New Haven), the anthropologist and attorney, Dr. Howard DeNike (San Francisco), the physicians, Dr. Edward J. Lefeber (San Antonio) and Professor Armond S. Goldman (Galveston), kindly read and commented helpfully on the manuscript, and nobody did more to improve its organization and prose than my dear wife, seasoned author and editor Sandy Granville Sheehy. Her inexhaustible enthusiasm and that of her literary agent, Charlotte Raymond, overcame my own skepticism about the possibilities of marketing this kind of book, the sound of which puzzled many a nervous specialized expert in publishing houses.

To all these friends and colleagues, my thanks. Their help and encouragement was vital, even if they could not protect me from my own errors.

Introduction

If medicine is or has been the "queen of the professions," what does that mean exactly? What *is* a modern "profession," and what has been the process—"professionalization"—that turned what had been a largely ineffective trade catering to the sick and wounded into the most admired or at least awe-inspiring and most highly rewarded learned occupation in the contemporary world? The term "professional" has recently come to signify something close to "businesslike," indicating a working person who is expected to live up to established standards of skill, competence, or character and to be qualified and experienced.[1] That is not, however, the sense in which the term will be used in this book.

One informal way of measuring the esteem of the various learned professions—the oldest being the clergy, law, medicine, and "arts and sciences"—is by searching for jokes about them. There are multitudes of jokes about lawyers, quite a few about clergymen, but relatively few about philosophers, scientists, and doctors. Even fewer of these jokes demonstrate the confusion between "learned professions" and more or less artisanal occupations. One American favorite cites a brain surgeon working in his office on a weekend. Driven to distraction by a drip in a sink, he finally calls in an emergency plumber. After replacing a washer with five minutes' work, the plumber presents a bill for $600. "Six hundred dollars for five minutes' work?" the surgeon protests. "Why, I'm a brain surgeon but I don't make that kind of money." The plumber laughs and says, "Yeah, that's why I got out of brain surgery myself."

Unfortunately social scientists (including historians) tend to define their terms without much sense of humor or irony—perhaps because they themselves hope to be taken seriously as professionals. I vividly recall my first university course in sociology in which the famous professor demanded that students read and repeat in class all the current definitions of "society." After spending most of the lecture hour painfully extracting what we recalled of reading a dozen different texts and writing them on all the blackboards in the room, the professor crossed them all out, turned to the class and said: "And now, gentlemen, *my* definition of society!" To save space, I will follow this method, warning, however, that there are many other definitions available.[2]

Modern professions can be understood as having at least eight characteristics: (1) highly specialized and advanced education; (2) a special code of personal conduct—"ethics"; (3) a spirit of altruism and public service; (4) rigorous tests of competence, such as examinations and licensing; (5) high social prestige and corresponding economic incentives; (6) occupational career patterns or "ladders"; (7) a drive to monopolize the market of services; and (8) autonomy.

There are of course other typical markers of "professional" status that one could easily wish away but must acknowledge, such as wrapping itself in a difficult, specialized jargon that not only mystifies outsiders, but also makes communicating clearly with patients difficult.

While the term "professional" is widely used today to imply some of these characteristics—such as the plumber in the joke—and often includes what some sociologists have called "the semi-professions," such as kindergarten teaching and some forms of information technology, the classical use can be restricted by the arduous, costly, and lengthy educational preparation, high social and economic standing, career ladders, and autonomy of what the Germans call *gelehrte Berufe*, or "learned, scholarly, or scientific" professions. The long and not always happy struggle of many worthy occupations, such as teaching and nursing, during the last century to "professionalize" by emulating the established classical learned professions reflects an even older struggle of, say, engineers and chemists to be recognized as "real professionals." (It is thus not to deny the importance of nursing, clinical laboratory science, or allied health professions—for which training is provided at health science universities like the University of Texas Medical Branch [UTMB]—nevertheless leaving them largely out of this book. Rather, it is because they were not a part of the Flexner reform initiative that effectively defined the "medical profession" in the twentieth century.) The "queen profession," the one most looked to by emulators as well as by historians and sociologists, had been in modern times medicine. It is the one whose "professionalization project"[3] has arguably been the most successful and acts as a bellwether for the health and prospects of all modern professions. And even its successes have been of fairly recent origin—a little more than a century—in the United States, and Galveston and UTMB are good examples of its spectacular career.

Still, to treat only the last century or two of the rise to high status of the medical profession is to lose an essential part of the story. Although one could not speak of a comparably normified, respected, and above all therapeutically effective medical "profession" before its emergence in the late nineteenth century, today's medical profession cannot be fully understood without reference to preceding centuries and even millennia. For that reason this book necessarily weaves selectively through the history of medicine, science, and culture to highlight the conditions promoting as well as hindering "professionalization." It does not pretend to be a history of Western medicine, even if the history of the "queen profession" cannot be understood fully without some glancing reference to the former.[4] Space limitations as well as the need to adhere to the central theme unfortunately militate against a more inclusive and discursive overview of the long and fascinating development of medicine as a whole. Thus, for example, much more space is devoted to characteristic physicians such as Hippocrates and Galen and less to broader and even more influential thinkers like Aristotle, who also left behind medical ideas.

I

From Healing Art to Scientific Profession: Medicine 500 BCE to 1850 CE

Chapter One

Swearing by Apollo

When I visited ancient Pergamon (today's Bergama, Turkey) a few years ago, I toured the ruins of the "Mayo Clinic of the Roman Empire," the Asclepion, named for the ancient demigod of healing and once directed by one of the world's first famous physicians, Galen. His fame resulted, in part, from his skill at sports medicine as the doctor to star gladiators. Even then, a couple of millennia before the Betty Ford Center and similar places, there were clinics favored by celebrities.

Today, little is left of Pergamon except the foundations, but my guide painted a verbal picture of what it had been like in its heyday. He told me that the words carved over the now-vanished portal had said "None who enters here leaves uncured." He went on to explain that there had been a back door to the building, bordering on a sheer cliff dropping hundreds of feet from this acropolis. To uphold the literal truth of the motto above the entrance, patients who died were quietly disposed of via the rear door in the middle of the night.

From what historians know or guess, most of the patients who came to the Pergamon clinic were wealthy men. They were treated to initiation rituals involving hallucinogens, religious incantations, baths in a sacred spring, good food, and luxurious pampering, and they probably experienced a hefty dose of the placebo effect.

Of course, most citizens of limited means—virtually all slaves (a large part of the population) and probably women and children—did not have access to this level of medical care. Home remedies, herbs, midwifery, nostrums, shamanism, incantations, prayer, and sacrifices in temples were the lot of ordinary people when they were sick, wounded, or giving birth. The ancient Egyptians set broken bones and developed the (sometimes) lifesaving technique of treating traumatic brain injury by drilling a hole in the skull to relieve the destructive pressure of brain swelling. The ancient equivalent of battlefield medics occasionally saved comrades by applying tourniquets or amputating limbs. The most skillful midwives used their hands to turn a breech baby to a head-first position. But for the most part, medicine in Europe, Africa, Asia, and the Incan and Mayan worlds relied on drugs concocted from herbs, roots, and minerals, many known since Paleolithic times, and on the knife, a distinctly unpopular and high-risk option in the days before anesthetics and antibiotics.

Up until the nineteenth century, few physicians qualified as "professionals" in the sense described in the introduction to this book, nor were all health care providers full-time or trained. In ancient Greece and Rome, many healers were in fact slaves, although not necessarily uneducated ones. (Wealthy Romans also had literate slaves teach their children and even keep their business accounts.) Other practitioners were part timers. Few had the benefit of any organized form of education and were at best trained through apprenticeships. They mostly lacked such characteristics of modern professionals as autonomy and high social standing. Such healers' cure rates were not significantly better than those of illiterate herbalists, "old wives," barbers, and the like—a situation that would largely persist until the late nineteenth century. It is true that from the time of Cicero at least, the term *professio* came into Roman use to describe something more than an oath in a legal matter. "Accordingly, the physician's profession [was] a promise to help, to serve the humanity of his patient with compassion (*misericordia*). It is, therefore, a solemn and sacred oath, and this is the way [the Roman physician] Scribonius Largus interpreted it." Similarly, the writings of Cicero implied that the role of physician was worthy of a gentleman.[1]

Galen of Pergamon was a notable example of that. The son of a wealthy architect of Greek extraction, Claudius Galenus was born in 129 CE ("in the common era," known in less culturally inclusive times as AD, short for *anno Domini*, "in the year of the Lord"). He benefitted from an elite and comprehensive Hellenistic education at the best schools in Greece and Alexandria. Historians disagree on the date of his death, some placing it as early as 199, others as late as 217. In either case, Galen lived a life that was long, prosperous, and prominent. He served as personal physician to several emperors. During his own era, his thinking influenced medical practice as far away as India, and it continued to dominate Western medical practice until the eighteenth century.

Galen was a great believer in drugs, the more the better. He compiled the first European formulary of medications. Of course, the tradition of dosing ailments predated him by millennia. In fact, seven of the eight plants discovered buried in a 60,000-year-old Neanderthal grave in modern-day Iraq had medicinal properties. Sumerian cuneiform tablets described healing potions 5,000 years ago. Among the personal effects accompanying the outstanding-ly well-preserved remains of Otzi, the Iceman, who suffered some fatal mishap in the Alps circa 3000 BCE, archeologists found herbs used to treat the intestinal parasites from which he suffered. In 1000 BCE Egyptians used castor oil, opium, garlic, and mint medicinally. The Hebrew scriptures mention medicinal plants, including mandrake root, a tricky but effective sedative. From ancient India, a 600 BCE text describes more than 800 medicines concocted from plants, minerals, and animal parts. Many of these naturally occurring compounds, albeit in their refined forms, line our bathroom cabinets today; 122 common drugs are modern versions of ancient nostrums. Until the development of anesthesia in the mid-nineteenth century, aspirin in the late nineteenth, and antibiotics in the early twentieth, the pharmacological arsenal was limited largely to laxatives, diuretics, hallucinogens, painkillers, stimulating tonics, and the occasionally soothing salve or poultice.

Alas, Galen and his professional brethren left an almost equally persistent but less helpful intellectual legacy: the humoral model of illness. Appealing to the ancients' passion for things numerological, this wrongheaded notion held that diseases resulted from imbalances in the four "humors"—black bile, yellow bile, phlegm, and blood. These humors were thought to wax and wane in the body, depending on inherited propensities and on diet and activity. A patient suffering from "bad humor" would show both physical and psychological symptoms.

In ancient Greek, black bile was *melan chole*; yellow bile, *chole*; and phlegm, *phlegma*. For some reason, the term that stuck for blood was the Latin *sanguis*. Individual temperament was attributed to a preponderance of one humor over another. That is why Shakespeare called Hamlet a melancholy Dane, our more recent ancestors said that a person quick to anger was choleric, we dismiss someone who habitually puts a damper on exciting ideas as phlegmatic, while we observe that an individual who responds enthusiastically to a plan is sanguine about it.

The theory of the four humors closely related to the Empedoclean theory that four elements—earth, fire, water, and air——made up everything in the world, as well as to the four seasons, with spring for blood, summer for yellow bile, autumn for black bile, and winter (for reasons even we moderns can understand) for phlegm. That was part of its lasting appeal: the ancient Greeks, Romans, and Jews, as well as their Muslim and Christian successors, liked things tied up in neat conceptual packages. Indeed, one of the great advances made by classical Greek civilization was the intellectual conceptualization of nature ("natural philosophy") that included medicine—but did not treat it as an isolated body of knowledge. The tendency to demark the sphere of medicine from that of transcendental explanations (magic, divine interventions, witchcraft, etc.) may be said to be the chief gift of ancient Greek thought to world medicine. The heritage of such Greek thinkers as Plato and Aristotle (also influencing medical conceptualization in profound ways) tended to be accepted for centuries as a whole, so that empirical questioning of, say, the writings of "the Master" Aristotle about medicine implied rejecting the wider foundations of Western thought. It followed that where the body was concerned, earth was predominantly present in the black bile, fire in the yellow bile (modern medical historians have yet no firm hold on what yellow bile was, but it was thought to involve the spleen), water in the phlegm, and air in the blood. Disease resulted from the humors getting seriously out of balance, with one predominating drastically over the others.

These humoral misconceptions led to such treatments as bleeding, purging, barely sublethal doses of toxic minerals and roots (primarily emetics and laxatives)—the "cure" often being worse than the disease. Such were the "best practices" for two millennia for physicians from the Middle East to the Atlantic and eventually to Europe's colonies. Nothing, including conflicting direct observations, could shake the authority of such ancient writings as the *Corpus Hippocraticum* and Galen's *On the Temperaments*. Not until the Berlin medical professor Rudolph Virchow (about whom we will learn more in a later chapter) discovered the cell pathology of illness in 1858 did physicians begin to abandon these ancient and mostly ineffective diagnostic teachings and the resulting treatments.

Of course there were other treatments available, with slightly less danger than bleedings and purgings: liberal application of milder medicinal herbs, minor surgical interventions on external parts of the body (from pulling teeth and setting bones to lithotomies and lancing boils). These remained in principle outside the province of learned physicians, left to the lower orders of surgeons, barbers, and so forth.[2]

One reason for the persistence of this approach to medicine was the reverence for ancient authority. In our own era of rapidly advancing technology, it may be difficult to imagine, but 2,000 years ago, the older a text, the more authoritative it was. None was held in more esteem than the *Corpus*, the surviving fragments of medical treatises allegedly penned by Hippocrates or his students.

Born on the Greek island of Kos around 460 BCE during the Golden Age of Pericles, Hippocrates was the first thinker, at least in the Mediterranean world, to define medicine as a field separate from religion and to attribute illness to natural causes, rather than godly ire or human sorcery. By doing this, he established healing as a practical art, one with elements of both applied science and social responsibility. His contemporary Plato mentioned him in the dialogue *Protagoras*, and Aristotle wrote about him a century later.

Despite serving a twenty-year prison sentence for defending medicine against the despotic government of his city-state, Hippocrates lived until at least the age of eighty-three, evidence that he had keen insight into the maintenance of health. He and his followers compiled and built upon the considerable medical knowledge developed by their predecessors, the ancient Egyptians and Sumerians. Although he didn't invent the theory of humors, Hippocrates promulgated it. However, unlike many physicians who followed him, he used medicines sparingly, believing that the body had the ability to rebalance the humors on its own, given bed rest, soothing surroundings, and a sterile environment. (He specified that only wine or clear water be used to clean wounds.) European physicians later suffered a 1,500-year lapse in the recognition of the importance of that last bit of medical wisdom.

Another precocious contribution that Hippocrates made to the field was the codification, in his monograph *On the Physician*, of what could be called appropriate bedside manner. The Hippocratic physician should be empathic, serious, calm, honest, and well groomed (down to his neatly trimmed fingernails). He should make a written history of each case, including observations such as the presence of fever, the quality of the pulse, and the color of the patient's skin, as well as noting the medicines and other treatments prescribed.

Hippocrates is remembered today not so much as a diagnostician or healer or even as the father of medicine as a profession (a title he may well deserve), but rather as a pioneer medical ethicist. As we will explore further in a later chapter, modern scholarship has cast some doubt on the authorship of the famous Hippocratic Oath, as well as on the degree to which it was known, administered, or honored in the ensuing two-and-a-half millennia. There are no records of the oath being used in the Middle Ages. Its earliest "rediscovery" was at the German University of Wittenberg, then-professor Martin Luther's school, in 1508! One can only wonder if the ethical ferment that led a few years later to the Protestant Reformation had anything to do with its rediscovery and reintroduction, culminating with its recognition by most medical school graduates in the Western world today.

Assuming that it is genuine (an assumption that does require a willingness to suspend insistence on strict provenance), the "rediscovered" classical version of the Hippocratic Oath begins, significantly, as follows: I swear by Apollo Physician and Asclepius and Hygieia and Panaceia and all the gods and goddesses, making them my witnesses, that I will fulfill according to my ability and judgment this oath and this covenant.

The appeal to the gods was itself not new and had been common for thousands of years in the various religions of the Mediterranean basin and the Middle East. The belief that higher deity circles determined health and illness continued long after the eclipse of classical civilization, too, as we shall see later. But Hippocrates and many of his followers did bring a fresh perspective of observation, curiosity, and even some experimentation into medical care. Much of the oath is in fact practical, laying out promises to respect one's medical teacher and his family, to look after the diet of patients, to sell no poisons or abortives, to avoid competing with surgeons or taking advantage of patients (e.g., sexually), and to safeguard their privacy.[3] Over the centuries, physicians, clergy, and medical educators have taken issue with everything from Hippocrates' alleged invocation of members of the Greek pantheon to its marked sexism and its separation of medicine and surgery. But however archaic some of the specifics may seem today, the underlying values of altruism, patient confidentiality, gratitude toward mentors, and commitment to transmit knowledge to future generations continue to inspire.

Virtually all U.S. medical schools now have their students take an updated version of this ancient pledge. Although the language may vary somewhat from school to school, in most cases the oath taken by today's medical students omits references to abortion and euthanasia, as well as mentions of deities and of the gender of the physician or patient.[4] Today's Hippocratic Oath has as little binding power as the original, and probably fewer of today's takers of the oath fear being struck down by Apollo or some other deity for bending it. State boards of medical examiners and state and federal courts draw on other documents when seeking to sanction physicians accused of infractions. But while the centuries have milked some of the gravitas from the original, both it and later iterations constitute guidelines for professional conduct. Indeed, since the early nineteenth century, the oath has been invoked in the Anglophone world as a common ethical basis for the medical profession, whereas it was probably, in the words of the renowned German historian of medicine Ackerknecht, "the reform program of an ethically disposed medical minority."[5]

Whether Hippocrates and his ancient Greek followers drafted the Hippocratic Oath or whether—as some scholars suspect based on suppositions gleaned from poring over the *Corpus*—an anonymous German classics student did so in the late fifteenth or early sixteenth century, the original oath specifically covers five of the eight characteristics of professionalism: highly specialized and advanced education, a special code of personal conduct, a spirit of altruism and public service, high social prestige (at least for those who conduct their practice honorably), and the drive to monopolize the market. The concepts of a career ladder—from student to practitioner to teacher—and of autonomy are strongly implied. Only the idea of rigorous tests of competence is missing, and in an age when the apprentice system was the rule, even in philosophy, no one sat for formal exams. As we shall see in the next chapter, medicine, at least in the West, would fall far from these norms; but at least for the age of Pericles and for our present day, Hippocrates rightfully deserves the title of the father of medicine as a profession.

Chapter Two

The Levant

Saving Grace of the Middle Ages

This chapter examines the passage of medical knowledge from the ancient world to what historians conventionally consider the dawn of the modern era—the sixteenth century. When it comes to scientific, including medical, knowledge, the turbulent period until recently called the Dark Ages in northern and western Europe extended roughly a thousand years from the fall of the Western Roman Empire in the fifth century to the Renaissance. (The eastern or Byzantine part lasted until 1453.) What little survived from the writings of ancient medical thinkers, including Hippocrates and Galen, we owe in large part to scholars in what we would now call the Middle East. It is no accident that the first medical school in Europe, in Italian Salerno, as well as such other medieval centers of medical learning as Toledo in Spain, owe their intellectual foundations to the brilliance and persistence of Islamic and Jewish scholars like the Iraqi Alkindus, the Persian Haly Abbas, and the Egyptian Isaac Israeli ben Solomon, as well as their translators. Christian monasteries also served as repositories of botanical texts and laboratories for herbal experimentation, such as those of the thirteenth-century nun Hildegard of Bingen. Even if so much of the buildings and libraries of such monastic institutions has been lost, intriguing evidence such as the Plan of St. Gall (from the time of Charlemagne in the early ninth century) shows that the idea of infirmaries that never got around to realization existed when political and social situations were briefly stable. Nor should we forget that civilizations about which Europe was almost totally ignorant—India, China, and even pre-Columbian America—developed medicine that was in some ways far in advance of Europe at the time.

If we know relatively little today about medicine in the ancient world, particularly that of Hellenistic and Roman Europe, it is because of what the historian Gibbon dubbed the "decline and fall" of that civilization. The sacking of Rome itself, the destruction of the library at Alexandria, the poverty, mayhem, collapse of trade and communications, even the decline of reading and education were part of what used to be called the "Dark Ages" of history in Europe. The roughly thousand years between the fall of Rome (or more precisely the western part of the Roman Empire) and the Renaissance, from the fifth to the fifteenth century CE, were characterized by political disunity, military insecurity, economic depression, depopulation, demographic upheaval, de-urbanization, and even anti-intellectualism. These were hardly the optimal conditions for the flourishing of any kind of empirical science, medical or otherwise.

Still, historians have recently been finding exceptions and spots of light in the Dark Ages. Although the Roman Empire may have ended in Western Europe with the arrival of "barbarian" Germanic tribes, it continued in the east in the form of the Byzantine Empire based in Constantinople (today's Istanbul) until its end at the hands of the Turks in 1453. Once a degree of political stability and settling down of such "wandering" peoples as the Vikings occurred, by around 1100 CE, monasteries, cathedral schools, and eventually universities began to encourage organized knowledge and even the study of medicine. And despite a widespread popular image today of Islamic schools (*madrasa*) as incubators of a certain type of fundamentalist, intolerant, and antiscientific brainwashing, that was far from the reality of Islamic schools established in the wake of the spread of Islam even into Europe (Iberia, southern Italy, the Balkans) after the seventh century CE. Nor were essentially religious schools the only seats of learning under many flourishing Islamic regimes, which protected the heritage of ancient Hellenistic culture. In a few cases, classical works here and there escaped destruction and oblivion. One was the herbal catalogue or pharmacopeia by the Greek physician to Roman emperor Nero, Pedanius Dioscorides, best known by its Latin name, *De materia medica*, uninterruptedly influential well into the nineteenth century.

Indeed, the little that survived as copies and commentaries of the writings of ancient medical thinkers from Hippocrates to Galen, plus many new and original works, came from Islamic scholars of the Middle East—today's Iran, Iraq, Egypt, and Syria, as well as Jewish scholars from all over. Of the latter, the one still cited in today's medical schools was Moshe ben Maimon (Maimonides), the eleventh-century rabbi, philosopher, and physician who was born in Spain and ended up in Egypt.[1] Their influence on Europe, not accidentally, came through the doors of such institutions as the first medical school in medieval Europe, Salerno, in what is today Italy but was then a multicultural meeting ground of Islamic, Christian, and Jewish knowledge, as well as further centers of learning like Toledo in Spain. The latter city thrived as a multilingual and multicultural scholarly center during the *Convivencia* ("living together," i.e., under Moorish encouragement of non-Islamic scholarship and translations) from the eighth through the fifteenth centuries. They owed much to the brilliance of Arab and Jewish scholars and teachers abetted by an air of tolerance for religious diversity. Abu Yusuf Yaqub ibn Ishaq as-Sabbah al-Kindi, known by his Latin name Alkindus, born about 800 CE in today's Iraq, was appointed by successive Abbasid caliphs to translate ancient Greek texts into Arabic and to synthesize Hellenistic culture (including medical knowledge) and spread it around the expanding Islamic world. Ali ibn al-abbas al-Majusi, Latinized as Haly Abbas, who lived in the late tenth century, was a Persian physician and hospital founder, but more importantly, the author of the *Kitab al-Maliki* (Complete Book of the Medical Art). Parts of it were translated into Latin about a century later. This in turn became (as the *Liber pantegni*) a central textbook of the Salerno medical school. It also preached the importance of professional ethics and was still being printed in Europe in the sixteenth century. And it was well known enough to be mentioned in Chaucer's *Canterbury Tales*.

The Egyptian-born Jewish scholar Isaac Israeli ben Solomon, a contemporary of Haly Abbas, wrote in Arabic a number of medical works of great influence on European schools of medicine. Perhaps even better-known figures influencing medieval European medicine were Abu Ali al-Husayn ibn Abd Allah ibn Sina (c. 980–1037), commonly known by his Latinized name Avicenna, and Abu al-Walid Muhammad bin Ahmad bin Rushd, Latinized as Averroës (1126–1198). The latter was perhaps more influential than any other in introducing Aristotle to Christian Europe via Moorish Spain. It is also worth noting that many of these Islamic scholars contributed greatly to the founding of modern mathematics, derived in part from India, without which what later came to be called the western Scientific Revolution would have been all but impossible.

One should not, to be sure, overstress the cultural advantages of mutual toleration of divergent religious traditions in the Middle Ages, such as the *Convivencia* in Moorish-ruled statelets of Spain or the vaster, later Ottoman lands of the Middle East. Periods of toleration and cooperation alternated with wars and violent persecution in the first cases, and little in the way of intercultural creativity appears to have emerged from the Ottomans after about 1300 CE.

Just as religious schools patronized by powerful rulers promoted the revival, amplification, and spread of knowledge—including medicine—medieval Christian institutions not primarily devoted to study became the nuclei of knowledge transmission—what we might today call "information technology"—in Europe. Christian monasteries also served as repositories of botanical texts and laboratories for herbal experimentation. Hildegard of Bingen (recently raised to official sainthood by Pope Benedict XVI), who lived through most of the twelfth century in western Germany, was one of the first women to spread healing knowledge through the use of herbs and tinctures. She authored two books on natural science and medicine, *Physica* and *Causae et Curae*.

It was also no accident that the "healing arts" of the time were associated with religious institutions, not only in the Middle Ages, but before and after as well. From Galen's *Asclepieion* at Pergamon through Hildegard's monastic medical center in the Rhineland, not to mention healing practices in the non-European world, the role of incantations (a variety of shamanism) and prayer should not be overlooked. If, as medieval people believed, illness was divinely ordained (whether as punishment or trial), it followed in theory that propitiating God by prayer could lead to recovery. As odd as it strikes us today, even the employment of certain kinds of stones and precious gems (as practiced by Hildegard and others) could be said to have met the main rule of the Hippocratic Oath, "first do no harm." And in practical terms, the patients' belief that recovery was possible probably contributed to what was later called the placebo effect. That belief is a powerful tool in treatment, as contemporary scientific medicine recognizes—even though how it exactly works remains a mystery.

The partial recovery and additions to the works of such ancient authorities as Aristotle, Hippocrates, and Galen, in summary, constituted a major foundation for the organized study of medicine in the later European Middle Ages. Unfortunately, as much later critics of "scholasticism" and dependence on ancient authorities in medical schools and universities in general would point out, much of the "book learning" passed down over the centuries was empirically wrong and sometimes harmful. Most of these traditions were based on similar wrongheaded notions about the origins of illness; that is, imbalances in the four humors: black bile, yellow bile, phlegm, and blood. Other additions to the mystique of the number four included Galen's insistence on the importance of the opposites cold and hot, wet and dry.[2] Even when later physicians challenged parts of such symbolic systems, they rarely attacked the authority of major ancient thinkers across the board.

All that said, it is important to recall that the transmission of ancient writings through formal education had little to do with the actual treatment of patients. We derive our honorific for physicians today—"doctor"—directly from the Latin word for a learned person, somebody who might not be able to cure you but could tell you why you were dying. And in the context of medieval Christian thought, the few who could afford such medical advice may have nevertheless preferred it to the standard folk wisdom. Why?

In medieval Christian Europe, as in many other cultures in other times and places, the etiology of disease was widely regarded as a divine judgment, the curing of which almost could be regarded as defying God. As a recent history of everyday life in this period put it, "The stillborn baby, the child born with defects and the chronically ill, but also the deaf, blind and dumb were the price to pay for God's wrath . . . for a sin committed by such people or their parents . . . [with] no remedy and no appeal to that judgment."[3] Thus the learned physician was required to be as up to date on theology as medicine, since both at the time aimed more for the salvation of the soul than the gravely ill body. Indeed, if a patient recovered from an illness, it was God and not just the physician who was to be thanked. Most of the influential medieval thinkers and writers already mentioned, whether Islamic, Christian, or Jewish, were polymaths, equally skilled in philosophy, theology, and other sciences as well as medicine. And there were conflicts among these fields of learning. Medieval Christian theology long forbade most investigations of the human body that could aid understanding anatomy, physiology, or pathology—for example, dissection. Medical schools taught a static form of book learning that for the most part discouraged scientific inquiry or challenges to orthodoxies that had very little effect on patient health. In other words, even when the characteristic of specialized higher education appeared, it was almost irrelevant to what we today understand as the primary stated goal of the medical profession: healing.

Chapter Three

Physicians, Barbers, and "Old Wives"

In terms of cures, the small minority of university-trained physicians emerging in late medieval and Renaissance Europe had little significant edge over their unlettered rivals. Only because they knew Latin and later some Greek (enough to read the ancient medical classics) could they share a common language and literary references with the tiny fraction of their contemporaries who were literate, including people of noble birth and high rank. Good manners and dress, plus the ability to quote scripture and the classics and to soothe the ill as well as the dying may have been more important skills for the doctors of the time than their armory of cures, paltry as it was. Indeed, the modern expectation of palliative care and hope for a cure only appeared in the wake of the Enlightenment. Offering medical hope to hopelessly ill "goners" was indeed regarded as unethical in medieval Christian Europe. The association of class and rank with different expectations about treatment explains the gap between the sort of learned physicians found at such places as the Asclepion, on one hand, and the separate class of practitioners employed to maintain the functionality of ancient Greek slaves, which one might call the predecessors of today's "physician assistants."

One might even speculate that the "doctors" (graduates of university medical faculties) from the late Middle Ages onward, deploying their erudition and class-appropriate comportment, may have provided a sort of expensive placebo for the ailing high-born and wealthy folk who could best afford their services. But the expanding prestige of "doctor medicine" in the high Middle Ages could not cope with frightening epidemics affecting all classes of society. The first European wave of the bubonic plague—the notorious Black Death of the fourteenth century—set back regard for professional medicine. Even the best-trained physicians were powerless against a baffling disease that killed twenty-five million people—a third of Europe's population—in six years.

This lack of therapeutic success in academic medicine may be contrasted with the continuing existence of popular or folk medicine. In the high Andes above La Paz, a peasant woman recently tripped and tumbled down an irregular staircase made of baked clay outside her modest hut. With no doctor for miles around and without money to pay if there had been one, she ordered her small son to beat some egg whites and tear a sheet of paper into strips. These were then made into a poultice to apply to her contusions and bruises on her neck and upper back suffered in the fall. The next day the poultice was replaced by wet coca leaves that numbed the pain. Such is folk medicine among the indigenous Aymara people living now at 15,000 feet above sea level in the Andes Mountains of South America. A few hours ride on a "chicken bus" could have taken her to the capital, where university-trained physicians would have applied very different remedies.

This small event, documented by the medical anthropologist Jerome Crowder, serves to remind us that even today more of the world's population probably depends on home remedies than the ministrations of trained health care professionals. Even in relatively advanced societies of Europe, even among some of the well educated, a standard home remedy for a cold or other ills is cupping therapy. This typically involves heating a number of small glass or plastic cups (similar to those used to hold a boiled breakfast egg), placing them on the skin of the back, and waiting as the cooling sucks the skin slightly inside. This alternative medicine was practiced in ancient China and Egypt, as well as by Hippocrates, Galen, and their followers. It can still be found in contemporary urban settings in Asia. And it is, of course, ridiculed by modern school medicine.

Twentieth-century school medicine fought tooth and nail against folk and alternative health care or at least against its practitioners. The attempt to limit medical practice to those licensed and certified by the state only began seriously in the nineteenth century. As we will see in later chapters, just as the modern state strives to achieve a monopoly on violence (through police forces and official armed forces), the modern medical profession has tried to create a monopoly on medical services. At its most successful it never completely succeeded in banishing its rivals. Most recently it has even acknowledged or at least tolerated some formerly ridiculed practices such as acupuncture. Others, such as homeopathy, remain on the list of "quackeries." But one only has to spend a couple of hours in a typical California spa to see how many people are attracted to what is essentially repackaged and often ancient "folk medicine." Warm rocks along the naked back may be just as suggestive of well-being as Hildegard of Bingen's applications of precious gems.

If we cast our historical eye back past the middle of the nineteenth century, we will discover very few "doctors" treating a tiny group of patients, but we will discover far more barbers, "wisewomen," tooth pullers, herbalists, oculists, pharmacists, midwives, priests, monks, nuns, and plain old mothers and grandmothers providing the bulk of medical care. Most people lived in the countryside where contagion, pollution, sewage-filled streets, and crime were less of a threat than in the relatively small number of cities. The then-dangerous and often-fatal process of childbirth was supervised by "old wives" or midwives. Work injuries or war wounds were the province of barbers, whose traditional professional emblem, the red and white striped pole, reminded the illiterate that this was a place for blood and bandages. None of these part- or full-time practitioners was trained academically. Apprenticeship and experience formed the basis of their knowledge.

The growth of European populations after the Black Death and the rise of guild-like organization of some mostly urban activities produced, for example, the first "Company of Barber-Surgeons" in the English-speaking world in 1540. Like guilds elsewhere, they attempted to regulate the apprenticeship training and standards of practice of their members, which in turn might give them a competitive edge over their unorganized rivals. Whatever their training, the barber-surgeons did not need much in the way of a medical kit beyond razors, scissors, and other barbering tools. A bleeding knife and pan, cupping glasses, and (by the nineteenth century) a clockwork-like scarificator were enough to carry out the most widely practiced "therapies" for centuries. Cauterizing tools might have rounded out the barber-surgeon's equipment and would be used to stop bleeding after an amputation (which, before the 1840s, was carried out without anesthesia beyond opiates or alcohol and was therefore definitely not "elective surgery"). Other widespread treatments followed the theory behind bloodletting; that is, removing excess material from the body ("plethoras") as the path to improvement. Inducing vomiting with emetics, urination, and defecation with drugs or enemas—"purging"—was also very common. Nor did these practices yield gracefully in the face of growing scientific and medical knowledge. One of the preeminent doctors in the young United States, Benjamin Rush of Philadelphia, for example, concocted the aptly named laxative pill "Rush's Thunderclapper." The active ingredients were mercury (itself, of course, a poison as we now know) and jalapeno peppers. Rush taught Meriwether Lewis the basics of medical science for three months before the Lewis and Clark expedition left to map the American West in 1804. Typically, Lewis was careful to pack fifty dozen of Dr. Rush's purgative pills.

Other ways of ridding the body of "plethoras" included fasting, sweating, and exercise, not unlike today.

Perhaps the most effective, or at least unharmful, medical treatment to develop by the late Middle Ages was herbalism. The use of plants to cure illnesses dates back to prehistory, to be sure, and here again the writings of Islamic, Jewish, and later Christian authorities already mentioned proved valuable. As catalogues and studies of herbal remedies made their way into medieval Europe, they were often put into practice at the very monasteries—especially Benedictine monasteries—charged with "the care of the sick . . . before every other duty," where translation and reproduction of medical manuscripts were also being carried out. The fictional character Brother Cadfael in the mystery novels by Ellis Peters sums up the combination of increased exposure to knowledge from the Middle East and monastic activity. Cadfael is portrayed as a former soldier and veteran of the wars of the Crusades in the Holy Land, where he came into contact with herbalism and (when not solving crimes) dispenses medical advice and medicines in a twelfth-century English Benedictine abbey. In historical fact, however, Benedictine monastics had relatively little to do with the local lay population, so their herbal knowledge did not often become socially available outside the community. Papal decrees from the twelfth century progressively forbade clerics in higher orders to practice medicine for gain, although it remains unclear to what extent this was aimed at preventing them from skipping out on their clerical duties or at responding to complaints by physicians about unfair competition. No doubt many clerics were unaffected by such decrees or ignored them, however.[1] Furthermore, the pious healing mission of the church developed vigorously through the saint and shrine industry. The overriding interest of the established church before the Reformation was to ensure that the terminally ill were visited by a priest for confession and extreme unction, since the rescue of the soul was far more important than the curing of the body.

In later centuries, though, the Roman church and its Protestant schismatics were equally capable of persecuting herbalists. Far more numerous than monastic gardeners, wisewomen (and sometimes "wise men" as well) also dispensed herbal knowledge and nostrums, especially to the poor peasantry of Europe. Indeed, the early struggle by a male-dominated "school" medical profession to eliminate rivals coincided roughly with the founding of other universities with medical faculties, all patronized by the papacy and royal governments. That development may have contributed slightly to the rise of witch hunts from the fourteenth through the seventeenth centuries. Dispensing herbal remedies might not in itself constitute evidence of witchcraft, but it was a frequent sign of suspicious activity, even if not linked to some kind of church sanction. The handbook *Malleus Maleficarum*, published in Germany in 1487 by the Dominican cleric Heinrich Kramer, was meant to guide magistrates in witch trials and was a popular goad for witch hysteria for centuries thereafter. Even though the Inquisition then as before often kept its distance from witch hunts, no amount of disapproval by theology professors could blunt the popularity of the *Malleus*. Given folk beliefs that illness was a punishment (or trial, as of Job) by God and that prayer or invocations were at least as potent as herbs or other medical interventions, all it took to cast suspicion on an herbalist was the unprovable assertion of her being in league with the devil. Quite often folk beliefs held that the "witch" was also having sex with the devil.

The misogyny apparent in such works as the *Malleus* (whose German title, *Hexenhammer*, or Hammer of Witches, is more vivid) reflected also a growing anxiety about sexual temptation. The book appeared just before the massive outbreak of syphilis in Europe, most likely brought from the New World by Columbus's crews (and a sort of ironic repayment for the "gift" of smallpox introduced into the indigenous populations of the Americas). It was largely due to accusations that bathhouses were fronts for prostitution that public bathing faced a much rockier history in late medieval Europe than, for example, in the lands that continued the public hygiene traditions of ancient Rome and the Middle East. We see here once again how a religious tradition—in this case from the Koran—encouraged frequent ablutions that were comparatively lacking in Christian Europe. Although the low state of personal hygiene in the late Middle Ages and early modern period may have been exaggerated by past historians, it would not be until the nineteenth century that even physicians learned the vital importance of cleanliness for themselves as well as their patients.

In terms of cures, the small minority of university-trained physicians emerging in late medieval and Renaissance Europe had little significant therapeutic edge over these abovementioned and often unlettered rivals. This may have been a reason there were initially so few of them. It has been estimated that the number of "physicians" operating in England amounted to a *total* of eight during the entire period from 500 to 1066 CE but rose to thirteen during the period 1066 to 1100, and then ninety in the half century from 1100 to 1154.[2] But from the eleventh century onward, more universities were established initially as communities of students or masters or both, later usually with a papal sanction and royal patronage. Within a century and a half after the first in Bologna as early as 1088, another dozen were set up in Paris, Oxford, Modena, Palencia, Cambridge, Salamanca, Montpellier, Padua, Toulouse, Orleans, Siena, and Coimbra. Another dozen were founded by the end of the fifteenth century.

As already noted, the mostly Aristotelian curriculum of the emerging European university system and the privilege of students and teachers to move around among institutions promoted a new level of thinking about philosophy, law, theology, and other fields, but it did not yet cause any revolution in medical practice. Indeed, the medieval medical "doctor" earned that title just as did his colleagues in theology or law, by putting in many postbaccalaureate years of learned study of texts, including not only philosophy and theology, but, because of the belief in the influence of planetary alignments on sickness and health, even astrology.

The revival of popular interest in astrology from the 1960s on may serve to demonstrate how ancient folk beliefs can persist even among otherwise highly educated and sophisticated populations. The fact that contemporary school medicine completely dismisses any connection between astral movements and organs of the human body and their disorders merely encourages those who are suspicious of it and seek "alternative therapies" to redouble its study. As is so often the case in the history of medicine, though, astrology was once not only a completely respectable part of higher medical education, but mastering its intricacies brought great prestige to its practitioners. We tend to forget that the seventeenth century not only accelerated what we refer to as the Scientific Revolution, it was also the heyday of astrology, when few important decisions of state, war, or commerce were made without consulting the propitiousness predicted by stars and planets. Each planet in the solar system, the sun, and the moon, as well as each of the twelve signs of the Zodiac was held to be linked to different parts of the body. A birth chart or horoscope could, it was believed, predict whether the patient was likely to suffer from this or that complaint or illness. Whether one judges this form of medical counsel merely harmlessly foolish or deleterious, it may also be that—like the placebo effect—being able to blame an illness on the (divinely ordered) solar system may have reduced the likelihood of the patient thinking she was possessed by an evil spirit or that he was the victim of a curse or the evil eye. In effect, then, deep knowledge of astrological lore dating back to the ancient world may have lent early modern *doctores* an intellectually respectable basis for making plausible-sounding diagnoses, even though their abilities to suggest effective therapies were not helped in the least.

What the title "doctor" meant was less a license to practice medicine than a badge of great learnedness, indeed the right to *teach* medicine. In hierarchical feudal societies, being certified to hold the correct opinions was as important as a good bedside manner and perhaps even therapeutic success.

Graduates of university medical faculties were far fewer in number than the theologians and lawyers needed to serve the expanding administrative apparatus of church and state. Nor is it surprising to find these "doctors" located mostly in urban settings or attached to princely courts and noble estates. Some achieved considerable fame, like Guy de Chauliac (ca. 1300–1368), a graduate of Montpellier and Bologna, court physician to a series of popes in Avignon. There he finished a seven-volume treatise on surgery, *Chirurgia magna* (1363), which became a major international text in medical schools. Yet even his advances in anatomical knowledge, anesthesia, and surgical techniques suffered from the widespread reluctance to resort to dissection.

That in turn reflected the powerful grip of religion and cultural and legal traditions. Roman law had outlawed dissection, and Jewish and Islamic law commentators generally regarded the invasion even of a dead human body as sacrilegious. There is evidence, though, that attitudes in late medieval Europe began to soften on this point. What is important to keep in mind as we track the rise of professional medicine, however, is the continued strong grip of organized religion on medical understanding and treatment. The unified church of Western Europe possessed a strong central bureaucracy (virtually the model for modernizing monarchies) and reached down into nearly all villages with a local priest. The church was also a major landowner and involved in production of goods and services. Theology was the "queen science," and all other professions, even learned ones associated with academic education like medicine, were expected to defer to church authorities.

While late medieval princely courts might flirt with courtly love poetry (troubadours) and Renaissance princes increasingly ignored religious preaching against luxury and other moral abuses, religious doctrine still painted the world as a place of sin and suffering. Health was not so much a goal to be pursued and achieved by better medical observation as a sign of the pleasure or disapproval of an inscrutable God. The Protestant Reformation beginning in the early sixteenth century probably intensified suspicion among churchmen about further challenges to their authority. A thinker who put forward a radical new idea about the universe before the Reformation may have been debated down and declared wrong but was not always perceived as a heretic or enemy of the hierarchy. But Galileo's famous recantation of his heliocentric theory of the solar system under pressure from the Counter-Reformation's inquisition demonstrated a growing force field of conflict between religious dogma and scientific discovery.

Chapter Four

Hospitals or Hospices?

As discussed in the preceding chapter, European medicine and religion were inexorably intertwined from ancient times until the eighteenth century. On one hand, this symbiosis held back the dawn of scientific medicine. Dogmatic respect for the authority of the ancients (even when they were wrong), suspicion of many medical investigations to promote understanding, such as dissection, or simply an otherworldly focus on the purpose and desirability of a long and healthy life on Earth counted among factors militating against developing accurate diagnoses and effective therapies. On the other hand, some of these post-pagan religious tenets also led to the expansion of institutional health care.

In Christian Europe, the etiology of disease was widely held to be a divine judgment and intervention, the "curing" of which almost could be regarded as defying God. Thus the learned physician was well advised to be as current on theology as medicine and to pray over patients (often in conjunction with the priest) as much as to examine them. Christian religious orders, starting early with the Cistercians, carried over the functions of treating the sick already present in some parts of the pagan world as a natural extension of religious incantation and expiation but augmented that with more material and active care of the ill.

The established church was, however, partly responsible for one of the medical innovations of the Middle Ages, the hospital. Sporadic attempts to attach hospitals to cathedrals and monasteries were made as early as Charlemagne, and here and there, starting even earlier than the eighth century, they became permanent local fixtures. Major cities in the Islamic world followed suit with charitable, secular institutions where treatment and education took place (*bimaristans*). Just as the Islamic world took seriously the pilgrimage to Mecca—one of the five pillars of faith ordered by the Koran—medieval

Christianity developed the pilgrimage to various holy sites. The European Crusades were justified by the notion that a pilgrimage to the Holy Land should be assured by the European warrior knights who invaded it, in principle to make secure the otherwise dangerous passage of pilgrims. Perilous it was, and survival was anything but certain. One of the oldest Christian orders was, indeed, that of the Hospitaliers, who provided way stations (only incidentally linked to medical care) to these pilgrims. The Knights of Saint John (today known as the Sovereign Military Hospitalier Order of St. John of Jerusalem of Rhodes and of Malta) did, however, set up a kind of hospice in Jerusalem in the eleventh century. European pilgrimages were not limited to the Holy Land, though. Any holy site, for example, a place where Christian martyrs had been executed, where miracles had occurred, or where some healing action had happened, attracted pilgrims needing housing and care if they became exhausted or ill.

An example or two may suffice. The Basilica of Saint Denis, a Metro ride from downtown Paris today and the burial tomb of the kings and queens of France early became a pilgrimage place. The eponymous saint had lost his head to early Christian persecutions in what later became Paris. His place of beheading is now one of the elevated parts of the city of Paris and a major tourist attraction, Montmartre (Mount of Martyrs). Denis was said to have picked up his head and walked the six miles to the site of the basilica later named for him, originally an abbey, which became an official pilgrimage site through centuries of the French monarchy. Chaucer's *Canterbury Tales* presents a kind of travelogue about a number of pilgrims to the site of the martyrdom of Thomas à Becket, famously murdered by vassals of King Henry II in 1170.

Even the short trip from London to Canterbury or Paris to Saint Denis was still often dangerous. Longer pilgrimages, for example, through France and northern Spain to Santiago or from all parts of Europe to Rome, required care of the pilgrims, provided by the established church. The "hospice," *hospital*, reminds us that the concept was more or less comparable to today's hotel, if one imagines a form of room service available for the bedridden ill. The oldest hospital of Paris recalls this link to the housing, feeding, and care of the poor and sick in its name Hôtel-Dieu (God's hotel).

As late as the eighteenth century, the populace regarded hospitals not primarily as places for people to be treated and cured, but as places for them to be quarantined or simply to die, albeit under relatively humane conditions, attended by sisters in holy orders.[1] Often called "pest houses," these refuges typically were located outside the city walls to isolate those dying of communicable diseases (e.g., bubonic plague or leprosy) from the rest of the population. More closely resembling today's hospices than modern hospitals, they offered people (mostly the poor) a chance to get right with God before dying, not the expectation of getting well, and almost certainly not getting cured by physicians. Indeed, some hospitals, such as the Hôtel-Dieu in Paris, were so rife with infection that they probably heightened rather than diminished their patients' chances of succumbing to some disease. Since the Middle Ages, the resources of the established church and many of its monastic orders were channeled into such hospitals. The powerful and wealthy were also encouraged to make financial contributions to atone for their own sins. In the wake of the Protestant Reformation of the sixteenth century, when most established church property was confiscated by the state and monastic orders dissolved, royal or local government had to assume the function of financial support. Also in the wake of the Catholic Counter-Reformation, novel charitable institutions such as the Company of the Holy Sacrament in France established care facilities for vagrants, the deserving poor, and the elderly. But even so, the hundred or so "general hospitals" (*hôpitaux généraux*) they established around the country by 1700 were more workhouses and senior homes than places of medical treatment. This situation remained until well into the nineteenth century. University-trained physicians typically treated their well-off patients at home—certainly a better place either to recover or to die than in the hospitals designed for the indigent.

The Spanish conquistadores and the monks who accompanied them founded hospitals in such places as Santo Domingo and Mexico City in the early sixteenth century, followed by a Hôtel-Dieu in French North America (Quebec) in 1639. Something approaching recognizably modern hospitals in the English-speaking world came into being only in the eighteenth century, with such examples as Guy's and St. Bartholomew's of London and Philadelphia's Pennsylvania Hospital in 1751. Even though an institution such as St. Bart's traced its origins back to the twelfth century, its transition from hospice to hospital began much later. The eighteenth century witnessed the redefinition of the hospital to mean a place primarily for the treatment of illness and staffed by physicians and surgeons rather than by monastic or lay caregivers. One of the best early examples of this trend was the Charité founded in Berlin in 1710. Although it was originally created as a pest house outside the city walls in anticipation of an outbreak of plague, the dreaded scourge did not arrive, and the building was refunctioned as a charity hospital for the indigent.

As we have seen, hospitals founded by Europeans were designed to deal with the consequences of the ride of three of the four horsemen of the Apocalypse (Book of Revelations)—conquest (e.g., of the Holy Land), famine, and death. The results of the fourth horseman—war—also required a medical response. The relatively small scale of military conflicts in medieval Europe began to escalate with the emergence of the centralized state (e.g., France and Spain) and the introduction of firearms starting about 1500 CE. Before the eighteenth century "royal" armies gradually replaced the short-term feudal levy, but they tended to be run partly as mercenary companies that could turn on their employers (and their employers' subjects) if their payroll was overdue. The dangers of relying on undisciplined mercenaries eventually led to the creation of the disciplined, uniformed, and fairly expensive professional armies characteristic of the eighteenth century. Since a royal soldier was contracted for a very long period of service and was drilled and trained thoroughly, it was only natural for the emerging ministries of war to protect the health of soldiers.

Two of the militarily competing monarchies of central Europe, Prussia and Austria, took steps in the mid-eighteenth century to upgrade and regulate the training of so-called *Wundärtze.* While the term had existed in the Middle Ages, it more or less overlapped with the other terms for "surgeons," such as barbers, bath-masters, and barber-surgeons. All these callings had in common the use of the first treatment offered to patients, bloodletting, but also (with regional variations) all sorts of physical interventions, usually with sharp instruments, for everything from treating glaucoma and kidney stones to setting broken limbs and pulling teeth—and, of course, patching up wounds. Ever since the thirteenth century, when the competency of the new European universities was circumscribed by established church councils, "academic" doctors were not supposed to do surgery—the origins of "internal medicine." Surgery was left, insofar as it was a regulated profession, to artisanal training, apprenticeship, and the guild system, but many itinerant "quacksalvers" practiced without such credentials.

Even with this minimal regulation and much scope for free-market medical practice, both the increasing size and complexity of Continental armies and the beginnings of faster population growth produced a shortage of *Wundärtze* for both the military and the general population. The upshot was the creation of special state schools where the pupils studied surgery for two or three years in a regulated semi-academic environment. The curriculum was of course less "learned" and more practical than that of traditional university medical faculties.

The rising importance of royal military forces also led to the creation of special hospitals for retired or injured soldiers and sailors, such as Louis XIV's Hôpital des Invalides (today better known to Paris tourists as the site of Napoleon's tomb) and the Royal Hospital for Seamen at Greenwich in London, both at the end of the seventeenth century. The first American military hospitals, mostly ad hoc buildings (in many cases, simply rented houses), date back to the American Revolution, but few of them were purpose-designed, substantial, and permanent until after the American Civil War. Standard floor and ward plans emerged in the era of World War I (e.g., Fort Bliss, Texas).[2] Perhaps the chief significance of the emergence of this branch of medicine was saving wounded soldiers and returning them to action. Increasingly, prevention of debilitating diseases among the troops (which historically caused far more casualties than battles) also became an obvious concern of governments. Since the American federal and state governments generally lacked the mandate to ensure similar services to the civilian population, the efforts of the military had significance for medical treatment generally. The discovery of the causes of yellow fever and malaria, for example, relied heavily on the work of military doctors such as the Frenchman Charles Louis Alphonse Laveran or the American Walter Reed, who with his army medical colleagues proved that mosquitoes were the vectors causing devastating tropical fevers. The army physician William Gorgas reduced the mosquito vector for malaria and yellow fever by sanitation practices in recently conquered Cuba and the Panama Canal.

Joseph Lister, though not a military surgeon, headed a hospital accident ward in London. There he discovered that carbolic acid for antisepsis and asepsis greatly reduced the major consequence of amputation (previously 50 to 80 percent of amputees, depending on the limb removed, died of post-operative infection). Nevertheless, many doctors in Europe and the United States rejected this innovation despite bringing mortality in Lister's own ward from post-amputation infections down to 1.5 percent. Notwithstanding this showing, many regarded Pasteur's "germ theory" explaining the action of bacteria as unproven. But the German army quickly adopted Lister's techniques and proved them effective.

The dramatic change in soldiers' survival rates as a result of such innovations naturally worked its way back into civilian treatment. Even such homely improvements as ambulances, field hospitals, nurses (Florence Nightingale in the Crimean War), and prosthetics began to make a major difference in survival rates. The French Revolutionary and Napoleonic wars (1815) caused the death of two and a half of the four and a half million soldiers involved from disease and complications from wounds, compared to only 150,000 killed in action. By the Franco-Prussian War (1870–1871), for the first time in history, more soldiers died from hostile fire than disease, largely because the German army overrode civilian doctors' skepticism about Lister's methods. Sterile first aid kits, medical "dog tags," systematic vaccination, and the use of sterile instruments, gowns, and masks, as well as rubber gloves in surgery, saved thousands of lives among the wounded. From that time on, one can adduce many other examples of medical innovations pushed through by military leaders, proving among other things that a standardized practice applied to a large, if captive, experimental population tends to override doubts about efficacy.[3] The lifesaving usefulness of military corpsmen and paramedics during and after the Vietnam War has worked its way into the manner in which emergency medical care is now delivered. Military experience thus often benefited civilian health.

Burgeoning population and the growth of cities also meant the growth of poverty and illness among that civilian population. Many European central, regional, and local governments, as well as private philanthropies, addressed these issues by building a new kind of hospital staffed by physicians, as we have seen. Even in the American colonies, America's first hospital, the Pennsylvania Hospital, opened its doors in 1751 to deal with all the poor people wandering the streets and becoming ill. Yet in contrast to the long-standing equation of "hospital" with "hospice" (i.e., somewhere to die), the creation aided by Benjamin Franklin specifically excluded admission to the incurable. Most of the members of its governing board were Quakers, whose religious sensibility and tolerance left a notable mark on the early American hospital movement. At the time of the American Revolution, Philadelphia was the second most populous city in the British Empire (with 40,000 residents), but the movement soon spread to smaller American cities such as New York.

The heightened interest of European and American governments as well as private philanthropists in providing hospital care of a new type derived from mixed motives. The very term "philanthropy" reflected the spread of values of the Enlightenment, and the "love" and improvement of "mankind" (*phil* plus *anthro*) and the possibility of better health through education, regulation, and the sharing of wealth constituted new ideas propagated by writers in France, Britain, and Germany, as well as by popularizers and amateur scientists like Franklin. But the mass rebellions of the American and French revolutions also showed that the poor, hungry, and sickly swarming into growing cities constituted a social danger. The newly retasked hospital was (in the view of the followers of Michel Foucault)[4] not only a place of treatment, but also a structure for imposing social discipline. The concurrent rise and reform of insane asylums and prisons can be compared in context to the rise of the new-model hospital, which has the additional purpose (in its "clinical" function) as a place for training young medical practitioners, as we will see in a subsequent chapter.

Not only governments and philanthropists, but also the wealthy and fashionable brought about changes in institutional health care. As early as the seventeenth century, wealthy and socially prominent Catholics, especially in France, supported the kind of "apostolic" outreach that combined missionary and educational work with nursing care. This is one reason for the founding of the oldest hospital in North America (after Santo Domingo and Mexico City), the Hôtel-Dieu de Québec (1639), funded by the French Duchess of Aiguillon. Catholic organizations for women serving in a nonconvented capacity allowing for interaction with the public produced, as offshoots, many of the hospitals in the colonial New World. Following the teachings of such Counter-Reformation leaders as St. Vincent de Paul (1580–1660), these orders of sisters differed from traditional nuns in that they did not get shut away in a monastic setting and did not usually take lifelong vows. And unlike traditional convents, no dowry was needed to join, so that young women with no money or marriage prospects could choose a path of religious service, including relatively unskilled nursing and hospital duty. Indeed, by 1900, half the hospitals in the United States were run by such religious communities of sisters, and in some places in North America and Europe, they were joined in the same activities by Anglican, Lutheran, and other Protestant orders devoted to nursing. As hospitals transformed into more high-tech and professionally dominated institutions and thanks to antifeminist trends in Vatican policies after World War I, many of these sisters were forced to shift their service focus to parochial education.[5]

In the context of the influence of fashion on medical care, one should mention the revival of "baths" in the form of spas. Despite the general decline of public baths already noted, some springs had retained an even pre-Christian reputation as being holy or at least healthy, such as the one at Spa in today's Belgium. Carlsbad in Bohemia likewise had a reputation well before the eighteenth century for beneficial effects of drinking as well as bathing in the mineral waters coming out of the ground. Scarborough in England had developed not only this kind of spa but, being on the coast, added sea bathing as well. But it took the transformation of the provincial English town of Bath (site of Roman colonial *thermae* centuries before) into a social hub of the English upper classes to begin the spread of "water cures" all over Europe and beyond. Bath owed its good fortune to the patronage of Queen Anne, followed by elements of the aristocracy and the promotion by the dandy and arbiter of British Georgian taste, Richard "Beau" Nash. The ostensible reason for the wealthy and leisured to visit them remained the reputedly salubrious internal and external treatments of "taking the waters," and no doubt rest, controlled diet, and mental distraction worked positively on the visitors' health. But spas became also notorious as gambling dens, places to arrange marriages (or cheat on them), and playgrounds of the wealthy.[6]

The popularity of spas promoted their growth or revival all over Europe and later in North America. Towns with names linked to baths, wells (e.g., Tunbridge Wells), or spa in Britain; *bains*, *thermes*, and *eau* in France (e.g., Vichy, Aix-les-Bains, Enghien-les-Bains); *Bad* in German-speaking Europe (e.g., Baden Baden, Bad Soden, Marienbad); *bagni* or *terme* in Italy (e.g., Taormina near Mt. Aetna); or various "hot springs" in the United States (including the bizarrely renamed Truth or Consequences, New Mexico) remind us of the existence of hundreds of these popular sites in an era predating modern tourist travel. They also provided a transition from one kind of relatively arduous and even dangerous travel (the religious pilgrimage) to the relatively luxurious and undoubtedly relaxing visit to a nearby spa. Both the pilgrims and the spa goers did incidentally give rise to new forms of medical care, though: from the hospice to the hospital, and from the morally condemned public baths to pathways, bandstands, and drinking fountains of the watering places of the *beau monde*.

And in all these cases, we should recall that medical care—and the profession of medicine itself—has always been conditioned by broader social, cultural, and religious beliefs. Many of these seem quaint if not downright toxic today. The pilgrim believed that his illness was a judgment of God that could not be lifted by a physician's treatment (or at least not alone) but might be by visiting a holy shrine and thereby gaining "remission" (a term still used to describe the halting of a progressive disease) of whatever sin he was being punished for. The Georgian dandy perhaps unconsciously revived the faith of his Celtic ancestors that certain wells (in a Christianized version, having come in contact with some saint) could cure ills. If contact with holy relics was one of the purposes of pilgrimages, it was not just to seek relief from pains and ills (as the metal and wax images of body parts—*milagros*—in Mexican and some Spanish churches today recall), but even more in the hope of entering heaven after the ills and afflictions of earthly life. The gouty nobleman at Bath may have had some relief from the results of excessive consumption of food and alcohol, and perhaps divine favor was sought at the gaming tables (although many, like Beau Nash himself, would end up bankrupt from gambling). Medical betterment, in these and other cases, was not the primary motive for the activity, even though some kinds of proto-medical personnel might be associated with it. Herbalist monks, caring "sisters of mercy," wisewomen or white witches, barber-surgeons, and even Latin-spouting physicians with the right to add "doctor" to their title (indicating a university degree, rather than a license to practice medicine) provided, along with midwives and family members, some form of medical care. But its intent was at least as much spiritual as physical, and in all cases its practice stood under the "professional" authority of the established church.

What spas signified for medical professionalization, however, was the linkage between medical care (prescribing waters, diet, exercise, etc.) and recovery from the stresses and overindulgences of normal daily life. Just as the hospital was evolving during the eighteenth century into something recognizable to us today, the spa became a new form of institutionalized health resort well into the twentieth century.

For a recognizably *modern* medical profession to emerge, new ideas about the etiology of disease and the possibilities of prevention, treatment, and cure had to come into play. These in turn required a different understanding of how the human body worked, especially as a part of the laws governing the physical universe. Reduced to the simplest terms, it required the transmission of new attitudes toward that universe and its workings to the medical profession. It required the Scientific Revolution.

Chapter Five

Gifts from the Sister Sciences

As we have seen in previous chapters, medicine is very old, but until some two centuries ago, "professional" medical care was limited to university-trained "doctors" equivalent to internists (with little practical training or effective remedies) and artisans armed with little more than knives, razors, and similar instruments. The "learned" part of "learned profession" was highly theoretical, based on ancient texts, and in many ways wrongheaded enough to cause actual harm to patients. If most people avoided this harm, it had more to do with their lack of money, opportunity, or contact with medical men and women than choice. As already noted, while theology remained the queen science in European civilization, the care of the patients' souls loomed much larger than the prolongation or salvation of the body, as revealed by the routine and usually mandatory appearance of priests along with doctors at the bedside of the gravely ill.

Questioning ancient interpretations of man and nature often was met with charges of heresy, as some Renaissance-era university professors (like Galileo) discovered. Of course, one should no longer think of a simple conflict between an orthodox "church" and forward-striving "scientists," as in the "Whig" interpretation of yore. Ecclesiastical authority found plenty of allied defenders of the Ptolemaic view among learned men within and outside the halls of academe, as well. Most of the newly curious early "scientists" of Europe indeed stood outside the disciplinary framework of the European university system that had evolved more or less fully by 1700 CE. They were often men of independent position or means or beneficiaries of wealthy patrons.[1] Patronage meant not only independence from the straitjacket of a poorly paid university post, but often courtly protection from accusations of heterodoxy or even heresy. This was important at a time when many scientists—especially those doing astronomy and astrology—had to be careful to shield their observations and findings from too much public scrutiny. A few, not so lucky, like Giordano Bruno, were burned at the stake for heresy, although scholars dispute whether Copernican cosmology was the main target of persecution. Insofar as a secular "scientific method" evolved beyond the activities of individuals like Tycho Brahe, Johannes Kepler, and Galileo Galilei, it did so through scientific societies or state-sponsored academies of science set up in major countries some three centuries ago. While these individuals, societies, and academies made great strides in describing the physical universe, the laws of nature, mathematics, botany, chemistry, and other disciplines, advances in medicine lagged far behind. The invention and perfection of the microscope (by van Leeuwenhoek and others at the end of the seventeenth century) enabled people to see cells (even if they were not well understood). And yet the greatest breakthrough in seventeenth-century medicine, William Harvey's discovery of the circulation of blood,[2] was not immediately accepted by his medical contemporaries. Marcello Malpighi's (1628–1694) microscopic confirmation of Harvey's theories of blood circulation happened well after Harvey's death. And even though they undermined Galen, and with that the continued justification of the practice of bloodletting, that practice continued many decades into the nineteenth century.

That so many of the advances essential to modern medicine came from other sciences, such as chemistry and optics, reflected in part the looser controls by established church authorities over many emerging scientific disciplines that did not directly involve the human body. Another factor was the encouragement and protection provided by some royal governments, the ministers of which became convinced of the practical utility of scientific discovery and even offered significant inducements—such as prizes—to encourage it. Behind this protective and promotional attitude lurked the promise of greater national wealth and power. The application of sophisticated mathematics to astronomy, for example, gradually resulted over the course of the eighteenth century in great improvements to navigation, enhancing the success of trade and naval power in European colonial expansion. Such advances could not have been made if the various royal and private learned academies and societies had simply accepted the established church's traditional Ptolemaic cosmology placing the earth at the center of the universe (the challenge to which had cost the monk Giordano Bruno his life).

Compared to the "new sciences" ranging from astronomy, physics, chemistry, and botany to mathematics and philosophy, the profession of medicine was glacially slow to abandon the ancient model of the four humors and to embrace scientific methods of inquiry. The main advances in medicine were made in anatomy, as already mentioned, through the application of observation to animal and human body structures and functions, starting with Vesalius and leading on through the likes of Harvey and Malpighi. The spread of the Enlightenment in the eighteenth century—especially in and from Britain into the countries of northwestern and central Europe and their colonies—brought into medical thinking such concepts as public health statistics (from economics), observation and measurement (from the natural sciences), and, perhaps most decisively, the dawning idea that the scientific method could actually improve life and even intervene in illness. Just as important, while early Enlightenment thinkers did not abandon religion, they recast God as a benevolent supreme being, by some descriptions as the "divine watchmaker" who built and wound up the universe but then let it tick away following eternal and rational laws of his devising. This deistic or pantheistic interpretation of the Judeo-Christian tradition resulted in a radically more optimistic view of the purpose of human life and the desirability of its protection and extension. The deity was no longer held responsible for daily, arbitrary, and often retributive interventions in human life (e.g., "miracles" both good and bad) but rather viewed as the hands-off maker of a rational, law-governed universe. And if science could explain phenomena that previously were thought to be signs of divine disfavor (e.g., natural catastrophes) as normal results of natural laws at work, then the dysfunctional human body could be diagnosed as being out of sync with nature's needs, as well.

Still, the brave partisans of the Enlightenment had to face long-standing teachings, prejudices, religious beliefs, and outright superstitions. It was all very well for scientists to figure out how to navigate better, build better instruments (such as reliable clocks), and improve merchants' profits, but challenging hidebound bureaucracies of church and state, let alone the suspicions of the still largely illiterate public, was an uphill battle. Not until the mid-nineteenth century, for example, was contaminated water recognized as the origin of pestilences such as cholera, and not until then could affordable technology provide the piping and treatment methods to deliver safe water to—and remove sewage from—cities.

It should also be mentioned that even the greatest of the revolutionaries in modern science had not completely shed many old beliefs. The application of the skeptical and inductive reasoning methods of Sir Francis Bacon or the mathematical proofs of the laws of the universe by Sir Isaac Newton did not turn them into unalloyed modern scientists. Newton adhered to Christian faith as well as a passion for alchemy and the quest for turning base metals into gold. Bacon himself, an advocate of the high-minded rule of law and a philosophical officeholder under King James I, fell from power because of a bribery scandal.

Even as experimental medicine began to apply Bacon's techniques of observation and deduction more often in the eighteenth century, it was not lacking in dangers. Inoculation (direct subdermal injection of variola from, say, a human smallpox victim's scab) entered Europe from Turkey in the early eighteenth century but could lead to infection and even death. Edward

Jenner's propagation of a vastly safer vaccination (with much weaker cowpox variola) against smallpox at the other end of the century still took decades to be completely accepted. As another example, how many decades did it take for Captain Cook's demonstrations preventing scurvy to be adopted by the British admiralty? Normally sailors on long voyages were much more likely to die of disease than enemy action or shipwreck, and most of the deaths from illness resulted from scurvy. Scottish ex-navy physician James Lind's *Treatise of the Scurvy* (1753) already promoted the advantages of citrus juice. Cook's 1761 circumnavigation of the globe delivered the empirical result of not losing a single sailor to scurvy. (The slang term "limey" for an English sailor refers back to their learning to suck limes during and after long sea voyages. Limes contained the vitamin C missing in sailor's diets once fresh fruit supplies had run out. Although Captain Cook had experimented with sauerkraut, the derogatory Anglo-American name for Germans—"Krauts"—it seems to have nothing to do with scurvy prevention.) Still the admiralty only began to recognize the scurvy-preventing advantages of citrus juice around 1800, a mere half century later.

A century after Cook's voyage, John Snow's correct explanation of the 1854 cholera outbreak in London's Soho district—from contaminated domestic water—did not result immediately in safer water supplies, even after the obnoxious and obvious "Great Stink" in its source, the River Thames, in 1858! Snow used a house-to-house survey and the resultant statistics to create incident maps localizing the source of the water contamination. But the economic interests of two private water supply companies and the persistence of the "miasma" (bad air) theory of cholera vectors bolstered resistance to his public health breakthrough. Habit, persistence of legends, threats to powerful economic interests, and political lethargy then—as now—delayed action that could have saved many lives. And even though Robert Koch had discovered the cholera pathogen in India in 1884, incidentally validating the germ theory, his findings could not prevent the loss of more than 8,000 lives in an outbreak in Hamburg in 1892—almost a half century after Snow's discovery.[3] Part of the reason for this failure was the popularity of a competing theory—essentially an update of miasmatism—by the Munich professor Max von Pettenkofer that took some time to disprove.

Many such medical discoveries were made haphazardly, without yet the full armory of experimental method, peer review, controlled testing, and wide publicity among practitioners (for example, through professional journals and conferences). The principle of reproducible experimental results, an increasingly common basis in the natural sciences, took longer to infiltrate the medical profession, even in the nineteenth century. Thus individual physicians might stumble on major lifesaving procedures without yet knowing the scientific reason why the procedure worked.

A few examples can illustrate this syndrome. The English eighteenth-century chemist Joseph Priestley not only is credited with the discovery of oxygen (and with that, the foundation of modern chemistry), but also with the discovery of nitrous oxide. This “laughing gas” and its close chemical relative, ether, became widely known to medical students, who used its behavior-altering properties in parties called “frolics.” A later American dentist and Harvard medical student, William T. G. Morton, used ether for a more serious purpose—a famous early surgery with general anesthesia in Boston General Hospital’s Ether Dome in 1846. It still took some time for this kind of surgical anesthesia to become common, partly because it could have serious side effects. Still, the alternative between unbearable pain and likely death (that had caused so many to choose the latter over the former) led eventually to surgery (under anesthesia) becoming routine rather than a grisly last resort.

Eventually the inhalable anesthetic chloroform supplanted ether, partly because it was easier to handle and did not explode around open flames. Its use spread into easing the pain of childbirth, although traditionalist doctors opposed it on the grounds that the pain of childbirth was a part of the curse of Eve. Only the glamour case of England’s Queen Victoria using it while bearing her last two children in and after 1853 began to overcome some of the medical profession’s skepticism about its use—and its potential toxicity to patients caused it eventually to be abandoned again for ether and other anesthetics.

A year after Morton’s experiment with ether, Ignaz Semmelweiss, working in Vienna General Hospital’s First Obstetrical Clinic, discovered that deaths from childbed (puerperal) fever could be cut from as high as 35 percent to 1 percent just by having the attending physicians wash their hands in an antiseptic solution. Physicians as well as surgeons were notorious for, even proud of, their bloodstained and soiled suits and frock coats, major unwashed vectors of infection to their patients. (The relative lack of the fever in wards run by sisters resulted from frequent handwashing, presumably as ablutions connected to prayer and worship services.) Semmelweiss’s proven success did not, however, gain wide acceptance until Louis Pasteur and others later provided a germ theory to explain *why* it worked.

Joseph Lister, a rare British surgeon who bothered to read French and German medical journals of the time, read about Pasteur’s theories and tried them out in actual surgery. Carbolic acid had recently been discovered by the University of Berlin PhD and Breslau chemistry professor Friedlieb Runge, another example of academic and industrial scientific discoveries slipping into medical doctors’ attention. Lister used it to make instruments and wounds antiseptic. Starting two decades after Semmelweiss’s discoveries, Lister managed to impress his contemporaries enough to win a knighthood eventually.

But other innovators were not so lucky. As a sidelight to the still-uphill battle faced by innovators like Semmelweiss, Runge, and even Pasteur, the first wound up beaten to death in a madhouse. Runge died in poverty after a string of major chemical discoveries including caffeine, the blue dye aniline, coal tar products such as the creosote used to prevent railroad ties from rotting, and many others with later medical applications. Even Joseph Priestley experienced the 1791 burning of his home, library, and laboratory by a mob whipped up by counterrevolutionary hysteria linking the French Revolution to modern science and religious tolerance. Indeed, the "Semmelweiss reflex" later became a scientific name for the common tendency, even among educated professionals, to reject new evidence or knowledge because it contradicts established norms, beliefs, or paradigms. In terms of Thomas Kuhn's account of how "normal science" rejects odd new findings until evidence builds up to validate them, these early pioneers rarely lived to reap the rewards of a paradigm shift in which their discoveries were integrated into a new understanding of the field.[4]

Even in the second half of the nineteenth century, a period in which faith in "progress" and science became almost a secular religion, the introduction of scientific method into medicine did not go unopposed. One of the era's most celebrated discoverers, Louis Pasteur, came from the discipline of chemistry. His many contributions to the betterment of public health and the economy flowed from his proving beyond doubt that the ancient theory of spontaneous generation was false and that microorganisms introduced from outside were the real cause of disorders such as the spoilage of wine and milk or the destruction of valuable silkworms' larvae. Having invented pasteurization and inspired Lister and others to adopt antiseptic surgical practices, Pasteur went on to consider immunization against invasive microorganisms while dealing with an animal disease called chicken cholera. Partly as a result of an assistant's mistake, he discovered that a cholera culture that had accidentally been left alone for a month caused mild symptoms in chickens but then produced immunity to further infection. We may recall that "vaccination" (from the Latin word for cow, *vacca*)—Jenner's discovery that cowpox could produce immunity against the much more dangerous smallpox—had been partly if not completely accepted by the 1860s, but nobody thought it was possible to produce an artificial version of the microorganism by weakening it (through aging in Pasteur's initial experiment) or killing it. By having a curious attitude about his assistant's mistake rather than letting the latter toss out the "aged" sample, Pasteur demonstrated the genuine scientist's openness to his assumptions being wrong. He later summed up this attitude in a famous quotation, "dans les champs de l'observation, le hasard ne favorise que les esprits preparés"—in the field of observation, chance favors only the prepared mind.[5] Having taken care of chickens' health, Pasteur then turned his attention to the sheep dying of anthrax, with similar happy results. By the mid-1880s Pasteur and his student Émile Roux had proven the effectiveness of a new rabies vaccine in a young human victim. His fame and new financial resources allowed him to create one of the world's first independent research institutes, the Institut Pasteur (1887).

Yet many contemporary physicians in France and elsewhere, far from hailing Pasteur's scientific discoveries, resented the fact that he was not a physician. Despite Pasteur's innovations he remained an outsider. Other examples abound of the personal cost to innovators in the area of medicine. Even Pasteur's friend (and questioner of the germ theory) Claude Bernard,[6] the first professor in the newly instituted chair of physiology at the Sorbonne and one of the major founders of modern medical research, faced the collapse of his marriage because his family could not reconcile his advocacy and practice of vivisection with their religious beliefs.

If Bernard's state-financed laboratory and Pasteur's privately-financed institute constituted Gallic innovations in the application of scientific method to medicine, across the Rhine in Germany another path was being developed. The career of Robert Koch shows the introduction of "scientific" investigative methods into university education (starting with the initiatives of the Humboldt brothers, Alexander and Wilhelm, founders of the new University of Berlin in 1810). Significantly, Koch first studied natural sciences at university before shifting into medicine and worked in an actual research project even as an undergraduate. His major professor of anatomy convinced him that infectious diseases were caused by living, parasitic organisms. And he learned to use a microscope to isolate and study those organisms, including ways of fixing them onto slides. Although he worked in his early career as a practicing physician, he was also a district health officer and maintained his own small personal research laboratory. Studying an outbreak of anthrax in the Wollstein district of Prussia, he demonstrated by fixing, staining, and photographing bacteria that anthrax could be spread not only by a live culture but also by spores in a dead one. (Parenthetically, he and his later students were still working out the applications of those aniline dyes discovered from the 1830s on by mostly German chemists from Friedlieb Runge to August Wilhelm von Hofmann and the latter's English student William Henry Perkin, the first to synthesize these dyes.) His work gained attention through lectures at related university institutes and publication in the burgeoning scholarly and scientific press of united Germany.

Indeed, the Imperial Health Office of the new national state provided him with an adequate laboratory where he managed to isolate the bacillus causing tuberculosis and developed rules for connecting specific bacteria to the etiology of specific diseases—"Koch's postulates." He then discovered the causative bacterium of cholera during a research trip to Egypt and laid down rules for the treatment of cholera outbreaks that are still in use today. As head of the University of Berlin's new Hygiene Institute founded in 1885, Koch tried to develop a cure for tuberculosis called "tuberculin," which, however, turned out to be ineffective and caused a public scandal. Koch's theories from that point on became more open to attack, although they more often than not proved correct later. Still, his next-generation protégés and colleagues in his institute, for example, Paul Ehrlich and Emil von Behring, respectively the fathers of treatment for syphilis and diphtheria, conclusively represented the triumphant march of scientific research into the etiology of human, animal, and plant disease that would become unstoppable in the twentieth century.

A fundamental breakthrough allowing for the integration of many individual scientific discoveries finally came in 1858 with the publication of cell theory by Rudolf von Virchow. Although trained initially to be a *Wundärtze* (a classification gradually abolished during his lifetime) in Prussia, he had studied chemistry and served as an assistant to great advocates of microscopy, particularly in both Berlin's Charité hospital and its new university. He was especially adept at microscopic investigations of human and animal pathology. Ultimately he came to believe that the cell was the basic unit of the body, that all cells came from the division of other cells, and that their study could reveal new insights into disease and cures. Aside from massive contributions to anatomical pathology, including laying down rules for autopsies, Virchow, although a very active liberal political leader, also helped found the subfield of social medicine. He was convinced that only public action and works (such as the sanitation projects he helped push through in Berlin) could reduce epidemics and contagions.

Virchow died in 1902, by which time the interconnection of scientific research, university teaching, and vigorous state and public intervention in both science and medical care constituted Germany's peculiar contribution to the professionalization of medicine. Virchow died, significantly, only a year after the first Nobel Prize was awarded in medicine, to his colleague Emil von Behring, already mentioned earlier. Compared to a century or even a half century before, support for scientific research in certain fields—and medicine and its related natural sciences was one of them—had made it into an attractive career with financial rewards, state recognition, and public esteem as previously unheard-of inducements. The same year as Behring's award, the Nobel Committee gave its first physics prize to Professor Wilhelm Röntgen for his discovery of X-rays. The accelerated speed of recognition may be gathered from the fact that Röntgen's breakthrough had only been announced in 1895, and he had already received three major international prizes before 1901. His apparatus also marked the spectacular debut of medical discoveries derived from the burgeoning revolution in electricity at the end of the nineteenth century.

This is not the place for further lengthy discussion of significant breakthroughs in the sciences related to medicine during the nineteenth century, but a brief time line will suggest the accelerating pace of discovery and may be kept in mind when we cast a glance in chapter 9 at the almost exponential march of discoveries.

1800: Humphrey Davy's use of nitrous oxide for anesthesia
1816: Laennec's stethoscope
1829: James Blundell's first successful blood transfusion
1846: William Morton and John Century Warren's first painless surgery with general anesthetic
1847: Ignaz Semmelweiss's countermeasures against puerperal fever
1867: Joseph Lister's *Antiseptic Principle of the Practice of Surgery*
1870: Louis Pasteur and Robert Koch's germ theory
1879: First vaccine for cholera
1881–1882: Louis Pasteur's anthrax and rabies vaccines
1890: Emil von Behring's passive immunizations against tetanus and diphtheria
1895: Wilhelm Conrad Röntgen's X-rays
1899: German firm Bayer markets synthetic aspirin

The rewards of organized scientific research had by 1900 become prizes and jobs, honors, and fame. But they also included unprecedented sway over the shaping of the wider medical profession, as we shall see in subsequent chapters.

Another characteristic of professionalization was still lacking until the second half of the nineteenth century: professional organizations to regulate and normify knowledge in the interest of controlling or dominating the market in services. Among the better organized of these, the American (1847) and British (1856) medical associations and their German equivalent, the Deutscher Ärtzevereinsbund (DÄV, 1872), all date roughly from the third quarter of the nineteenth century. These and similar organizations elsewhere more or less openly saw their mission as "representing the interests of the estate" of physicians—what would in a later time be called lobbying. Nevertheless, their regional and national conventions, regular and occasional publications—especially journals—and organized pressure on legislation and regulation undoubtedly contributed to shaping something like a unified profession. In addition, the extraordinary wave of founding private associations of people sharing common interests—so characteristic of the nineteenth century—carried to prominence many a general or specialized learned society involved in medicine. These, too, held regular meetings, maintained journals, and interacted with the public. An early example was the German Scientists and Physicians Society (Gesellschaft Deutscher Naturforscher und Ärzte [GDNÄ]), starting in 1822. This was, however, perhaps the earliest *modern* European national interdisciplinary association for promoting science and medicine, both for exchange among members, but also to awaken understanding and acceptance among the public. England's Royal Society dated, to be sure, back to the seventeenth century, when scientists and physicians had also joined it in large numbers, and it published its journal *Philosophical Transactions*, but it required considerable overhaul in the mid-nineteenth century to update it into an important multidisciplinary scientific organization with more medical and scientific members than politicians and other lay worthies. Similarly, the Royal Medical Society (Edinburgh) and the Royal Society of Medicine (London) had older roots, maintained libraries, but had certain regional limitations. Similarly, the Société de Médecine de Paris had a geographic limitation and underwent abolition by the French Revolution as well as reforms later in the nineteenth century, but it also included mostly local physicians as well as some scientists. Later in the nineteenth century many societies were founded in western Europe and North America to promote the circulation of knowledge about medical specialties, again with their own meetings, journals, and public activities. Nearly twenty of these were founded in Britain alone by the eve of World War I, to be merged finally into the Royal Society of Medicine in 1907. They represented the major medical specializations at that time, from pathology, ob-gyn, and anesthesiology to ear, nose, and throat and dermatology.

The trend continued through the twentieth century, with a proliferation of societies with missions and methods that overlapped to some degree. But they ranged from board interdisciplinary associations with some interest in medicine to extremely specialized ones usually spawned by the latest breakthroughs in medical knowledge. They correspondingly organized their communicative activities ranging from public lectures and demonstrations, accompanied by publications for lay audiences, to arcane journals largely indecipherable to nonphysicians (and even to some physician nonspecialists).

These organizations all, in one way or another, contributed to professionalization in the sense of promoting continuing medical education (CME) as well as indirectly raising public consciousness not only of health issues but of the way the organized profession addressed them. Insofar as they adopted a high-road approach to spreading, debating, and validating new medical knowledge, they also tended to demonstrate the expert mode compared to the more popular and older methods of hawking care and nostrums at medical shows and local fairs, and simple peddling by unscientific or empiric practitioners. In an age that subscribed to an unprecedented faith in science and "progress," the claims of medical societies to hitch their memberships to the triumphant star of therapeutic effectiveness fueled the claims to superiority by physicians trained in university-level medical schools. These claims also resonated with state bureaucracies and legislatures being pressured to forbid the "harmful" activities of "quacks" and "snake oil salesmen."

II

The Making of a Doctor: The Evolution of Medical Education

Chapter Six

Acolytes and Apprentices

From prehistory through the early Middle Ages, aspiring physicians learned medicine by apprenticing themselves to experienced practitioners or by joining a pre-Christian sect or, later, a religious order such as the Benedictines. The required technical knowledge pertained primarily to therapeutic compounds of herbs and minerals combined with shamanistic incantations. As Christianity spread across Europe, spells were replaced by prayers to appropriate saints, but astral influences were still thought to be important, so physicians often required background in astrology.

Although some people insisted that medicine was an unsuitable occupation for a Christian, since curing afflictions amounted to denying God's will, members of the Benedictine order considered care of the sick to be their primary work. As already noted, the character of Brother Cadfael, portrayed by Derek Jacobi in the eponymous BBC series, was based loosely if not always accurately on the Benedictine practitioners who passed down diagnostic and herbal wisdom to novitiates.

What few medical texts existed in medieval Europe entered as copies or translations, largely via southern Italy and Moorish Spain, then were copied by hand and preserved in monasteries. Other works were recaptured from the Near East by Crusaders; the transmission of relatively advanced medical knowledge was furthered by some knightly orders involved in medicine.[1] Chief among these precious volumes was the *Canon of Medicine* by the Persian polymath Avicenna (Abu Ali al-Husain ibn Abd Allah ibn Sina). Although this compilation of Hippocrates, Galen, and Islamic medicine was penned in 1030, it took another century for a translation into Latin. The translation was worth the effort, though, since the book was still being used in European medical schools in the mid-seventeenth century. Such was the glacial speed of the spread of knowledge.

"Apprenticeship" strikes most twenty-first-century readers as a quaint or alien term. And yet it was the dominant educational system, at least in practical trades, from the beginning of human society until quite recently. Indeed, it survives very well in the developing world and even as a successful supplement to formal secondary education in some highly advanced societies (e.g., the German system of dual vocational training). The latter combines the theoretical curriculum common at all vocational secondary schools with practical experience at a real work site.

Apprenticeship had the obvious advantage of close personal supervision of the learners by the already skilled, the masters of the trade. In medieval and early-modern Europe, indeed until most guilds were abolished or marginalized during the nineteenth century, training in the trades and professions (and in most lines of work, including farming) was hands-on, personal, and often imbedded in the social network of a larger family. In the guild system, a more organized and urban variant of the apprentice system, young people were usually taken into the combined workshop and home of a master, who (with his own family) operated in loco parentis. Apprentices, like interns in today's ultra-capitalist societies, were not only unpaid for their as-yet-unskilled work, they often had to pay the master for room, board, and education. Once an apprentice had done his (or in some trades, e.g., seamstress or baker, her) stated years of work (a typical term was seven years), depending on the trade, he could become a wandering "journeyman," allowing for exposure to other variants of the practice of the craft in other locations—a substitute for today's equivalent of journals, workshops, and conventions, all forms of "continuing education." The lucky few could aspire to becoming masters in their own right.

What set medical education apart from this system? Most medical practitioners (until about a century ago) were indeed trained as apprentices, whether in a formal guild-like setting recognized by some civic or state authority or in an informal way, like village wisewomen. The odd difference compared to other trades lay in the availability of an alternate high and scholarly path to medical "knowledge" as incorporated in university medical faculties. One could not become a doctor of baking or carpentry, but one could become doctor (literally "teacher") of medicine.

A major difference between apprenticeship and university education lay in the tendency of the latter toward cosmopolitanism. Guilds and masters were by definition locally privileged and to some degree hereditary. A medical apprentice in Cologne would not be likely to be able (linguistically, culturally, and perhaps even technically) to compete with one trained in Seville or Warsaw, in his own region. Everything from techniques of bleeding and bone setting to different regional herbs and minerals would make medical care by apprentice-trained practitioners highly localized. Except for the time of "journeyman" continuing education (a phenomenon restricted to the late Middle Ages and later, largely to German- and French-speaking wandering *Gesellen* and *compagnons*), and then only for certain trades, finishers of apprenticeships did not for the most part wander far from home. By contrast, universities were from the beginning linked by a common language (Latin), often used the same textbooks, and drew many of their students from abroad (giving rise to the multiple "nations" into which students were frequently organized). Ironically, few "doctor" graduates of universities could generally boast of greater therapeutic effectiveness than the often-illiterate practitioners trained through apprenticeship, but they could move about Europe and be accepted by patients much more readily than the latter.

As mentioned earlier, yet another path to some form of medical knowledge wound its way through the institutions of the established church. It should be emphasized that the pursuit of medical knowledge or the care of the ill were never the primary objective of Christian institutional organizations. Even though universities often developed out of cathedral schools and hospitals out of Jesus's example that faith can heal and that believers should aid lepers and the sick, the central focus of institutionalized Christianity in Europe and elsewhere, aside from palliative care for the dying, remained the salvation of the soul. It does not go too far to argue that the main reason for hospitals and nursing care, for example, was to offer a last chance for sinners to repent and find their way to God before their physical demise so that their chances of entering heaven would be augmented.

That said, as with other unintended consequences of social organization, the desire to be saved from hell often led to saving others from the pain, fear, and loneliness of serious illnesses and softening their usual final outcome, death.

Meanwhile, the beginnings of urbanization in late medieval Europe, the need for literate and numerate administrators in church and state as well as the first reappearance of such economic surpluses as lead to luxury and the support of arts and sciences also started the process of multiple paths to the healing arts. The apprentice system continued to be the mainstay of training in the practical application of medical knowledge for several more centuries. But, sporadically at first then increasingly institutionalized by the sixteenth century, a second path to medical knowledge and training, rare in a global context, opened with the founding of medical schools and their attachment to universities. It was from that happenstance that some medical healers became more than *medicii* (the plural of the Latin for "physician") and could call themselves doctors. The latter were, if anything, possibly less able to treat and heal patients than their apprenticeship-trained rivals. But from the newborn distinction of theoretical learnedness—and its attachment to the circles of wealth and power—came many of today's notions of professional hierarchy and value. Let us now turn to the emerging branching of paths to medical knowledge by the late Middle Ages.

Chapter Seven

Starting with Salerno

Europe's First Medical Schools

Rigorous, lengthy, and costly formal postgraduate education is one of the undisputed characteristics of the learned profession of medicine as we know it today. Yet university-level medical studies could not begin until there were universities. Put another way, physicians could not become "doctors" (ironically rooted in the Greek word for "teacher") until there were degree-granting institutions.

As we have seen in previous chapters, there were of course places where medicine was taught in the ancient world and outside Europe for centuries before the first "universities," properly speaking, were founded. It might therefore be just as accurate to refer to early European medical faculties as centers of learning (and some healing). They were not normally equipped with permanent campuses, buildings, bloated administrations, or many of the other characteristics we tend of think of when the term "university" is mentioned today. They were instead small bands of scholars and adepts with highly variable organizational modes. The oldest continually operating European university may be Bologna, founded as early as 1088 CE and later formally privileged by the Holy Roman Emperor and nominal ruler of much of Italy, Frederick Barbarossa. The original *universitas*, as it called itself, amounted to a collection of students organized into "nations" to protect themselves from municipal authorities' attempts to control and often punish these foreigners. The students in turn hired (and disciplined) their teachers. Their academic freedom rested primarily in the students' ability to hire and fire teachers and to threaten to leave the city en masse—taking their money with them—if they felt mistreated. Indeed, many other universities got established through these walkout strikes, for example, Oxford from Paris and

Cambridge from Oxford. Bologna, like many very early universities, resembled more a specialized professional school (in this case, for the teaching of Roman and canon law) than a full university offering degrees in theology, arts and sciences, and medicine as well as law.

The presence of what is claimed to be the first medical school in Europe, Scola Medica Salernitana, dating from the eleventh century in this region, had much older roots going back to ancient times. Significantly, this part of southern Italy constituted a fertile crossroads of ancient Greco-Roman as well as Islamic and Jewish scholarly and medical traditions, with important translations of older texts being produced in Salerno and the nearby monastery of Monte Cassino. Monks such as Constantinus Africanus Latinized many of the fundamental texts of ancient Greek medicine that had in turn been rescued and translated into Arabic before. Salerno's faculty collaborated to write *Ars Medicinae* and other fundamental texts such as the *Liber Ysogogarum* (Book of Introduction). Stressing Galen's idea of the "non-naturals"—healthy living through attention to nutrition, exercise, sleep, moderation, and so on, these served as primary medical texts that spread northward in Europe during the following centuries. The twelfth and thirteenth centuries followed suit with further translations from Arabic, notably in Toledo (Gerard of Cremona) and also Italy. Further universities appeared in Paris and Montpellier with medical and the other faculties. The university curriculum began to unite study of the classics and general subjects, often followed by a few years of specialization in law, theology, or medicine, depending on the profession to which the student aspired. Then as now, medicine required the longest commitment to university study. Earning an MD generally required ten years, with students enrolling as early as age fourteen.

Only nobles and wealthy merchants could generally afford to send their sons for this prolonged university residence. Sons of the emerging middle class could join a medical guild and learn the healing arts as apprentices, as discussed in the previous chapter. Women could become nuns or learn more informally from others (e.g., wisewomen or midwives) and focus their service on medicine or nursing. Even in later Protestant Europe, where the Reformation generally included the expropriation of monastic property, sisters often continued to exist as caregivers. But under almost no circumstances were women allowed to attend universities with the object of attaining a medical degree.

Before the founding of European universities, probably as many women as men practiced "medicine." The most famous of these was Trotula of Salerno, whom some authorities regard as the first European woman medical professor, an innovation doomed not to be repeated until the late nineteenth century. A few early Italian universities, notably Bologna, allowed women to attend lectures, and Dorotea Bucca taught medicine there as late as the beginning of the fifteenth century. Generally, though, females were denied access to higher education and declined in number and professional standing. Women, however, still predominated as midwives and gynecologists, partly because sexual mores forbade male physicians from examining women intimately. Most aspiring midwives learned through apprenticeships, but some studied under their physician fathers. In order to apprentice herself, all a woman needed was a statement from her parish priest vouching for her good character.

The evolution of European universities, it should be noted, lasted many centuries, during which time generalizations are slippery. Yet by the end of the Middle Ages, there were dozens of them, all sharing some sort of official papal or royal charter and privileges and many boasting the characteristic division into four faculties. To be sure, one could practice most of the learned professions for which the university prepared without attending one or getting a degree. The guild system and other forms of apprenticeship, including in the law and clergy, not just medicine, continued to exist side by side. Already by the thirteenth century, "the practice of medicine had changed from a right to a privilege with the introduction of medical licensure and the development of medical and surgical guilds that sought and obtained monopolies . . . in exchange for guarantees of high ethical standards and requisite training for all practitioners, . . . the basis for the assurance of competence."[1]

The establishment of university courses in medicine marked the emergence of another form of professionalization than had been known before. Significantly, this form of professionalization also implied male dominance of the higher and more socially prestigious forms of practice. The tendency also seems to have pointed in the direction of *learned* medicine (connected with medical schools), becoming markedly more secular. From decrees and papal orders after the Council of Tours (1163 CE) on, monastic and later secular clergy were prohibited or discouraged from studying medicine (and law as well).[2] It is also worth repeating frequently that the medical "doctors" produced by this new professional track were probably in no way therapeutically superior to the artisanal medical practitioners ("empirics") who continued to bleed, purge, and set bones. What was changing was the increasing luxury and sophistication of some cities and courts, where each wealthy merchant or feudal notable might find himself socially challenged if his retinue did not include a "learned" physician, a token of wealth and power rather than a sign of heightened health consciousness. The urban or court physician of the centuries after the founding of university medical faculties might therefore be regarded similarly as other protégés of the powerful and wealthy, embedded in a late medieval and early modern system of patronage. Significantly, the first solid signs of what one might call "doctor licensing" appeared in the mid-thirteenth century at the hands of the last of the brilliant Hohenstaufen emperors, Frederick II. His law code issued for the Kingdom of Sicily (1231 CE) formally entrusted the examination and licensing of medical practitioners to the "masters" of the Salerno medical faculty.[3]

Although statistical estimates remain largely guesswork and based disproportionately on urbanized and more prosperous areas of Europe, the proportion of medical practitioners who had attended a medical school or university faculty (and the significantly smaller number who actually completed master's or doctoral degrees, which more or less automatically conveyed the right to practice) might have been only as high as 40 percent in all of France as well as in Florence before about 1500. These figures shrink almost into insignificance when we realize that the medical faculties were almost everywhere the least popular among students—only 1 percent at the University of Cologne in the first half of the fourteenth century, for example.[4] If one adds in the unknowable numbers of village empirics and non-organized (e.g., rural, non-guild) practitioners, the percentage of medicos having had some brush with scholastic medical instruction would presumably be much smaller.

Until the mid-nineteenth century, as already mentioned, medicine and surgery were formally separate occupations, with surgery given lower status and requiring less training. A few universities, to be sure, offered courses in surgery (e.g., Bologna, Padua, and Montpellier), carrying on traditions established earlier by Salerno, and the separation of academic medicine from surgery was never as pronounced in Italy as elsewhere. An example of the results can be found in the life and works of Theodoric Borgognoni, a Bologna student and Dominican friar who became a favorite at the papal court (and ultimately a bishop). He wrote *Cyrurgia*, a four-volume tome filled with theory and techniques developed by actual practice and often questioning wrongheaded authorities such as Galen. He experimented with partial solutions to some of the perennial surgical problems such as anesthesia and antisepsis. And yet his career also lacked one of the hallmarks of a modern learned professional: he was at once a surgeon, monk, clerical administrator (as bishop of Cervia, near Ravenna, for thirty years), courtier, and expert in falconry. This form of multitasking remained characteristic of many later generations and has come down to us in the term "Renaissance man"—a concept that contains admiration for versatility but also points to deficits in focus and specialization.

The fate of medical science in European universities during and after the Renaissance and Reformation remained wedded to the religious ideologies of the time more than the advancements in knowledge of the physical universe that we conventionally call the Scientific Revolution. As late as the 1730s, even the creator of the first arguably modern university in Göttingen, Germany, Baron Gerlach Adolf von Münchhausen, was more interested in teaching young members of the elite to be good lawyers and clergymen than in preparing them to be physicians. When he somewhat grudgingly added a small medical faculty to his new design, his colleague in planning, J. G. von Meiern, referred mordantly to "the creation of ten or fifteen young exterminating angels [per year], so that people can be delivered methodically to the cemetery."[5]

It was a dangerous undertaking to establish new universities in the eighteenth century, as Münchhausen did. The many new ones set up in the wake of the Protestant Reformation, the Catholic Counter-Reformation, and even in the New World by assorted religious sects (e.g., Puritans at Harvard and Congregationalists at Yale) promulgated their interpretations of scripture, philosophy, law, and some other theoretical subjects, but they afforded little scope for new thought about medicine. Indeed, the growing gap between an ossified university curriculum stuck in centuries-old classical texts and the spread of new knowledge derived from the investigative habits and sensational discoveries of scientists became increasingly a reason for some radicals of the eighteenth century to argue for the abolition of traditional universities (and their medical faculties) altogether.

One need only to read the memoirs of Edward Gibbon or the denunciations by French and German Enlightenment critics to savor their contempt for the hoary, feudal, and corrupt ruins of the medieval universities of Europe. Gibbon's fourteen months at Magdalen College were summed up by Adam Smith's observation that "in the university of Oxford the greater part of the public professors have for these many years given up altogether even the pretence of teaching," and that his time there had been "completely lost for every purpose of improvement."[6] The German pedagogical reformer Johann Heinrich Campe, writing after the outbreak of the French Revolution, declared that "the best young people are, if not destroyed completely, at least made wild at universities and return from them weakened in body and soul, lost to themselves and the world."[7] Contemporary fiction, for example, Goethe's *Faust*, parodied the hollowness of traditional university learning. And the culmination of years of complaints about the rotten state of French universities, colleges, and faculties was their outright abolition by the revolutionary governments between 1789 and 1794. The spread of French revolutionary ideas to most other parts of Europe via the conquests of French armies, particularly under Napoleon, meant the closing of many other European universities or, at minimum, the shake-up and reform of existing ones.

New-model institutions replaced the decayed old universities in most European countries invaded by the French, Britain being the notable exception. The French reform model consisted of a welter of professional schools (such as the schools of medicine in Paris, Strasbourg, and Montpellier, or the dozen law schools scattered across the country), that is, specialized training schools (for teachers, engineers, military officers etc.). Ultimately a "university of France" created a fairly rigid bureaucratic hierarchy encompassing not only the former colleges and the faculties of theology, medicine, arts, and law, but also the secondary and primary schools. This system lasted until the end of the nineteenth century. Across the Rhine, however, new-model universities had been founded during the eighteenth century, notably Göttingen, and these not only survived the French conquest, but provided models for new ones (e.g., Berlin and Bonn) or reformed older ones (e.g., Heidelberg and Munich). The German university model emerging in the early nineteenth century retained the traditional division into four faculties, but these were increasingly expected to do original research and to expand knowledge, not merely to transmit static textbook learning. Not only professors but, in principle, students also were rewarded for pursuing a dynamic *Wissenschaft*, the expansion of scholarly knowledge by applying variants of scientific method. To be sure, some fields of investigation—such as philology, philosophy, and history—were quicker to realize the advantages of original research well before the fields of law and medicine. By the middle of the nineteenth century, though, even these fields were beginning to bear the fruits of investments in collections and laboratories.

These developments appear important for the professionalization of medicine (as well as other learned professions) but primarily in retrospect. We must recall that the predominant linkage of advanced medical practice to university education, as widespread and common as it has become, did not become firmly established, even in central Europe, before the middle of the nineteenth century. And even there (as in France, finally, during the Revolution), those eighteenth-century reformers who saw no possibility of shaking hidebound universities out of their torpor created other types of medical training institutions. The "enlightened despot" Emperor Joseph II created the Josephinum in Vienna in 1785 and gave it the right to award doctorates in medicine and surgery. Prussia, for example, developed a *Collegium medico-chirurgicum* in the 1720s to oversee and administer the training of all sorts of medical personnel, partly connecting it with the Charité hospital. In 1795, observing the failures of military surgeons in the first conflicts with revolutionary France, Prussia went further to establish a "Pépinière," a "nursery" not for plants, as the name implied, but rather for military surgeons. Unlike university or guild training, this institution was free and highly selective, expecting only a term of service in the armed forces in return for free education. Thus, for the first time, gifted but poor children could obtain a medical education. Another venue for medical education emerging in the eighteenth century was the hospital. As we have seen, "God's hotels" (*hôtels de Dieu)* had been established, in the Middle Ages primarily by religious orders, as refuges for the terminally ill, poor, or those afflicted with dangerous contagious diseases. Their purpose lay less in the curing of the body than in the salvation of the soul. But new foundations of the Age of Enlightenment tended to be more secular (funded by the state), staffed by paid physicians (yet still by medically untrained nurses or sisters, some hailing from nonconvented Catholic and even Protestant religious orders), and here and there including physicians taking students on rounds to teach by bedside example rather than the pure book learning of yore. Some few European university medical faculties actually had used bedside teaching in the past, such as Padua and Leyden, the latter of which stimulated a similar program at the University of Edinburgh. But these innovations tended to remain local or spread very slowly. By the eve of the French Revolution, again under the aegis of Emperor Joseph II, Vienna opened its General Hospital (*Allgemeines Krankenhaus*) in 1784. At that time and for long thereafter, this hospital was the largest in Europe and had the first dedicated lunatic wing, still standing today as a museum (the *Narrenturm*, or Fools' Tower). It not only treated patients, but gradually became a research and teaching center as well.

Finally, the eighteenth century began to pioneer what might be called modern outpatient clinical care. Of course, patients had long been treated by all manner of medical personnel in their homes (or in the surgery of the local doctor). What set off the strong emergence of clinics in the nineteenth century was their attachment to hospitals or university medical faculties. They not only dispensed outpatient care and medications—those cases not requiring hospitalization—but gave medical personnel in training an opportunity to observe many different kinds of illness.

It was indeed the innovation of combining clinical experience and theoretical learning available up until then primarily at universities that began laying the foundations for the effective reform of higher medical education, at least in Europe, by the mid-nineteenth century. Self-taught or apprenticed lay practitioners continued to practice in Europe and, until much later, America with few if any restrictions. They were popularly known as "leeches" because of their fondness for that particular therapy. But the opportunity for medical trainees, masters of theory, the scientifically curious, and wider circles benefitting from circulating new knowledge and experience (for example, through learned journals) would require clearing a path for such knowledge to be sheltered from negative social sanctions.

Chapter Eight

From Sacrilege to Science

Dissection and Observation

Religious taboos long forbade most direct investigations of the human body that could aid understanding of anatomy, physiology, or pathology. Although some ancient Greek physicians (e.g., two famous ones working in Ptolemaic Alexandria, Herophilus of Chalcedon and Erasistratus of Chios) used dissection of human cadavers and, apparently, even vivisection of criminals to study the body,[1] the law of the Roman Empire soon prohibited the practice, and even such ancient authorities as Galen had to use dead apes rather than humans to formulate guesses about anatomy. It remains unknown or controversial to what extent medieval Christian Europe and the Islamic world forbade or discouraged human dissection and the pursuit of post-mortem pathological examination ("autopsy" from Greek for "seeing for oneself"), but the weight of evidence suggests that the practice, when not absolutely forbidden, was not much encouraged. There were many cultural and religious reasons for this but also the practical one of the rapid deterioration of corpses, especially in warmer weather. When the Vatican did once authorize an autopsy in the early sixteenth century, it was to determine whether two Siamese twins had one or two hearts: Galen had taught that the heart is the site of the soul.[2] The issue was not what the children had died from, how their health could have been maintained, or anything resembling a modern autopsy outcome. It was rather to determine if one or two souls might go to heaven.

In the same century, Andreas Vesalius, professor at Padua and court physician to Emperor Charles V, was discouraged from exploring anatomy by dissection. His famous book, *De humani corporis fabrica* (*On the Fabric of the Human Body*) may stand as one of the earliest correct challenges of Galen concerning anatomy. But his influence largely waned after he was driven out of university teaching by stubborn defenders of the sacred texts of Galen. He wound up as court physician to Emperor Charles V and later his son King Philip II of Spain.

Remarkably, though, knowledge of anatomy received a significant and irreversible impetus from visual artists from the Renaissance on, best exemplified by Leonardo da Vinci.

The "doctors" continued to defend the static form of book learning that had limited practical applicability to patient health. There is little evidence that the very limited practice of human cadaver dissection in the late Middle Ages had any other purpose than instruction—almost certainly not to promote a better understanding of the body's functioning by questioning or challenging ancient received teachings. Even medical schools, like Padua, that did carry out dissections did only a couple a year.[3] And even those who practiced dissection and autopsy out of curiosity, defying public and religious opinion, admitted that it was a messy, disgusting business. There were no preservatives like formaldehyde, so cadavers had to be autopsied as soon as possible after death, before the stench of decomposition would overcome the investigator. When dissection eventually became a sort of wink-and-nod crime comparable to other breaches of social ethics (such as the sexual infidelities of the upper classes), hanged criminals might be accepted as proper "material" for curious scientists. (It was considered in some places a proper punishment for their crimes, beyond merely being executed.) As a last desperate resort, when the advantages of cadaver dissection as a part of medical education had become obvious, hiring grave robbers literally to dig up the recently deceased became, if not common, at least the theme of much lurid fiction, including, of course, Mary Shelley's *Frankenstein* (1818).

Thus, even when specialized anatomical studies were available to a few select medical students (like those of Vesalius in Padua), the question remained: why bother? Even Vesalius was looking for the "correct" blood vessel for applying bleeding, not in fact to abandon bloodletting altogether in favor of something like Harvey's theory of the circulation of blood. The sturdy opposition of all the doctors who had spent years and fortunes getting their MD degrees from European universities militated against such heretical speculation against the authority of Galen. The goal of the majority of the medical profession was indeed what Vesalius himself achieved—a lifetime pension from a patron (the Spanish monarchy in this case)—and this was not achieved by trying to overturn the authority of the ancients, particularly among those educated in the values of the Renaissance.

The history of medicine, like the broader history of science, has often been written as a tale of heroes breaking through the limits of prejudice and superstition to lead humanity to better paths of knowledge. Only gradually during the last half of the twentieth century did scholars like Thomas Kuhn begin to ask questions about the social mentality of the "discoverers" themselves. Why, for example, did it take thousands of years for the medical profession to discover, or once discovered, to promote the study of anatomy and its necessary corollary, dissection? In any era when life was "solitary, poor, nasty, brutish, and short" (as Thomas Hobbes commented in his *Leviathan*), the proper disposal of dead bodies took priority over asking what killed them. It may seem astonishing to us, in an era where popular entertainment (e.g., cop shows) involves massive numbers of autopsies, that these were not a standard part of medical education until the nineteenth century. The first great work on the subject, Giovanni Morgagni's *De Sedibus et Causis Morborum per Anatomen Indagatis* (*The Seats and Causes of Diseases Investigated by Anatomy*) was published only a few years before the American Revolution in 1769. It would not be until a century later, when Rudolf von Virchow set down the standards for proper autopsies, that the establishment of the cause of death began to become a standard part of medical education.

The autopsy has become important, of course, for criminal justice as well as for the advancement of diagnosis. And yet one of its primary benefits remains resisted today by many medical practitioners, insurance companies, and other interested parties. Routine autopsies can reveal, among other things, flawed physicians' diagnoses. It is almost a joke that every human dies of "heart failure," because it is so easy, safe, and obvious to sign a death certificate with that "diagnosis." It is unknown and probably unknowable how many deaths are the results of malpractice, that is, flawed diagnosis, and it is questionable how many doctors or their medical malpractice insurers even want to know.

But what if the purpose of medicine is not to consign the dead in an orderly way to the cemetery? The dissection of humans who had died under unnatural circumstances, especially if having exhibited signs of physical abnormality, led to further questions about why this or that internal organ was deformed or otherwise looked odd. Knowing the difference between a normal and an abnormal body part is of course a foundational element in any doctor's training today. Yet the social conventions, pruderies, and fears of centuries overpowered the rare curiosity of medical practitioners. They are still a powerful force today and perhaps even more pronounced in the Jewish and Islamic traditions than in Christian or other cultures.

The development of forensic medicine in the nineteenth century and after provides a vivid example of the changing forces on medical professionalization. The emergence of the police state, so to speak, made it possible and desirable for the first time systematically to link criminals to punishment. The creation of national and urban police forces after the French Revolution made it possible, for the first time in modern history, to sanction and punish lawbreaking in a reliable and orderly way. Indeed, the very word "police" refers to the original notion of public policy, derived from Europe's oldest police force, imposed on Paris by Louis XIV. London's bobbies (named for their creator Robert "Bobby" Peel) came later, but the German term *Polizei* smelled a little like a top-down imposition of welfare state order on society.

It is therefore no surprise to see Virchow developing the method of determining the time frame of a corpse's death using a liver thermometer. His laboratory was not only set up to answer such scientific questions, but to help the Prussian police and the criminal forensic system to arrive at defensible determinations about the time, cause, and responsibility for deaths.

Experimental medicine began to appear more often in the eighteenth century as the techniques of observation and experimentation initiated philosophically by people like Sir Francis Bacon had made headway in such areas as astronomy, physics, chemistry, navigation, and warfare. It was not without dangers.

As already noted, Edward Jenner, observing that milkmaids did not contract smallpox, invented human vaccination by employing the cowpox vaccine. (Indeed, the term vaccination comes from the Latin *vaccinus*, pertaining to cows.) But his discovery met with decades of resistance. Why? An earlier inoculation, "variolation," had proved dangerous, as the president of what later became Princeton University, Jonathan Edwards, discovered when his self-inoculation—meant to encourage his students—ended in his death in 1758. Jenner's safer method took another half century. Like many such discoveries, it was made haphazardly, without the later full armory of experimental method, peer review, controlled testing, and wide publicity among practitioners. Still lacking at this juncture was one of the telling characteristics of *modern* professionalization: organizations to regulate and normify knowledge so as to control or dominate the market in services.

Indeed, the tendency to list an ever-expanding series of breakthroughs and discoveries by medical science can obscure the more complex truth that even the careers of heroic pathfinders often contained embarrassing blunders and wrong guesses. Without the kind of careful, time-consuming testing of new treatments that only gradually became the norm during the twentieth century, the number of theories about diseases and their treatments could almost amount to the number of physicians asked. Such professional disagreements (and the variety of the kinds of physicians involved) were well ridiculed, for example, in George Bernard Shaw's *The Doctor's Dilemma*, first performed in 1906.

The spread of the "Enlightenment" in the eighteenth century—especially in and from Britain, into the countries of northwestern and central Europe and their overseas colonies—brought into medical thinking such concepts as public statistics (from the economists), observation and measurement (from the natural sciences and the many recently founded royal academies of science that promoted exploration, observation, and scholarly communication), and perhaps most decisively by the dawning idea that scientific method could actually improve life and even intervene in illness. It is hard for us today to imagine the brave battles partisans of the Enlightenment had to face against long-standing teachings, prejudices, religious beliefs, and superstitions. There was no victory, merely an arc of persuasion, with many reverses—right up to our own day. It was all very well for scientists to figure out how to navigate better, build better instruments (such as reliable clocks), and improve merchants' profits. But challenging hidebound bureaucracies of church and state, let alone the still largely illiterate public, was an uphill battle.

We have already noted how many decades it took for Captain Cook's proof of scurvy prevention to be adopted by the British admiralty as well as John Snow's explanation of cholera in London to result in decontaminating drinking water. The very Enlightenment notion of a universal right to "life, liberty, and the pursuit of happiness" was a striking innovation by the Founding Fathers that might be denigrated as socialist or worse by today's radical American conservatives.

While the American Founding Fathers (and mothers) participated in this movement, establishing some of the first real American universities, medical schools, and hospitals, the incipient professionalization of medicine in the United States received a setback in the form of the Jacksonian populist and antigovernment rebellion against elites. As we will explore more fully later, the incipient professionalization of medicine and many other fields was nullified for many decades in the new United States, roughly until the "closing of the American frontier" in the 1890s, according to Fredrick Jackson Turner. The closing of that frontier coincided with the expansion of American economic and military/naval power overseas, with the invasion and occupation of Cuba and the Philippines (Spanish-American War), Hawaii, Panama, and—with World War I—Europe.

The founding of an American overseas empire had heretofore little-studied repercussions on medical care at home, as will be explored later. But to give one example: the successful building of the Panama Canal could not have been carried out without the epidemiological work of American medical researchers. It is fair to say that the normal regular practitioner produced by the festering shallow and research-averse proprietary medical schools could never have produced such results. The demand to shut out graduates of such schools and follow German (Johns Hopkins) university paths to medical training was in a way a side effect of the United States jumping on the already well-launched European imperialist bandwagon.

The success of the professionalization project among physicians up until that time was, to be sure, not a lot greater across the Atlantic. The Royal College of Physicians licensed doctors in London (and tried to maintain a monopoly for all England), for example, and compulsory apprenticeship and formal qualifications for general practitioners (GPs) was introduced by the 1815 Apothecaries Act. But only in 1858 did Parliament create a General

Medical Council (GMC) to register and regulate doctors. A decade before, Prussia had abolished a two-class system of physicians, those with university degrees and successful licensing exams on one hand and the lesser-trained group of military surgeons (*Wundärtze*) who also served a wider public. About the same time as the founding of the American Medical Association (AMA) in 1847, German physicians began organizing their first national medical association. But as in France and most other Continental countries, it was the state (sometimes with prodding from the doctors) that had the most influence on all the eight markers of professionalization that we have mentioned.

We can return later to some of the important differences between Continental versus British and American professionalization patterns, but for now it is enough to note them. A major difference that affected medical professionalization was the invention of legally mandated health insurance for ordinary workers in Germany in 1883—an achievement the United States has still only been able to approach one and a quarter centuries later. And it is highly ironic to hear the American reform described by the historically ignorant as socialist, since it was initiated in Germany by a conservative leader—Count Otto von Bismarck—with the intention of wooing the rabble away from following socialist revolutionaries! As we will see in greater detail below, what eventually came to be the world's first system of seamless state medical insurance for all was thus a conservative, paternalist, and royalist plot not a socialist one. And let us note that medical professionalization might remain relatively meaningless without a significantly large clientele for professional services, such as that provided by near-universal health insurance. Put another way, and in purely economic terms of motivation, Germany's lead in mass health insurance expanded opportunities for newly graduated physicians. A tiny minority of fashionable doctors could be sustained by private, fee-for-service practice. (The richest were legendarily found around spa and resort towns like Wiesbaden, called "Pensionopolis" because of its large number of retired, wealthy, and often gouty residents, which counted 2,200 doctors per million inhabitants compared to 300 nationwide).[4]

As we shall see in the next chapter, the growing interaction of medical and public health education and professional regulation (including self-regulation) between Europe and the United States began to erode the legacy of the radical free-market ideology dominating the latter in the Jacksonian era. Let us make a little detour to one of the frontiers of the United States in the second half of the nineteenth century to illustrate this point. One of the major entry points for the settling of the West was the port city of Galveston, the largest city in Texas at the time and the "Ellis Island of the West." Immigrants were attracted by the free or cheap land available in Texas and westward, although many remained in the growing urban areas as well. One of Galveston's most famous sons was Albert Lasker, credited (for better or worse) with creating the modern American advertising industry. We will have a little more to examine regarding that in a later chapter.

But what does Albert have to do with medical professionalization? His parents emigrated from Prussia, and although Albert grew up in Galveston, he was born in Germany, too, while his parents were back on a brief visit. The founder of modern cellular pathology and later the exemplary Berlin medical historical museum, Professor Rudolf Virchow, was not only a world-class medical researcher and public hygiene hero, but also an active and influential politician in the Prussian state legislature and the German national congress (*Reichstag*). One of his collaborators on so many projects—including support for modern medical education—was another leading political figure of the 1860s and until his death in the early 1880s, Edward Lasker. Who was Lasker's brother? Morris Lasker, who founded the Galveston family. Who was his nephew? Albert Lasker. Last not least, Albert's own family philanthropic foundation (which today supports the Lasker Prize and similar encouragements of medical innovation) just may have come about in part from guilt about the vast sums he made successfully peddling products of dubious salubrity, such as cigarettes. He coined the motto "Reach for a Lucky instead of a sweet"—a slogan that increased the cigarette brand's sales 600-fold!

The ease with which people could sail back and forth between Galveston as well as other American ports and Europe (and elsewhere), in relative safety and comfort, might be compared, as an information highway, to the Internet of today. Of course the first effective transatlantic telegraph cable (1868) and the spread of telegraphy across both the linked continents greatly improved the speed and dissemination of news, and cities such as Galveston were ready to be hooked up to it through Western Union. But telegraphy was expensive, and the affordable spread of new knowledge—such as medical journals—tended at first to rely on transport by ship, later supplemented by rail freight distribution. Port cities like Galveston were entrepots for news and information, including scientific news in an era that showed a high regard for scientific progress. The steamships and railways that carried the Laskers and others and transported mail and printed matter like journals back and forth across the Atlantic and the continent related to medicine in an indirect way. The invention of the steam locomotive (Stephenson's *Rocket*, 1829) and the stethoscope (Laennec, 1816) lay a mere baker's dozen years apart.

The first chemistry lab at a university was founded about this time by Justus von Liebig in Giessen, Germany, resulting in both science-based agriculture (with the discovery of nitrogen for fertilizers) as well as the modern bouillon cube (protein for the poor and ill). As we shall see later, Liebig's students revolutionized modern chemistry, including that of human physiology. Soon medical schools began founding laboratories on a modest scale, such as Johannes Muller's in Berlin, where the microscope came to be used routinely by medical researchers. The rapid improvement of such nonmedical technologies as glass, metallurgy, ceramics, steam and electric power, transportation, printing, communications, and so on, quietly furthered the introduction of science into modern medicine on a massive scale. The mere fact, for example, that physicians and medical professors could travel easily to congresses and purchase affordable journals containing the latest medical news immensely accelerated the spread of new methods of treatment. It was not just that the origins of pestilences such as cholera were discovered by medical scientists (John Snow's London public water study in 1854)—and finally grudgingly accepted—but that modern, affordable technology could at last provide the piping and treatment methods to deliver safe water and to take away sewage from cities that colluded to make a population explosion. The simple introduction of hygiene (doctors washing hands, antibacterial cleaning products), trained nurses instead of prisoners or ex-prostitutes as hospital attendants, and even the widespread adoption of cheap (and washable!) cotton clothing made hospitals relatively safe for the first time. The *applied* results of science—including in medicine—lent legitimacy to the claims by men learned in theoretical expertise to public trust and high rewards.

One almost revolutionary result of all these innovations was the rapid transformation of the hospital from a place for the mostly poor to be warehoused prior to death into a place more sanitary, scientific, and supervised than the private bedroom. Not only did the number of hospitals boom from the late nineteenth century on—from 1,500 to 27,000 between 1904 and 1927 in the United States alone. Medical schools scrambled to be associated with hospitals, which came not only to treat (and cure) many more patients but to be extensions of postgraduate medical education via internships. Whereas lay philanthropic hospital boards had selected local physicians for hospital privileges, increasingly, medical boards composed of senior physicians made these choices in hospitals. The ability to have admitting and treatment privileges in a good hospital greatly enhanced the career prospects of doctors and became eagerly sought after. The presence of interns (also selected by the hospital medical boards) allowed for round-the-clock medical attention to patients, which they highly prized. Finally, the addition of residencies in the burgeoning specialties developing rapidly from the early twentieth century enhanced the care of patients, the continuing education of young MDs, and, not least, the authority and power of the elite of the local medical profession. The latter effectively controlled access to full physicians' practice through the selection of interns and residents. A further shift in professional power, at least in the United States, lay in the direction of dominance by surgeons. The American College of Surgeons (founded 1913) gained considerable organizational experience during World War I and managed to impose uniform norms on many hospitals where surgeons increasingly dominated the scene.

"In 1918 the ACS began a decade-long effort to inspect, grade and standardize hospital-based surgery as a precondition for its ultimate goal, the elimination of most surgery by general practitioners."[5] By the onset of the Great Depression, more than 90 percent of American hospitals had been graded by the ACS standards.

Successfully funneling the seriously ill into hospitals, once they were sanitary enough to reduce rather than increase complications, infections, and other life-threatening outcomes, made possible the observation and monitoring of ever-larger numbers of patients. Outpatient clinics and dispensaries added their quotas to the number of ill people who could be systematically observed, tested, and treated. As we will see in the following chapter, the opportunity to use the hospital, clinical setting, and (finally) laboratory to further the education of physicians went hand in hand with the development of modern scientific medicine during the course of the nineteenth century.

Chapter Nine

Three Paths Leading to Modern Medical Education

Colonial America, like the imperial mother countries (e.g., Britain, Spain, or France) got by with very few "doctors," that is, physicians with some kind of higher education. Insofar as these existed, they were concentrated mostly in larger cities such as London or Paris. In 1790 the biggest cities in the thirteen former British colonies (New York, Philadelphia, Boston, and Baltimore) had respectively 33,000, 28,000, 18,000, and 14,000 inhabitants. It is worth noting that all these were port cities and relatively wealthy commercial centers, explaining why they early on established medical schools and hospitals, as would such coastal or inland port cities as Chicago, San Francisco, New Orleans, or Galveston later, when the latter two were the major ports of the Gulf Coast.

But even the fairly weak and premodern kind of professionalization characteristic of the (London) Royal College of Surgeons, a breakaway guild from the much older Worshipful Company of Barbers, struck only feeble imitative roots in the early American Republic. The revolutions of the late eighteenth and early nineteenth centuries may have freed medicine from the strictures of organized religion. They also laid the groundwork, especially in America, for a populist rebellion against "elites," attended by a movement against privileging and licensing of any kind of expert skill. As a result, the incipient professionalization of medicine and many other fields was delayed for decades, roughly until the closing of the American frontier in the 1890s.

As broadly a part of the Romantic rebellion against the Age of Reason, this movement also reflected the raw values of American expansion westward, with "heroes" such as Andrew Jackson and Davy Crockett. Brave as their legends paint them, they were also fleeing the law and order of settled East Coast cities rather than face the consequences of stealing another man's wife (Jackson) or creditors' money (Crockett). Despite several notable foundations and beginnings in medical education and treatment before and just after the American Revolution, the further professionalization of medicine in the new country was held back by many factors, not just the radical populism during and after the Jacksonian era. Aspiring American physicians who wanted something better than an often slipshod apprentice system were tempted in growing numbers in the early nineteenth century to study first in Britain, then in France, and finally in Germany.

In England, although one could get an MD degree after many years of theoretical study from the ancient universities of Oxford and Cambridge, effective medical education was relegated by the turn of the nineteenth century largely to teaching hospitals as a sort of extension of the apprentice system. Scotland, by contrast, anchored training in its major universities, in medicine especially at Edinburgh, but also at Glasgow. While Edinburgh had been teaching some medicine since the sixteenth century, it organized a formal medical school only in 1726 in the wake of the Scottish Enlightenment. Many of its early faculty carried on the traditions they had learned as students at the Dutch University of Leiden, where Herman Boerhaave had pioneered the application of Newtonian physics models to illness and developed clinical teaching and the modern academic hospital in the early eighteenth century. One of his pupils, Gerard van Swieten, became court physician to Empress Maria Theresa in Vienna and a major reformer of medical training and care there.

The French university system in the eighteenth century had not escaped the charges of ossification, corruption, and irrelevance to modern science and life that swept Europe along with the Enlightenment critiques. Thoroughly reformed in the wake of the French Revolution and Napoleon, it rested on France's then-leading position in scientific research and medical innovation. Above all, the Paris school opened new paths to diagnosis (through the stethoscope and its obvious advantages in dealing with diseases of the thorax) and pathology (with emphasis on autopsies).

The second half of the nineteenth century then saw France eclipsed by German-speaking Europe, where governments instituted licensing requirements and medical students had to do laboratory work and to learn to treat patients in their schools' affiliated clinics and hospitals.

These three models of modern professionalized medicine were far from identical, although they all rested on some version of advances in scientific method and hands-on medical instruction. Each of them tended to break down the age-old distinction between medicine as theoretical book learning (the province of university medical faculties) and practical observation, diagnosis, and even therapy for patients (the former province, mostly, of barber-surgeons and other empirics lacking higher Latin learning and sometimes even the ability to read). The emerging English system grew largely out of hospitals and, like the French, was heavily based in the capital, with its wealth of case material. Medical education in England (similarly to the study of law) was by now no longer principally anchored in the traditional universities, Oxford and Cambridge. In a comparable way, effective legal education was consigned to London's Inns of Court rather than the ancient universities. Serious medical education was carried out mainly in London's teaching hospitals, such as the eighteenth-century foundings of Guy's, St. Bartholomew's, and London hospitals, although an old-fashioned apprenticeship system persisted side by side. Only with the creation of the University of London, the first British "red brick" in the 1830s, were university training and a clinical hospital finally linked. (The first major operation under ether was carried out there in 1846 by its clinical surgery professor Robert Liston.)

Medical training at a university otherwise could be so totally divorced from practical experience that one might wisely have run the other way from an Oxford MD. People trained as surgeons, apothecaries, or midwives—with widely varying and unregulated training—dealt with the wider populace. Not even after the stricter licensing laws under the General Medical Council (1858) could one confidently describe English medicine as a coherent system with uniform standards. Scotland (with its two major universities at Edinburgh and Glasgow) was of course different, much more rationally organized, and most similar to the German system to be described later.

The French system had been thoroughly reformed in the wake of the 1789 revolution and Napoleon, with serious medical schools in Paris and three in the provinces (Montpellier, Bordeaux, and Strasbourg). Medical students were allowed to observe and sometimes assist at hospitals. France came to be seen by many ambitious American medical students as offering better solutions than Britain, perhaps partly because France then held the lead in international scientific and medical innovation during the first half of the nineteenth century or partly because Paris was so much more pleasant to live in than, say, smoky, expensive, and dangerous London. The French state—unlike its British or American counterparts—regarded it as a duty to organize the medical care of the population, creating *officiers de santé*. France can make a legitimate claim to having established the modern clinic on a wide basis as well as numerous breakthroughs in technique, from Claude Bernard's *Study of Experimental Medicine* (1865) to Louis Pasteur's discovery of microbes. Or consider the almost universal symbol of physicians next to the white coat: the stethoscope, invented by the French hospital physician René Laennec, who later became a professor at the College de France. Not only did it greatly enhance auscultation by amplifying sound, but it overcame the sexual prudery that up until then made it virtually taboo for (male) doctors to listen to the torsos of women patients (which would have required putting their ears on naked female flesh!). Now the first adequate diagnoses of the ills of half the human race became possible, beginning the process of rolling back the bizarre gynecological beliefs of the Victorian and previous ages.

Unfortunately French medical education and the profession itself became increasingly conservative and class-bound during the nineteenth century, so that Pasteur remained an outsider despite all his important innovations. So deeply hostile to his kind of empirical microbiology did large segments of the French medical establishment remain that he was forced to found his own institute with the income he earned from his discoveries. One sign of this resistance lay in the astonishing fact that the Medical School of Paris offered no instruction in microbiology as late as World War I. Many French doctors even opposed vaccination against diphtheria because its Pasteur Institute developer, Gaston Ramon, was a mere veterinarian by training. To this day one can say of France that its *grandes écoles*, including to some extent its medical faculties, originally set up as meritocratic institutions, have also hardened large parts of French elites and made them tend toward smugness, provinciality, and a sense of entitlement. The French themselves did begin to recognize the superiority of German higher education in the wake of their defeat in the Franco-Prussian War (1870–1871). But French society was probably too polarized during the Third Republic to do much about it.

Certainly the change of direction of the continuing stream of American students of medicine to Europe endorsed this alteration of prestige. The second half of the nineteenth century, especially after about 1870, saw the rise to world leadership in medicine pass to Germany (if we loosely include Austro-Hungarian centers such as Vienna). Here the influence of the state was decisive, as Prussia and other central European states following its example unified the medical profession via control of education (university medical faculties), hospitals, physician licensing, and—partly to overcome Germany's economic backwardness—a heavy investment in science. More than elsewhere, German professors of medicine set the standards, and they were able to set them high, thanks in part to a decentralized and competitive cultural and scientific regime in the federalized German Reich, established in 1871. Increasingly after mid-century, German medical students (and numerous Americans) were forced to do hands-on laboratory work and learn to treat patients in the university's own ambulatory outpatient clinics as well as affiliated hospitals. They were expected not only to be able to practice but to know how to do original research as well—just as all the professors were expected to make original contributions to knowledge. The universities of the German Empire were, in a way, the first to adopt a completely dynamic attitude toward education, with the expectation that today's certainties will be undermined by tomorrow's further discoveries. Last not least, universities became engines of upward social mobility in an otherwise rigid society, and the expansion of the medical profession was helped along enormously by the introduction of mandatory health insurance for the working masses (Health

Insurance Bill of 1883), which Bismarck originally called "practical Christianity."

What made the German medical system so superior that it attracted so many foreign—and especially American—students, who then returned home to introduce some of its elements in their own lands, from Japan to Texas? One can identify perhaps three important elements in roughly the half century before World War I.

The first important element was a conscious government will to invest heavily in modern science as a way of leapfrogging an economically backward country into prosperity and power. The stunning breakthrough discoveries of German scientists, including medical ones, and their location mostly in universities encouraged further investment in university facilities, chairs, and laboratories. This worked out well until shortly before World War I, when strains on government budgets plus the heavier research demands made by burgeoning industry (including the chemical and pharmaceutical ones) produced a shift in the way basic research was carried out, with less funding for university labs.

One must interject here, however, that German medical professionalization based in universities remained (as elsewhere) limited in principle to males. For a brief period around the 1848 revolutions in central Europe, women were for a time considered for medical study, but the conservative reaction and co-optation of German liberalism over the second half of the nineteenth century put a stop to such experiments. Curiously, though, one woman student, Maria Elisabeth Zakrzewska (1829–1902), who graduated from the Charité midwifery school in Berlin in 1851, was even being considered as successor to her patron, the director of the Charité, Josef Schmidt, until his untimely death in 1852. Like many Germans during that period, Schmidt had a highly colored and admiring image of the new United States and suggested to his pupil that her chances of pursuing a medical career would be better there than in increasingly reactionary Prussia. That advice, which turned out to be wrong, nevertheless propelled her to New England, where she founded the New England Hospital for Women and Children and its nursing school, one of the first and most important in the country.[1] Along with the first native-born American woman physician, Elizabeth Blackwell (who wound up emigrating to England), she is celebrated as the founder of modern American women's medicine.

The second important element in Germany's increasing leadership lay in the decentralization of cultural and educational policy in a loosely federated German Reich after 1871. Given the academic freedom of students to wander freely among the two dozen universities in the German-speaking world before 1914, even smaller states with limited budgets found it worth their while to compete with such powerful rivals as Prussia, Austria, and Saxony so that their own students would not be tempted to abandon the local higher education system. This rivalry promoted keen competition for the best researchers, professors, and students, ratcheting up the value of experimental science, including in medical fields.

The third important element lay in the expansion of affordable medical coverage for the working poor (and finally for everybody), giving a great impetus after 1883 to the expansion and modernization of medical education, a flood of new physicians, greater competition, and the ratcheting up of standards, requirements, and rewards—in short, both the professionalization and the "scientificization" (*Verwissenschaftlichung*) of German medical practice. Every physician was now trained, at least in principle, as a scientist and expected to keep up with the dynamic development of a science-based occupation. This lent the twentieth-century medical profession its special claim to surpass all other modern learned professions in importance and value.

Medical innovation could and sometimes did lead to immense fame and considerable wealth, a relatively new incentive for medical practitioners to follow a path of scientific training. A glance at the list of medical Nobel Prize winners from German-speaking Europe after the creation of the lucrative and famous award at the beginning of the twentieth century vividly demonstrates the success of the German model of medical education and professionalization:

Emil von Behring (1854–1917): 1901, diphtheria cure
Robert Koch (1843–1910): 1905, cause of infectious diseases
Paul Ehrlich (1854–1915): 1908, Salvarsan, the first chemotherapeutic agent against syphilis
Emil Theodor Kocher (1841–1914): 1909, physiology, pathology, and surgery of thyroid gland
Albrecht Kossel (1853–1927): 1910, work on nucleic acids
Robert Bárány (1876–1936): 1914, physiology and pathology of the vestibular apparatus
Otto Fritz Meyerhof (1884–1951): 1922, relationship between the consumption of oxygen and the metabolism of lactic acid in muscles
Julius Wagner-Auregg (1857–1940): 1927, value of malaria inoculation in the treatment of dementia paralytica
Karl Landsteiner (1868–1943): 1930, discovery of human blood groups
Otto Warburg (1883–1970): 1931, nature and mode of action of respiratory enzyme
Hans Spemann (1869–1941): 1935, organizer effect in embryonic development
Otto Loewi (1873–1961): 1936, chemical transmission of nerve impulses
Gerhard Domagk (1873–1961): 1939, (denied by Nazi government) antibacterial effects of Prontosil

Werner Forssmann (1904–1979): 1956, cardiac catheterization (work done in 1929)[2]

How could this university-based, unified medical profession have enjoyed such temporary world stature until the arrival of the Nazi wrecking ball in 1933?[3] The German equivalent of the American Medical Association operated in cooperation with state funders and regulators, even though many physicians were unhappy about the high numbers of practitioners and about lower average incomes than they would have liked. An authoritarian, professionally trained, and largely incorruptible bureaucracy sought to set up a fair system, strict but without excessively minute regulation. Although ancillary expenses for studying medicine were higher for students than in other fields, university tuition was virtually free, offering in principle meritocratic access to the profession of medicine. (Of course, the educational requirements for admission to universities meant in practice that families had to be able to finance the postponement of a child's income-producing work for the thirteen years of pre-university schooling, so few proletarian children and virtually no women enjoyed access before about 1900.)

For certain social groups such as Jews, who were nominally equal but in fact practically excluded from many state-based professions like military officer commissions, the clergy, and the bench (if not the private bar), medicine offered a rare chance for social mobility. The ostentatious loyalty of many German Jews to the empire reflected this relative social openness, until the racist and exclusionary resentments of the interwar years helped the Nazis to power by 1933. It might well be arguable, as the last living granddaughter of Kaiser Wilhelm II, Marina Victoria (1917–1981), by then an American citizen and comfortable with democratic values, told me, "The empire under my grandfather was a well-run enterprise." If it strains the imagination to think so after Hitler, we should nevertheless recall that this was the Germany—with its medical professionalization system, excellent universities, laboratory experience, and bedside diagnosis in university outpatient clinics, internships, and continuing education—that Abraham Flexner encountered as a student from Kentucky when he went to Berlin. And from there, we can perhaps better understand both the Flexner Report of 1910, to be discussed next, and Flexner's high regard for such new medical schools as that of the University of Texas in Galveston or its near-contemporary new founding, the Johns Hopkins University medical school and hospital in Baltimore.

Especially in London, the older English model of teaching in large urban hospitals, augmented by a renewed linkage to university studies as in France, and finally the German model incorporating theoretical, clinical, and research elements successively set the standard for much-needed reforms in American medical training after 1890. As we shall explore further later, the patent failure of an often primitive, inexpensive, cursory, and unscientific free-market medical training system that in most cases rarely transcended a short and shallow apprenticeship coincided with the closing of the American frontier and the tipping of the United States from a predominantly rural to an urban, industrialized society drove the perception that a radical overhaul was needed. The central contribution of the German model, which continued to attract the most ambitious American medical students right down to the outbreak of World War I, lay in the combination of research within a teaching institution. The aim was no longer merely to pass along static traditions through commentaries on ancient writings, but to write and rewrite new and improved guides to effective practice. To vary slightly a quotation attributed to the Berlin philosopher Georg Friedrich Hegel, "A great university is measured by the number of its students who have surpassed their professors." Although this remained a goal that never could be perfectly attained, resetting the goal posts alone put American medical education and research on a path that would lead, in the twentieth century, to world leadership.

As we shall see in later chapters, however, that leadership has come under question as the function of American medical schools—almost all attached to notable research-oriented universities—has ceased to be medical education exclusively and has instead become a "profit generator" in a postindustrial and finance-capital-oriented society.

Chapter Ten

Money Talks

Abraham Flexner's Reforms

The Emmy- and Golden Globe–winning HBO television series *Deadwood* offers a vivid depiction of a physician in a gold rush Dakota Territory mining camp in the 1870s. Although the show's creator and major writer, David Milch, based the character of Doc Cochran on the journals of real-life frontier physician Lyman F. Babcock, the scientific sophistication, social and ethical sensitivity, and technical skill Cochran exhibits in the show's episodes—set a mere decade after the American Civil War—feels closer to fiction than fact. Not that there were no physicians at the time who understood the importance of sanitation and smallpox vaccination, the wisdom of having prostitutes in a brothel checked regularly for sexually transmitted disease, or the ethical complexities of treating a grieving widow addicted to opiates, but those physicians were few and far between, and they were almost all located in large cities, not in frontier outposts. Boomtowns like Deadwood would be very lucky to have a competent former Civil War army surgeon not too addled by drink as its health care provider.

Still in the throes of Jacksonian anti-elitism, nineteenth-century America largely left professional training up to local initiative, with ample room for abuse of the totally unregulated market. Lawyers like Abraham Lincoln prepared themselves by "reading the law" on their own by the fireside. Minimally trained, all-but-illiterate men received licenses as physicians, and most states and territories were free of sanctions against those without licenses or imposed such sanctions sporadically. Frontier self-reliance rather than fancy medical degrees and licenses positioned my great-grandmother, for example, as the sole medical practitioner in Hale County in the Texas Panhandle in the

1870s. She served in this capacity without any formal medical or nursing training until a proper MD showed up around 1900.

When members of the upper crust in New York, Boston, New Orleans, and San Francisco fell ill, they just might be able to call in a doctor educated at a university in France, Austria, or Britain. The rest of Americans had to rely on physicians who had taken cursory courses in small proprietary medical schools run for profit by local physicians, typically in rented rooms downtown.

It may be hard to believe today, but the status and respect accorded doctors in colonial and nineteenth-century America was less than that of teachers, lawyers, or clergymen partly because, unlike these other professionals, American physicians were often almost illiterate. Few had any college education, since it was not required, and therefore almost no exposure to modern science. In the early years of the republic, apprenticeship continued to be the normal path for a would-be physician. But instead of the traditional seven years mentoring by an established doctor, it was usually reduced to three. Much like an indentured servant, the young student "learned to make pills, mix potions and powders, cup, bleed and do bedside nursing," as one historian noted. "Not a few of these half-fledged youths were also expected to act as sweep and stable boy for the doctor," and maintaining the physician's horse or buggy was often a major part of medical training.[1] Naturally the precepting physician demanded fees for this training, and these may have comprised a major part of the income of some less scrupulous practitioners.

Still, the opportunity for a poorly educated youth to learn a few useful tricks as apprentice to a seasoned, conscientious physician did exist. Observation of actual illness under the guidance of wise and experienced practitioners had been the norm for medical training for centuries all over the world. But the professional organizations that had here and there enforced standards, such as guilds, had largely disappeared or been abolished in the wake of the American and French revolutions. What gradually replaced apprenticeship in nineteenth-century America was collective endeavors of a half dozen or so local doctors banding together as founders and proprietors of small for-profit medical "schools." These were not, as we think of medical schools today, extremely advanced institutions of higher learning and research often attached to prestigious universities. Indeed, there had only been three of those in 1800 (at today's Harvard, Columbia, and Penn), and even they resembled the better "proprietary" schools of their day more than they did modern medical schools. The proliferation of proprietary medical schools advanced (twenty-six founded between 1810 and 1840, then forty-seven more by 1876) even as more states dropped licensing of physicians and recognized anybody as a doctor who had an MD degree from one of dozens of dubious shops. Insofar as a few of them were attached to famous colleges, they were long run as separate businesses with their own faculty members, admissions, teaching and graduation standards, curricula, and fees.

In many ways, however, the education they offered differed little from that of the most mediocre colleges or even night schools. American college education at the time was characterized largely by rigid attention to classical texts and memorization. Instruction was almost entirely by lecture, supplemented by some reading. It astonishes people today to think that a barely literate teenager without a high school diploma could attend a sixteen-week lecture course given by a few local doctors, often in a second-story room above the neighborhood pharmacy, for several hours each winter (a second "semester" was normally required, but with the identical courses and material, presumably to reinforce memorization) and emerge at the end as an MD, ready to hang up his shingle. (Some schools did require a minimum age of twenty-one for the degree, however.)

Entrance requirements were virtually nonexistent. The main paper document needed for matriculation took the form of the currency to pay the tuition fees. Virtually the only control of students was attendance, although that was not always certain. What final examinations were administered were usually oral and elementary. Since many schools did not require even the rudimentary elements of high school education, there was no real exposure to modern science. And lacking that, there was no expectation of work in a laboratory, learning from dissection, or much hands-on training. Nor were most medical schools closely affiliated with hospitals or clinics, and aside from the occasional cursory tour of a hospital ward that some med schools offered, it was not unusual for a graduating American MD rarely or never to have touched, let alone diagnosed, an actual patient. The use of available "new technologies" such as the stethoscope and auscultation, thermometers, and more advanced diagnostic tools was unknown to many American physicians even near the end of the nineteenth century. The success of a proprietary medical school rested on its degree output and profitability, not on the cure rates of its graduates. Medical schools were, in the words of one medical historian, "businesses rather than educational enterprises," and with such primitive overhead costs, the more students, the greater the profits.[2]

Thus in this most deprofessionalized, mercantilized, and unregulated market, virtually anybody armed with the average tuition fee (perhaps a hundred dollars, the equivalent of a few thousand by today's standards) could become an MD and practicing physician after thirty-two weeks (at most) of sitting through lectures. By the 1880s, enough hucksters were offering MDs for little more than the price, and "degree mills" made American medical education internationally notorious. Did anybody within the American medical profession object? With laudable concern for the public (but also for the reputation and incomes of proper doctors), a minority of the latter founded the American Medical Association (AMA) in 1847 and, among other things, began demanding reform of medical education. But these remained voices in the wilderness for decades. In the 1860s, during the American Civil War, when the federal government introduced written examinations for MDs aspiring to serve with the army or navy, only one in four of those who took the relatively modest exam was able to pass. Even a decade after the war, as one of the frustrated reformers with a new and reputable med school, president James Angell of the University of Michigan lamented, "The present state of education in the [medical] profession is as disgraceful to the practitioners as it is dangerous to the patients."[3] His Harvard colleague, president Charles Eliot, went even further a few years later, claiming that "an American physician may be, and often is, a coarse and uncultivated person, devoid of intellectual interests outside of his calling, and quite unable to either speak or write his mother tongue with accuracy."[4] When Eliot had been a student earlier at Harvard, the MD was awarded to candidates who could pass ten-minute oral exams in five of nine principal subjects. Tellingly, both Eliot and Angell had spent a couple of years studying in France and Germany.

The situation in England in the mid-nineteenth century was presumably not much better. As the English scientist Thomas Henry Huxley ("Darwin's bulldog") recalled his own medical training, "It was possible for a young man to come to London and to spend two years and six months of the time of his compulsory three years 'walking the hospitals' in idleness or worse; he could then by putting himself in the hands of a judicious 'grinder' for the remaining six months, pass triumphantly through the ordeal of one hour's *viva voce* examination, . . . all that was absolutely necessary . . . to be turned loose upon the public, like Death on the pale horse . . . as a 'qualified practitioner.'"[5] Huxley, like most others involved, approved of the 1858 Medical Act and the creation of a General Medical Council (GMC) to supervise medical licensing. But the act was a compromise, and it by no means made medical training and licensure uniform or guaranteed a minimum standard of practice. It conferred examining and licensing privileges to the ancient Royal College of Physicians (the RCP dated back to the early sixteenth century), as well as to newer entities such as the Society of Apothecaries (since 1815). The act in effect allowed the RCP—originally a tiny band of London-based physicians—and a few other medical corporations to examine and license practitioners and place their names on a medical register, but it did not grant them monopoly status. In effect, and in accordance with contemporary liberal free trade ideology, it also allowed unlicensed practitioners to continue working, even if under greater constraints. But the advantage to the RCP and similar corporate members was that they had from the start been associated with the London-centered crown, court, and aristocracy, giving them a social cachet that the typical provincial general practitioner or bleeder lacked. As Huxley's comments underlined, licensed or not, English physicians, surgeons, and apothecaries did not yet as a group have much more leverage as therapeutically effective practitioners than unexamined or unlicensed practitioners.[6]

Literary conventions bear out the skepticism of the public about therapeutic efficacy. From ancient Roman through modern European plays and novels, the doctor was depicted as "a comic type, one of a variety of professional men [which includes lawyers, clerics, and academicians] in the argument of comedy against pedantry, . . . one of a number of larger groups of pretentious characters. . . . It was not until well into the nineteenth century that the medical doctor became a hero in dramatic literature."[7] And even at the start of the next century, granting British physicians at least honest belief in their therapies based on the latest scientific discoveries, Shaw, as already mentioned, could still lampoon their inability to agree on diagnosis and treatment.[8] The absurdities of medical mistakes, superstitions, pretentions, guesswork, and arrogance have even been wittily updated by the British physician and writer Richard Gordon, a useful antidote to the temptation to apply the mentality of Whig history to the healing professions.[9]

A half century later, amid galloping improvements in medical science as well as the success of foreign (e.g., German) medical insurance plans for the masses, Britain passed the National Health Insurance Act (1912). It offered virtually free medical care to low-income workers who signed up for it. Most did, joining a local panel of health providers and choosing among them for their personal care. The physicians were reimbursed by a per-head (capitation) fee from a central fund or by a salary if they worked as a hospital consultant. As effective state employees, the caregivers had to be licensed by the General Medical Council as a part of the 1858 Medical Act, so that the participating doctors wound up, despite initial doubts, with the offer of free services to patients, "a powerful competitive device [for doctors] within the open market."[10] The expansion of government-supervised medical care under the National Health Service Act (1946) via the National Health Service (since 1948) covered hospitalization and dependents—in effect, the entire British population—through taxation and simplified the patchwork of fee-for-service, government-insured, municipal, eleemosynary, and voluntary services. Although it never attracted 100 percent of the population (tiny percentages preferred to pay fashionable doctors out of their own resources), the NHS cemented the licensed physicians' monopoly over medical services. One price the doctors paid was recurring dissatisfaction with the economic rewards offered (steady if low, compared to American colleagues). Indeed, the British Medical Association has been recognized since 1971 as the official bargaining agent for doctors' pay and working conditions—in effect, as a professional labor union. Objectively, their efforts appear to be fairly successful, since physicians' incomes in the United Kingdom average higher than all other European countries, if only about two-thirds of American averages.[11]

It must be mentioned in this context that, unlike the United States, medical and other forms of higher education in the United Kingdom, as elsewhere in Europe, have until recently been accessible without the heavy burden of tuition costs, loans, and student debt that Americans have had to bear. English universities began charging significant tuition fees from 1998 on. There are still a few European Union countries that charge no or very low fees, for example, Finland. Most now charge very low fees for students from the Union and usually for those from the European Economic Area (Iceland, Liechtenstein, and Norway) plus Switzerland. Students from other countries usually wind up paying higher fees, but even the highest do not compare with the top fees of American universities (hovering around $40,000 per year). Not counting postgraduate residency training, many European Union students are able to obtain an MD degree only six years after completing the equivalent of a *Gymnasium* or *lycée* secondary education, compared to eight years in the United States. Considering that the debt load on European (and many other non-American) medical graduates is incomparably lighter, the lower incomes of practitioners in Europe (and also the lower costs of medical care) have at least something to do with the continued public financing of most higher education there.

Even if the AMA's reform goals—to restrict medical practice by raising the standards of certified knowledge and licenses—had been realized before the early twentieth century, originally it did not entail such a radical departure from the status quo. Stronger admission standards, extending the course of instruction, and serious doctoral exams were among the reforms demanded, but the changes would have been so modest that significant numbers of existing medical schools already met them. In the decades of ineffectual floundering during most of the second half of the nineteenth century, the AMA attempted to convince the public that doctors who did not belong to it therefore were suspected of not endorsing its ethical code and therefore were unethical.[12] It would take nearly a half century after its founding before the AMA began agitating for major qualitative, rather than mere quantitative, changes in medical training. In the end, the public acceptance of an MD degree—from even the most threadbare proprietary medical school run at night at the local pharmacy—as a badge of competence ran against the aspiration of AMA members to monopolize the right to provide service for fee (and even the growing promise of therapeutic success) to an expanding and affluent middle class.

It may well be that the reforms advocated by the AMA and others would have made little difference to the health of the American people at the time. Given the sorry state of primary and secondary education in the country, requiring high school diplomas themselves would not have guaranteed much more than literacy in a few classics and certainly not a firm grounding in science. Lengthening the course of lectures in traditional fields such as anatomy, physiology, pharmacy, chemistry, internal medicine, surgery, and obstetrics/gynecology—all usually taught exclusively by lecture and textbook, almost never with lab work or clinical experience of patients—would, many critics sensibly objected, merely add to the load of impractical memorized baggage. Nor would more stringent testing of the aspiring physicians' memory of this baggage enable them to treat patients with any greater success. The sad fact remained: medicine as taught and practiced in America was largely therapeutically ineffective. Molière's quip, "Nearly all men die of their medicines, not of their diseases," remained as true in 1860 as two centuries earlier.[13]

This is not to deny that some beginning efforts in preventive medicine, notably in areas of public sanitation and vaccination, began to cut death rates from epidemic diseases, nor to deny that occasional skilled physicians (including increasing numbers with postdoctoral training in Europe) might affect the chances of a patient, once ill, to recover. But otherwise it is hardly exaggerated to say that the majority of Americans who had little or no contact with doctors probably stood as good a chance of overcoming an illness as those treated by MDs. Even if the diagnosis might be right, it was rarely because of the accuracy of the theories memorized in medical schools. Standard cures such as bleeding and purging did more harm than good; many standard medicines were dangerously toxic (like mercury) or addictive (like the opiate laudanum); and surgery was uncommon because (before safe anesthetics) it was too painful and (even after ether but before Lister's antisepsis) still dangerously likely to lead to complicating, often deadly infections.

Insofar as physicians denounced each other, as they often vehemently did, it was not for killing off patients so much as for applying the wrong sectarian theory (all of them equal nonsense from today's viewpoint). Some that flourished (and have even survived into marginal respectability by adopting elements of scientific training) include osteopathy, naturopathy, homeopathy, and chiropractic, but there were many more. Like religious sects, they began with sets of statements not subject to empirical proof but susceptible to dogmatization and notably at variance with accepted mainstream belief (in the medical case, with allopathic medicine). The proprietary schools especially liked sectarian labels, which enabled them to denounce rivals as heretical and advertise their own supposed superiority. Except for the high degree of mumbo jumbo, this form of negative advertising did not differ much from today's political campaign attack ads, but, similarly, appears to have been somewhat effective in attracting suckers.

In short, the approach to medical education by proprietary medical schools was recognizably similar to the age-old apprentice system but lacking the benefit of the standards sometimes enforced by medieval guilds. Even as late as 1900, the reputation of many American medical schools lingered in Europe as degree mills, some dispensing with lecture attendance altogether.

You paid the tuition; you got the certificate. Even legitimate ones accepted most students without high school diplomas, put them through a few months of formal lectures, and unleashed them on the free market. Some of the better-educated MDs—for example, those who organized the AMA—tried to fight this system, but their efforts remained remarkably ineffective for most of the nineteenth century.

Some private and new state or land grant universities did include medical schools, but the teaching also tended to rely on lectures and demonstrations by part-time local physician-professors. Even at the best university medical schools, students rarely spent significant time in the laboratory or at the bedside. They observed dissections rather than conducting them themselves.

Criticism of the state of medical professionalization in America did not have to wait for the Flexner Report, to be sure. To revert to our Texas example: after Galveston Medical College's faculty resigned en masse to protest the poor administration of their typical proprietary school—inept, underequipped, hasty—and a subsequent Texas Medical College took its place for a few years, it lasted only until the teachers had the chance to yield to the newly established University of Texas Medical Branch (UTMB). The problem with instituting the new model of medical education that doctors well before Flexner's report were advocating was *money*, for—as European experience already showed—setting up a modern, scientifically oriented medical faculty was the most expensive item by far in a university budget. Texas also did not wait for Flexner to reverse decades of weak licensing and professional enforcement. In the 1870s the state became the very first in the union to create a state board of medical licensing under the nominal control of medical societies. But it (like many established in the 1880s and 1890s) remained a feeble and under-organized restrictor of practice, since it basically allowed doctors to register licenses accorded by local medical societies or by virtue of their medical college diplomas. As long as, say, MD degrees could, in effect, be purchased cheaply and easily at the burgeoning number of local proprietary medical schools, medical licensing remained no warranty of the quality of the practitioner's skills.[14] Recognizing this, the Texas legislature in 1901 greatly beefed up the nation's first such board (whose 1876 powers many regular physicians deemed insufficient to deny licenses to irregulars like chiropractors) as a State Board of Medical Examiners. It stated that "no member shall be a professor or teacher in any medical school," so licensing decisions were removed from faculty members, killing off their only advantage for med students.[15] In 1907 the legislature required candidates for licenses to attend medical schools offering a total of 4,000 instruction hours during four years of college. The schools would also have to offer laboratory experience. Admissions would no longer be administered by the medical faculty but by a central university admissions office with uniform standards. It was, after all, around this time that European and especially

German medical school professors were developing "miracle" treatments and diagnostic tools in the laboratory (vaccines for anthrax and tuberculosis by Robert Koch; rabies vaccine by Louis Pasteur; tetanus and diphtheria vaccines by Emil von Behring; X-rays by Wilhelm Conrad Röntgen; aspirin by Felix Hoffman; blood typing by Karl Landsteiner; a cure for syphilis by Paul Ehrlich; etc.).

The generally sorry state of preparation for the profession so alarmed the AMA's new Council on Medical Education that it asked the Carnegie Foundation for the Advancement of Teaching, established by Scottish-born steel tycoon Andrew Carnegie in 1905, to investigate the extent of the problem and recommend remedies. Like other self-made robber barons of his generation, Andrew Carnegie climbed to the top of the capitalist heap—becoming the second-richest man in the world, bested only by John D. Rockefeller—without the help of higher education. But unlike many of his peers, he believed that it was key to the country's future and that it should be both of high quality and accessible. The mission of the Carnegie Foundation for the Advancement of Teaching was to improve and support teaching at all levels but especially in higher education.

Andrew Carnegie himself may have been the second-richest man in the world, but he was personally erratic in his philanthropy. For example, when he visited Princeton and looked around, he decided what the university needed was a "loch" so the rowing crew could practice. As the college president of the time, one Woodrow Wilson, remarked, "We asked you for bread and you gave us cake." Carnegie was eventually persuaded to delegate many decisions about how to identify priority needs and funnel resources into their fulfillment by hiring a staff of trusted administrators, of which Flexner was the chieftain for medical education issues. It was these kinds of administrators, often virtually acting alone but with documented research, who made such innovations as the founding of TIAA-CREF, to provide secure retirement for educators, and the Educational Testing Service, which standardized admission tests for colleges and universities, via the Scholastic Aptitude Test (SAT) and, for graduate and professional schools, the Graduate Record Exam (GRE), the Law School Admission Test (LSAT), and its medical school equivalent, the MCAT. The Carnegie Foundation set out to examine the chaos of American institutions calling themselves colleges and universities, which ranged at the time from not much more than bad high schools and professional degree mills to centers of scholarship and research poised to become some of the world's best.

The experienced reformer retained for examining the "chaos" of medical education by the Carnegie Foundation was Abraham Flexner, a successful secondary school founder and reformer. Flexner had been a teacher at Louisville Male School, then founder of his own successful Ivy League–oriented college-prep school. Although lacking an MD, his expertise in school reform seemed to qualify him to study existing medical schools, to identify those doing a good job, and to make recommendations for overhauling—or in many cases closing—the rest. The son of Jewish immigrants, Flexner was born in Louisville in 1866. He had indirect knowledge of the medical profession from his physician brother, Simon. By the first decade of the twentieth century, Simon had become a friend of oil baron John D. Rockefeller and was appointed the first director of the new Rockefeller Institute for Medical Research in 1901. Both brothers had studied at the new-model Johns Hopkins University, which was in the process of revolutionizing American higher education. Abraham had also been deeply influenced by his graduate school professor at Harvard, Hugo Münsterberg, who was from Germany, and had followed his recommendation to study in Berlin. Flexner returned to the States convinced that the German university system was the world's best model for higher education.

When the AMA's new (1904) Council on Medical Education (CME) asked the Carnegie Foundation to study the deficiencies of American medical education, Flexner, although no MD, was recommended by his older brother Simon at New York's Rockefeller Institute for Medical Research. William Welch, the pioneering professor of medicine at Hopkins where both Flexner brothers had studied, was an influential board member of the institute and seconded the choice of Abraham.

Published in 1910, the Flexner Report set rigorous standards that largely followed the German model and have guided medical education to this day: among them, a high school diploma plus at least two years of undergraduate university study (then required by only sixteen of 155 medical schools), a further four years of medical study in a scientific (university-affiliated) environment, under full-time faculty rather than moonlighting private practitioners, and *active* clinical experience in hospital settings. His criticism condemned interminable lectures and recitations by local MDs moonlighting as part-time instructors, followed by weary evenings of textbook reading. Students either had little or no access to hospitals and even when they did, observed rather than interacted with patients themselves.

In Flexner's view, as well as that of the AMA's Council on Medical Education, a gullible public was unable to differentiate between good physicians and the host of badly trained quacks from degree mills. The reforms demanded a radical cut in the "overproduction" of MDs. Designed to protect the public, this move would, as a handy coincidence, also reduce competition for fee for service, thus raising doctors' incomes. (Overproduction of MDs was a worldwide worry by 1910.) Thus, in following the guidelines of the CME, as well as Abraham Flexner's even more stringent standards, American medicine would arguably be raised on at least five of the eight criteria of a profession mentioned earlier: highly specialized and advanced education, rigorous tests of competence, a spirit of altruism and public service, high social prestige and income, and market monopolization. And remember, much of what was meant by "medical ethics" in the nineteenth century pertained to suppressing "bad" medicine by competitors outside the profession, rather than criticizing fellow members of the profession for failure to put patient well-being above their own pecuniary interests.[16]

Hitting the scene at the height of the Progressive Era, the Flexner Report received widespread public discussion and generated considerable political pressure. The result was dramatic. For example, whereas only sixteen of the country's 155 medical schools required at least two years of college for admission in 1910, more than 90 percent of the surviving ones did by 1920. As much as 40 percent of proprietary medical schools closed, merged, or affiliated with universities as a result of Flexner's harsh criticisms.

Even medical departments at major universities suffered Flexner's lashing. In Louisiana, only Tulane was deemed worthy, in Texas, only the University of Texas Medical Department (now UTMB). (Significantly, both were located in swampy port cities—New Orleans and Galveston—affording ample opportunities to study tropical maladies and other infectious diseases.) Arkansas, Alabama, Colorado, and Mississippi lacked a single institution that passed Flexner's muster. Furthermore, despite their scale, age, funding, and size, the premier medical schools in cities like New York, Philadelphia, Boston, and Ann Arbor had significant demerits. And in terms of medical education, woe betide Chicago, "the plague spot of the country." Only the University of Chicago's Rush School of Medicine escaped unscourged by Flexner.

On the positive side, Flexner's highest marks went to Johns Hopkins School of Medicine, a division of his own alma mater. Thanks to a bequest from the eponymous Baltimore and Ohio Railroad magnate, a Quaker bachelor, that established Johns Hopkins University in Baltimore in 1876 and the generosity and civic zeal of Baltimore and Ohio Railroad heiress Mary E. Garrett, internist William Osler, pathologist William Henry Welch, surgeon William Stewart Halstead, and gynecologist Howard Atwood Kelly founded the Johns Hopkins School of Medicine in Baltimore in 1893. Their contribution was recognized in 1906 by John Singer Sargent, the foremost portrait painter of his generation, who had painted Mary Garrett two years earlier. Sargent depicted *The Four Doctors* in full academic regalia, posed in front of a large globe turned to North America, visual testimony that their collective achievement had put American medical education on the map.

Johns Hopkins balanced formal lectures with hands-on work dissecting cadavers and conducting experiments in laboratories. Osler himself noted: "To study the phenomena of disease without books is to sail an uncharted sea, while to study books without patients is not to go to sea at all."[17]

Of all the medical schools in the United States, Johns Hopkins most closely approached Flexner's German model: a bachelor's degree required for admission, a four-year course of study in basic and then clinical sciences, full-time professors in charge of laboratory and clinical departments, superbly equipped laboratories, a top-notch hospital controlled by the medical school, and—as introduced by Osler—clerkships (later called "internships"). And it had one additional qualification: ample financing.

Money talked elsewhere, too. One of the reasons that Abraham Flexner's report had such an impact was that in 1912 Flexner himself went to work for the Rockefeller Foundation, putting him in a position to channel huge amounts of grant money to schools that reformed medical education his way.

Since Johns Hopkins, UTMB, and a forward-thinking minority of other medical schools had been tending toward ever-higher academic standards for two decades, the Flexner Report failed to change them much. But the shutting down of small proprietary schools, the sharply elevated stringency of entrance requirements, the reduction of the number of physicians per capita, and the increased control of doctors over medical care resulted in higher incomes and greater prestige for licensed physicians. So did the medicalization of illness and even pregnancy. Instead of dosing their children with home remedies when they had a cold, parents began phoning the doctor (who still made house calls). Rather than seeing pregnancy as a natural process, handled well by humans since their simian ancestors climbed down out of the trees and relying on midwives for everything except the most complicated deliveries, women rushed to obstetrical specialists at their first missed period.

All of this was not without serious social costs. It became much harder for people of limited economic means—women, immigrants, and people of color—to attend medical school. (Nursing was an almost completely female occupation and not yet as fully professionalized as doctoring or pharmacy.) Motivated by early Victorian prudery (he didn't like the idea of male physicians assisting women in childbirth) as much as by feminism, Samuel Gregory opened Boston Female Medical College in 1848. Although he held a degree in English from Yale, his formal medical training consisted of a summer course in anatomy and physiology. In short, his was a proprietary school producing midwives. In 1850, a consortium of Quaker businessmen and clergy founded the Women's Medical College of Pennsylvania, which after several iterations became part of Drexel University. English immigrant Elizabeth Blackwell, the first American woman to earn a medical degree (conferred by Geneva Medical College in upstate New York), established the Women's Medical College of the New York Infirmary in 1868. African American Howard University College of Medicine (founded 1868) and Meharry (1876) survived scrutiny by Flexner and continue to be respected to this day. These and other historically black institutions educated 85 percent of African American physicians until the mid-twentieth century, when predominately white medical schools dropped discriminatory admission policies, either voluntarily or by court order.

Flexner himself was in favor of training women, and for that matter, minorities, to become physicians, but he was against underfunded schools that could not provide them with a first-class education, and American social mores were not yet wholly prepared for medical coeducation and ethnic integration. As a 2011 work on modern professions puts it, "The professionalization of medicine was founded on a hierarchization of gender produced by excluding women from the care roles which they had performed until the eighteenth century, their appropriation by doctors, and the restriction of midwives and nurses to secondary roles."[18]

Criticisms of Flexner have included the fact that his decisions in distributing an immense amount of Carnegie and Rockefeller money to various educational enterprises—some $600 million in the harder dollars of then, worth perhaps $12 billion in today's money—were made almost entirely by him with little peer review. His largesse also brought about consequences that he surely never intended. The rise of federal and state funding of medical education and medical care since the 1940s shifted the focus away from private philanthropy. After half a century of increasing dependence on public money, health sciences universities, the poor and the very ill, and physicians themselves have found themselves faced with the current national mood against adequate public sacrifice for education and social welfare.

The immense wealth thrown off by new philanthropists will not pick up the slack. Take the Bill and Melinda Gates Foundation, which counts among its major goals the eradication of malaria. Laudable though this may be, the foundation has tossed so much money (by some guesses, more than $15 *billion* since 1994, but certainly $3.5 billion alone in 2010–2011)[19] to its Global Health Initiative that it is virtually impossible to find disinterested experts to provide independent peer review. Almost anyone competent to pass judgment has received support from a Gates Foundation grant.

Abraham Flexner's background and training made him a true believer in the independence, altruism, and general potential for improvement of society if only professionals (like himself) called the tune, and especially if American medicine was professionalized. Despite his good acquaintance with Europe (his last major book, still worth reading, was a 1930 comparison among American and European universities), he missed the significance of a shift toward bureaucratization and state control on the continent. This trend eventually came home to the United States and bedevils the professional lives of medical practitioners here, not just in Europe, today.

Chapter Eleven

High Tech, Low Touch?

The revolution in medical education launched by the turn of the twentieth century was brought about by rapid scientific and technological advances and social change. Suddenly, thanks to the breakthroughs rewarded with Nobel Prizes already starting in 1900, further progress in such areas as antibiotics, safer anesthetics, statins, insulin, chemotherapy agents, the artificial heart, and scores of other new drugs and devices, physicians could be taught to cure diseases rather than just to treat the symptoms. As a consequence, the volume of biomedical science that students had to master increased every year, and the faith their professors placed in medical technology got transmitted clearly, often at the cost of teaching the interpersonal healing arts.

Meanwhile, social change and increasing cultural diversity opened the doors of medical schools, first grudgingly (less so during wartime) and then as a matter of course, to women and minorities. Even otherwise scientifically progressive reformers such as Flexner, as we have seen, proved ambivalent about expanding opportunities for the latter two groups. The new American medical elite of the interwar years and beyond would be better trained, better organized, better remunerated, and more therapeutically effective than its predecessors. But it would also be more male or at least hierarchically dominated by Caucasian males.

On the other hand, the expansion of the circle of social inclusion in medical care, direct or indirect, constituted one of the greatest shifts in the conditions of life in many centuries, especially for the poor and minorities previously all but excluded from physicians' care. Among other techniques, the combination of vastly expanded pathological knowledge through dissection and autopsy with laboratory examination resulted in the discovery of means of detection, diagnosis, cure, and prevention of some of the great perennial killer diseases and epidemic illnesses. A focus on public hygiene and simple preventive measures from vaccines to sterilization enabled scientific medical discoveries from the late nineteenth century on to save millions of lives, especially among the densely packed poor of burgeoning cities.

The faith of so many reformers we have mentioned, for example, Flexner and university presidents Eliot and Angell, in European and especially German science and medicine pointed inexorably to an emphasis on laboratory work and its attitudinal concomitant, "objectivity." As hospitals became safer and likelier places to recover than to die, as much treatment for serious illness moved out of the home into clinical institutions, the physician rose in power and authority. "The doctor knows best" might be called the most apt motto of the medical profession, underlining the widening gap between the professional armed with knowledge, tools, and remedies and a lay public as yet little exposed to advanced education or information. Patients nowadays hooked up to monitors and other devices might go for days without speaking to an attending physician or seeing her only amid a mob of medical students and residents more interested in readouts from the monitors than in looking at the patient. The depersonalization of medical care has become again recently a major concern to parts of the medical profession.

And yet skepticism about overdependence on the benefits of science- and technology-based medical education was present even among some of the most illustrious advocates of reform a generation before Flexner. An outstanding example of advocating for patient-based medical care even before the scientific basis for it was being adopted can be found in Sir William Osler. As noted above, Osler helped found the Johns Hopkins medical school in the early 1890s before moving on to Oxford for the rest of his career until 1919.

It is useful to compare Osler's medical school with one on the about-to-close American frontier (Turner) in the 1890s. Arguably the most successful model of a modern American medical school may be said to be Johns Hopkins in Baltimore, which with its affiliated hospital dates from almost exactly the same time as the University of Texas Medical Department (later University of Texas Medical Branch [UTMB]) in Galveston. Interestingly, the two cities had other things in common: both were important ports and then railheads, adjoining what can be described as the largest and second-largest bays in the United States. (San Francisco Bay proper is smaller, unless one counts sub-bays like San Pablo). In the pre-automobile pre-road transit era, port-and-railhead cities like Baltimore and Galveston, as well as older sisters like Boston, New York, and Philadelphia and new ones like Chicago, St. Louis, and San Francisco, shared urban characteristics that promoted modern health care, hospitals, and scientific medical teaching. Compared to the landlocked backwoods, they both had great prosperity and wealth, as well as lots of poor people and immigrants (as potential patients), were crossroads for diseases (some of them exotic, from tropical and other zones), and had laboratories of public hygiene, industrial accident and injury treatment, and—by the dawn of the Progressive Era in America—playgrounds for experiments in philanthropy and reform.

Although even Flexner found it a little odd that Texas had established its university medical school in Galveston rather than the inland capital city Austin, such anomalies were not unknown at the time. Territorial New Mexico established its university in 1889 in Albuquerque rather than Santa Fe, the capital, mostly because legislators anticipated more patronage jobs if they located the state prison in Santa Fe (and the state madhouse in Las Vegas), leaving the tiny new university in the smaller town of Albuquerque. California's state university was located in Berkeley but its medical school in San Francisco, at the time the main urban center. And decisive in Galveston's case was the willingness of a local family to donate the money to build a modern teaching hospital, John Sealy, without which a medical school was no longer considered complete. The same was true of Baltimore and Hopkins. Even the oldest seats of learning in the United States, such as Harvard, Yale, Columbia, and Penn—all located in port cities linked by rail to the interior—might have had some sort of medical faculties and hospitals before, but they had to struggle to modernize and keep up.

Thus the combination of creating a viable state university and the local initiative of what at the time could be called the most up-to-date city in Texas brought into being a hospital, a school of medicine, and one of nursing incorporated in 1896 into the University of Texas system (incidentally as the first university-affiliated nursing school in the United States), all tending toward the introduction of laboratory science, with most of the senior instructors being full-time professors and researchers rather than local doctors (as in the still-extant proprietary medical schools elsewhere in Texas and the rest of the country).

These new and ambitious medical faculties, integrated with (rather than being merely loosely associated with) new or reformed universities, typically hired their full-time leading professors from as far away as other countries rather than recruiting among whatever local MDs were at hand. Typically, these new professors had spent some time doing postgraduate training in Europe and had considerable experience in laboratory work. William Osler, for example, had trained after an MD degree at McGill in Montreal by studying for two years in Berlin, Vienna, and London. William Keiller, the founder of UTMB's anatomical collection, had trained in Edinburgh and Glasgow before being recruited to Texas. Abraham Flexner's brother Simon was a rare exception in this generation (born in a fifteen-year span roughly ending with the termination of the American Civil War) *not* to have done postgraduate work abroad, but by the time he finished medical school, he was at Hopkins doing original research under another of the founding professors and colleagues of Osler, William Henry Welch (who had done postgraduate studies in Germany). All these men were deeply interested in anatomy and pathology (Osler did thousands of autopsies for scientific reasons, Welch taught it as a field, and Keiller introduced formaldehyde to preserve cadavers used for dissection). Welch helped promote his student and young colleague Simon Flexner to run the first eminent medical research laboratory in the country, the Rockefeller Institute.

All of these professors made significant contributions to medical education. Osler is generally credited with imitating and spreading as a worldwide phenomenon the clinical clerkship, with third- and fourth-year students not only observing patients in ward settings, but being taught there rather than in lecture halls and having increased responsibilities for record keeping, diagnosis, and other duties previously left to attending physicians. Diagnosis, especially of still widespread and deadly epidemic diseases, depended increasingly on quality pathological work and examination, as the Pasteur, Koch, and Virchow institutes in Europe had demonstrated. All of these professors also published and illustrated widely. Osler's *Principles and Practice of Medicine* (1892) was one of the first textbooks not only to incorporate the most recent scientific discoveries, but to update the information in new editions, the last of which was still being published more than a century after the first. Keiller made a similar textbook contribution in neural anatomy; Simon Flexner edited an important journal on experimental medicine that had been founded by Welch. It is worth noting that from this point on, graduated MDs were expected to keep up with new developments by staying abreast of the expanding periodical literature and other means of continuing medical education (now widely abbreviated CME). Although all the reformers mentioned held broadly the same aims and worked generally in the direction of realizing all the previously surveyed attributes of modern professionalism for the medical fields, it would be misleading to think they all agreed completely on priorities. William Osler, for example, still defended bloodletting as a therapy, and he gently questioned the overemphasis on laboratory science and physician authoritarianism as learned from his acquaintance with German academic medicine. Indeed, what distinguished Osler and his followers (especially in North America, where he was born and taught, and Britain, where death ended his career in 1919) was his insistence on humanistic values and close dialogue with patients. This emphasis fit well with the structure of higher education emerging in North America and Britain, which added components of the much-admired German education system rather than copying it entirely. Thus the typical American undergraduate education included a far more varied and humanistically oriented curriculum than that at German universities, where the arts and sciences were assumed already to have been mastered by students by the time they had finished secondary school. While these pedagogical differences may not have been as significant as violent upheavals in politics, economics, and social fragmentation that differed in intensity and violence in the Anglophone and continental European worlds after World War I, they were nevertheless important. The simple difference between a fee-for-service system in North America and Britain versus an almost universal health insurance scheme in Germany implied radically different relationships between physician and patient as well. Both systems made the hospital a place where those who could afford it, and many who could not, would go for more than the purpose of dying in comparative comfort.

But World War I and its disastrous consequences for Europe sent two continents onto differing paths for the professionalization of modern medicine.

Let us glance for a moment at the further evolution of the vaunted German medical system taken as Flexner's primary model. A couple of years after the Flexner Report, German doctors began organizing to confront the financial disadvantages imposed on the profession by the ever-expanding state-mandated system of medical insurance, even striking in 1913. On the whole they were successful, but World War I pulled the rug out from under the German (and many other European) physicians' professionalization project. Revolution, war debt, and chronic financial crises checked progress toward medical professionalization in the sense of raising the profession.

As already noted, one of the main reasons for Germany's excellence before World War I was that strong and fairly enlightened governments were willing to invest heavily in universities, especially medical schools. Yet even in 1910, the year of the Flexner Report, the Prussian government, ruler of two-thirds of the German federal Reich, found itself no longer able to finance the heavy costs of research, including what medical schools were doing. The needs of the arms race took precedence, and medical and scientific discovery suffered in the end. Even the "winners" of World War I were unable to carry on scientific and medical research in the way they had before. The United States, however, was the only World War I combatant that actually profited from the war.

It was no accident that, among all German professional groups, physicians gradually became the most strongly attracted to the siren call of Nazism. Once in power the Nazis eliminated or curtailed the right to study or practice medicine for women, Jews, and political opponents. And of course they gave the world its most horrible lessons in the abuse of medical ethics with extreme, even insane invocations of eugenics, cruel medical experiments on human subjects, and finally the Holocaust. We will look more closely at this in later chapters. In terms of the impact of the depredations caused in the wake of World War I on Germany, the Nazi leaders were extreme "deprofessionalizers," even though they initially promised gains in the opposite direction for professions, including medicine. Instead they brought their national wreckage to many other parts of Europe and its populations, including finally Germany itself by 1945. The expulsion of so many excellent Jewish and liberal medical people and teachers was only a part of the intellectual purge carried out by fascist regimes, and it is interesting that Flexner himself went on to found the Institute for Advanced Study in Princeton, offering a haven to many refugees including Albert Einstein. America's gain was Germany's long-term loss, and one can say without qualification that Germany lost its model character probably forever, just as the United States surged ahead to become what it is today, the world leader in medicine.

Ironically, the prestige and rise in wealth of the American medical profession after the Flexner Report led for the first time to the dominance in medical policies of the American Medical Association (AMA), which had been weak and marginal before the reform of American medical education. But the rise of "scientific" medicine changed that. "A major tenet common to both progressivism and professionalism was the belief that scientific knowledge was the principal domain of experts. Progressives believed that science was too complex for public consumption, that only experts with advanced education and technical training could grasp its features . . . elevating the status of physicians and distinguishing medical work from commercial and business pursuits. Self-regulation was a logical outgrowth of progressive ideas."[1] Because of their advanced knowledge and training, physicians were presumed to be the only ones capable of determining their own technical standards. Its Council on Medical Education (especially from 1904 on) successfully lobbied for raising the educational level (and not accidentally, lowering the number of competing doctors) even before the Flexner Report and foundation funding sped up the process. By 1901, all American states had created licensing bodies that more or less "delegated authority to the medical profession to set standards and to police itself."[2] Although the AMA's national house of delegates foreswore setting fees (one of many ways it was exempt from the Sherman Antitrust Act of 1890 and supervision by the Federal Trade Commission created in 1914), nothing kept regional medical societies from doing so.

From the viewpoint of protecting the professional interests of "scientifically trained" and state-licensed "regular" American physicians, the AMA did a great job and has gone down in history as one of the most successful professional lobbying organizations in the world. In Eliot Freidson's judgment, it raised American medicine to a golden age (1945–1965) when it enjoyed "a historically unprecedented peak of prestige, prosperity and political and cultural influence—perhaps as autonomous as a profession could be."[3] Whether what it lobbied for was in the best interests of the public or even the profession remains a controversial matter, however.

Sustaining the push for pure foods and drugs of the Progressive Era, the AMA established in 1905 a Council on Pharmacy and Chemistry (later called Council on Drugs) that maintained its own testing lab. During the 1920s and

1930s, no drug could be advertised in the *Journal of the American Medical Association* (JAMA) if it did not have the AMA's seal of approval after testing in that lab. The long-term purpose constituted a part of the drive to eliminate quackery from American medicine, but this could deteriorate into questionable practices. By 1955, the AMA, under commercial pressure, discontinued the "seal" and finally quietly disbanded the council in 1972.[4] Once the Progressive Era had passed, physicians had retreated from their initial open attitude about national health insurance, and as the era of Harding/Coolidge "normalcy" began, the AMA largely rested on its laurels of having restricted practice to graduates of the reformed medical schools.

From the mid-1920s until the threshold of the 1950s, the primary guiding light of the organization was an MD who had never practiced, Morris Fishbein. He was editor of the organization's main journal, *JAMA*, until his ouster in 1949. During this time Fishbein managed to derive half the AMA's income from journal advertising, including the use of some practices that would be considered unethical today. Even as far back as the 1930s these resulted in Fishbein and the AMA being hauled into courts under the Sherman Antitrust Act. Fishbein's personal specialty was denigrating rival providers of unorthodox medical care such as chiropractic, but his financing methods came to include selling expensive advertising space to pharmaceutical companies and even cigarette manufacturers. (One may recall here the role of Albert Lasker, already mentioned, in promoting smoking with the implied approval of the medical profession.) AMA members did not have to pay dues, since Fishbein garnered all the revenue needed for lobbying from advertisers. The latter were especially glad of AMA "seals of approval" handed out by Fishbein for medications and products that the AMA no longer bothered to test. The combative Fishbein survived indictments and citations before committees of Congress and, if any single person can be cited for the achievement, led the fight against expanded third-party payers of doctors' fees (including public and initially even private health insurance).

In its 1903, 1912, and 1949 medical ethics statements, the AMA for the first time "attacked what later was called 'contract practice,' in which doctors were salaried to provide unlimited services to all members of a voluntary organization," an attack reinforced in its 1912 *Principles of Ethics*.[5] From then until 1949, the AMA was additionally confronted with health insurance plans from private industry, Blue Cross and Blue Shield, prepaid plans like Kaiser Permanente, and such group practice clinics as the Mayo (Minnesota) and Scott and White (Texas). Indeed, the origins of Blue Cross/Blue Shield go back to a hospital insurance plan concocted for schoolteachers in Dallas by educator Justin F. Kimball in 1929. In 1934, the AMA's Bureau of Medical Economics formulated ten principles meant to head off the creation of health plans:

1. All medical services must be under the control of the medical profession.
2. No third party must be permitted to come between the patient and his physician.
3. Patients must have absolute freedom to choose a legally qualified doctor of medicine.
4. A permanent, confidential relationship existed between the patient and the family physician.
5. All medical phases of all institutions involved in the medical service (e.g., hospitals) should be under physicians' control.
6. The immediate cost of treatment should be borne by the patient.
7. Medical service must have no connection with any cash benefits.
8. Any form of medical service should include all willing, legally qualified doctors of medicine of the locality.
9. Relief of low income classes should be limited strictly.
10. There would be no restrictions on treatment or prescribing not formulated and enforced by the organized medical profession.[6]

These points are worth recalling here if only because they have remained standard demands of opponents of expanded medical insurance and care by non-MDs over the last eight decades—even after the AMA itself yielded on many of them.

The 1949 *Principles of Ethics* attempted to address the growing intervention of such third parties between physicians and patients in such a way as to "create a one-way flow of resources into the profession by covering costs . . . of delivering services."[7] The example of expanding socialized medicine in Europe (e.g., the recently inaugurated National Health Service in Britain) clearly played a role in this tactic. The postwar American government at the same time had tried to introduce a federal universal health insurance program, just as it had attempted and failed to include some such provision in the 1935 Social Security Act. AMA lobbying had been decisive in defeating both. The advent of the Cold War gave further fuel to paint universal health coverage as somehow alien and subversive.

Prefacing the 1949 AMA *Principles of Ethics* statement was a speech to the house of delegates summarizing the organization's official attitude toward "the cancer of socialization," also known as health care reform: "The greatest emergency any of you has confronted in all your years of practice. Not just one life hangs in the balance, but the life of the nation is in your hands."[8] As one might guess, the AMA had hired a public relations firm to write this overblown verbiage so tellingly soaked in McCarthyite paranoid rhetoric.

An anecdote may serve to illustrate how powerful (and often ruthless) the AMA had become by the middle of the twentieth century. Although still relying on *JAMA* cigarette and pharmaceutical advertising for its income, the AMA levied a one-time $25-per-member assessment (about $250 in 2012 dollars) to defeat the "socialized medicine" proposed by the Truman administration. At the time it was the biggest and most expensive lobbying effort in U.S. history.[9] For an example of the kind of demagogic smear tactics these funds produced, one need only refer to the "news story" linking reforming U.S. Senator Claude Pepper to the "communist negro" singer Paul Robeson or the 1950 "redneck speech" by Pepper's successful challenger for his Florida seat, which candidate George Smathers reportedly delivered to a poorly educated audience. The speech turned out to be an exaggeration but was close enough to reality to be believed. As it was reported in *Time* magazine:

> Are you aware that Claude Pepper is known all over Washington as a shameless *extrovert*? Not only that, but this man is reliably reported to practice *nepotism* with his sister-in-law, he has a brother who is a known *homo sapiens*, and he has a sister who was once a *thespian* in wicked New York. Worst of all, it is an established fact that Mr. Pepper, before his marriage, habitually practiced *celibacy*.[10]

The power of the AMA waned by the 1960s when it lost its bid to crush Medicare legislation. Its declining membership (currently about 15 percent of U.S. physicians)[11] may reflect the centrifugal forces of specialty organizations, the decline of individual or small group practices, and many other factors. But even its detractors, who regard it as primarily an economic lobby dedicated to minimizing the number and maximizing the incomes of practitioners, concede that it was probably the most effective in those professionalizing goals of any comparable medical organization of the twentieth century. And it was effective especially in the period when the individual family physician constituted the backbone of the AMA. In this respect it may have met needs paralleling the teachings of William Osler and his followers, with special and individual care to the patient. The sort of mechanical and even industrial processing of patients that increasingly accompanied expanded and technologically driven mass care and approached assembly-line impersonality (if not necessarily efficiency) has made many Oslerians uncomfortable during the last few decades. "Taylorism," or the industrial ideology of manufacturing efficiency appropriate to making Ford Model T's, has finally arrived in the American medical profession.

Whereas the typical encounter between patient and physician in the golden age of doctoring (mid-twentieth century) lasted fifteen to twenty minutes, for example, by the end of the century it had been reduced to six to eight minutes. Not only did physicians previously have more time to get to know the patient individually, but the relationship tended to last many years. More recently, patients (now renamed "clients") are likely to encounter multiple and changing health care providers (including specialists) during their medical lifetime.[12] The availability of computerized medical records, for example, however useful for the patient's welfare, also enlarges the ability of actors outside the doctor-patient relationship to peer into and monitor what transpires within it. The claimed confidentiality of the relationship is likewise called into question. "With the phenomenal growth of corporatized medical care the average physician's administrative, economic and even clinical autonomy has been challenged."[13] Osler had long before anticipated and warned against the depersonalization of care made possible by high-tech testing, monitoring, and specialization: "The good physician treats the disease; the great physician treats the patient who has the disease."

As mentioned earlier, Osler is credited with founding the system of residencies for medical students at Johns Hopkins University in 1889. Ironically, part of the current tensions within the profession in the United States derives from contradictions in the way medical personnel are educated. Since the 1970s, the model type for physician education has come to include the following: First comes a bachelor's degree (with some required basic science courses and, as a rule, high academic achievement). Then follows a four-year stint at medical school (undergraduate medical education or UME), divided roughly into two years of mostly theoretical studies and two more with clinical experience of patient care. After the completion of this course with an MD degree, a physician can theoretically (as in the decades before 1970) go on for a postgraduate year (as an intern) and proceed to be licensed to practice. But in fact very few do this any more and instead the (post)graduate medical education or GME includes at least three years as a resident (the first year sometimes still called internship) treating patients in a clinical or hospital setting. In effect, GME trains MDs in various specialties. The ones requiring the fewest years of residency include family medicine, internal medicine, pediatrics, and ob-gyn. Others such as surgery take many more years of training. Finally, there is subspecialty training for which physicians do fellowships.

The effect of all this training on the energy, finances, and professional ethics of doctors will be examined in greater depth later. At this point, let it suffice to point out a few significant peculiarities of the American system. First, the costs of undergraduate medical education (UME) are borne largely by medical students themselves, the vast majority of whom need financial aid, usually in the form of loans. Currently they emerge with their MD degrees at roughly the age of twenty-six, with years of further training ahead of them and deeply in debt. (In 2013 it averaged \$170,000.)[14] Some of the costs of their education are provided by state or local governments and endowments, but the average contribution of American states toward this amounts to a mere 6 percent. By contrast, "in many European Union countries that achieve better health outcomes than does the United States, medical students pay little or no tuition."[15]

Second, the costs of GME are largely provided by Medicare and Medicaid. It is the insured, aged, and poor who constitute the clientele for hospitals and clinics where the majority of GME goes on. Indeed, rising each year to a new level of diagnostic and therapeutic independence while still kept on grueling schedules and relatively paltry salaries comparable to those of public schoolteachers, the residents are the sine qua non of American medical centers. There is little doubt that American GME is among the best in the world, as evidenced by the large percentage of residents who come for it from abroad and without whom the treatment system would be crippled. But it is also clear that the primary consideration in allocating the residents' time and attention is, less and less often, in response to their need for a structured set of exposures to many different types of illness and treatment and more to the accidental and haphazard supply of patients' sicknesses. In other words, it is not always the medical school and teaching hospital faculty who are free to determine the best balance of training for the upcoming specialists, but the market driven by one or another aspect of the health insurance industry or the hospitals' needs for more revenue.

Third, faculty at most of the country's academic medical centers rely more and more on treating patients (e.g., through "faculty practice plans") to generate revenue for the center or university than ever before—an average of one-third of total medical school revenue in seventy-six public ones and 42 percent in the remaining fifty private ones (2009). To relativize these huge contributions of faculty to nonteaching activities, appropriations from government are miniscule (less than 1 percent from the federal government, the same to private medical schools from the same source, and a mere 12 percent to so-called state-supported ones). So are income from tuition and fees (less than 4 percent), endowment (1 to 3 percent), and even more than the second-largest source, grants and contracts (e.g., for research).[16] This explains the medical professors' quip, "I'm not paid to teach." The obvious danger is that, in making medical schools and the nearly 130 surrounding academic medical centers (including faculty practice plans and owned or affiliated hospitals) into "profit centers," quality teaching may suffer. Although Flexner's demand that medical schools be staffed by full-time faculty is still technically met, in some ways, the present situation represents a slippage back into the pre-reform era of proprietary medical schools. Then, local practicing physicians, in their spare time after treating patients, looked after the education of their successors. This growing aberration is largely the result of the unique, historically patched-together American system of financing both medical education and patient care since the arrival of Medicare in 1965.

By contrast, before Medicare, "medical schools were small organizations with few faculty members; clinical practice revenues accounted for less than 3 percent of total school revenues."[17]

This radical and rapid transformation in the size and function of medical school faculties cannot fail to have an impact on the shape of the future medical profession as a whole. How this may look will be taken up again in subsequent chapters. It has become a cause for concern about the distortion of the "formation of professional values." Given also the reallocation of resources from public (taxpayer) funding to other, quite large sources of support such as faculty patient care and research grants, one must also consider the impact on the entire American higher education system. The vast majority of medical schools are parts of universities. Insofar as the latter still respect the faculty's rights to determine curricular matters and participate in the governance of the institution, the sheer number of colleagues with MD degrees can threaten an overweening influence by the latter on broad matters of curriculum, governance, and mission of the whole university. Only a few decades ago, the largest collection of professors at most universities was to be found in the arts and sciences, and they tended to promote thorough grounding in the humanities and social and natural sciences. It is of course not certain that the professors in medical schools, faced with conflicting demands between profit-oriented patient care and teaching or mentoring medical students and residents, will necessarily opt for high-tech and low-touch initiatives. But insofar as any of them do, they will have resounding backing from representatives of newly organized economic, political, and social special interests who regard STEM (science, technology, engineering, and mathematics) programs as the most deserving candidates when universities must make painful decisions about allocating or begging for resources.

How such lopsided "university reforms" will affect what are widely perceived as threats to the humanitarian aspects of medicine will be taken up in part III. It suffices to note here that a growing tendency to apply business models and a corresponding management style to most institutions of higher education, especially in the United States and Britain, constitutes a worrisome threat to the professions involved in teaching and research there. Just as many teaching members of the medical profession complain about the forced commercialization of their professional activities, their fellow professors in other disciplines complain of the growing reduction of autonomy, security, and reward structures that formerly made their occupations also "learned professions." A management style that declares them to be mere employees like interchangeable cogs in a corporate machine but at the same time denies them the right of collective bargaining is already launched down a path that may destroy the very modern university system that all proclaim to be one of the greatest achievements of the twentieth century.

III

Medical Ethics

The first two parts of this book took us on a rapid tour through the centuries when a few, but by no means all, of the characteristics of a "medical profession"—as now defined—emerged. We sped from the classical Greco-Roman innovations of scholarly observation (departing from purely religious approaches to illness), exemplified by Hippocrates and his successors, through the founding of special clinics like the one at Pergamon (Galen), through the poorly documented dimness of the early Middle Ages, the advent of hospitals and university medical schools, and the accelerating tendency since the Renaissance to augment and eventually substitute scientific method for the fanciful but orthodox notions of illness represented by the theory of humors. The second section then picked up from the transformation of medical study and practice in Britain, France, and Germany by 1900, around which time the German model arrived in the United States in such varied forms as Johns Hopkins and the University of Texas Medical Branch. The scathing 1910 report on the old-model proprietary medical schools across the country by Abraham Flexner effectively put these schools out of business or forced them to upgrade into university-level faculties of medicine. By the 1920s we had reached a point where one could begin to see the characteristics of a modern medical profession emerging in a systematic way. As the American medical profession became more scientific, therapeutically effective, and prestigious, its social and economic stature as well as its increasing interdependence with high technology and the introduction of quasi-industrial models of organization and treatment techniques made medicine overall a profession increasingly alienated from its patients. What defines a health professional has increasingly come to revolve around questions of proper behavior—of ethics.

A central concern at many of today's medical schools is to reinforce the wider humanitarian aspects of medicine—such characteristics as professional ethics, altruism, and well-grounded judgment based on values beyond the parameters of science and technique. Aside from being elements of best practice as taught by Osler and others, maintaining such values is essential to justifying genuine professional autonomy. Let us dwell in this section on professional ethics only. This is, of course, not an easy topic. The bewildering intricacies of contemporary medical ethics issues require the insights from many learned professions, from the humanities and social sciences to the law and even the fine arts. The narrower range that we are able to explore here can merely consider how medical ethics adapted to social, economic, and cultural environments through history. To take just one illustrative example: how do societies as superficially similar as the United States and many in Europe differ in approaching patient rights? A major difference lies in the obvious litigiousness of the United States, where accusations of ethical violations can easily be transformed into lawsuits. Different societies do—and have in the past—put on offer different ethical solutions to conflicts and doubts. And just as three of the learned professions, theology, law, and medicine, evolved as separate university faculties, each one evolved its own set of ethical mandates. All three, incidentally, needed such requirements if for no other reason than that each dealt with highly charged existential issues—the well-being of the eternal soul, of liberty and property, and of life and death.

Chapter Twelve

A Sacred Trust

Roots of Medical Ethics

Of the eight qualities we have cited that define a professional, two fall under the rubric of ethics: a special code of personal conduct and a spirit of altruism and public service. For physicians these trace their ancient roots to three concepts. Historians of medical ethics (*Ηθική*) often refer to two or three types of behavior for healers: those derived from decorum, from deontology, and (maybe) community-shaped ("politic") ethics.

The first, decorum, is not limited to good manners but encompasses as well habits of behavior thought to reflect the moral integrity of the personality—courage, constancy, respect for others, but also punctuality and politeness. These are widely shared among many learned professions and can, of course, be taught as well as faked. As a reminder of decorum, many residues of dress and other markers of office that were more pronounced in earlier ages remain with us, for example, the robes and (in Britain) wigs worn by judges, the caps and gowns worn at academic graduation ceremonies, and of course the white coats of physicians (to be discussed more fully later). Whatever the clothing, it should be clean and its wearer well-groomed, calm, reflective, and reassuring.

The resulting self-assurance has incidentally provided writers and playwrights with endless fodder for drama and comedy, and not only regarding the medical profession. Even some of the best doctor jokes depend on the images of professional decorum. For example: A famous surgeon dies and goes directly to heaven. St. Peter welcomes him and asks him to come back in a couple of days for a regular orientation but tells him that meanwhile he is free to roam around on his own. He is surprised that food service is provided only in a cafeteria. While the food is OK, there is always a line. While standing in it, more than once he notices a tall, older man in a white physician's coat cutting to the head of the line to get his food. Nobody protests, but the surgeon does mention this seemingly unholy behavior to St. Peter when they next get together. "Oh," St. Peter says, "that's not really a doctor. It's actually God. He just *thinks* he's a doctor."

The second concept is deontology—behavior guided by sense of duty (*deon*), for example, the duty to help the sick or the duty to keep promises. Others include the duty to avoid harm (the first duty under the Hippocratic Oath), to improve oneself by keeping up with developments in the field, to refuse to take a life (including assisted suicide and direct involvement in executions) or to perform an abortion, to respect patient privacy, and so on. These rules have tended to be set by members of the profession themselves and promulgated by noted teachers. Of course these duties have not at all times and in all places constituted an unbending set of absolute commandments. And debates about the ethics of abortion or assisted suicide today may remind us of how flexible deontology may have been in the past, as well. Abortion, for example, changed from being a mere sin in public consciousness to being criminalized by canon and civil jurisprudence between the twelfth and sixteenth centuries.[1] Nor is the profession alone in laying down the duties of health care providers: increasingly these are legislated and supervised by public bodies, from legislatures and state bureaucracies to giant corporations. One of the main experts on medical ethics today, Albert Jonsen, also denotes a third kind of ethics, "politic ethics," involving obligations between the professional and the community.[2] For example, should doctors flee or stay when a calamity like plague in the Middle Ages or a hurricane today befalls a region? Is a physician obliged, for example, to treat victims of a highly contagious, deadly disease, such as bubonic plague in the Middle Ages or Ebola in our own time? In essence, this form of medical ethics involves the recognition of physicians' obligations to the community as a whole (or its representative, the state) as a quid pro quo in return for privileging the profession with special status and prestige. While this term may cause more confusion than clarity, it does point to an area of mutual responsibility between the profession and the larger society that has often been missing from discussions in the Anglo-American world. There, more than in continental Europe, the profession has attempted to use the state to bolster its monopoly on medical services without, however, granting the state the right to police and regulate the profession beyond a token level. It is worth bearing in mind, therefore, that continental models of a more balanced set of mutual obligations between community and profession do not necessarily imply "deprofessionalization" as much as they express another dimension of professional ethics.

One can describe a kind of historical arc here. Initially decorum served as an outward sign of inner goodness and reliability. With higher levels of social organization (e.g., urbanization), the ever-increasing rules of deontological ethics in the form of a code, provided either by the profession and its organizations or negotiated with outside civil or economic forces, laid down specific norms of behavior. With even more complex levels of social organization, politic ethics has come to be an evolving gray area subjecting professional behavior to shifting and sometimes contradictory or ambiguous societal expectations.

In the ancient world, the sense of duty for any profession was considered to be imparted from on high by the gods. In medieval and Renaissance Europe, restrictions imposed by the established church, even if not firm points of doctrine, often clashed with what physicians considered their duty to relieve suffering. For example, as late as the mid-nineteenth century, when administration of the newest pain-relieving drugs, ether or chloroform, to mothers in childbirth became possible, controversy arose from religious fundamentalists who insisted that the biblical "curse of Eve" demanded that women "bring forth their children in pain," making such relief unethical or heretical.

The more historians research the history of medical ethics—not exactly a previous beehive of activity—the more they wonder how, whether, and when such ethics were actually invoked and followed. The Hippocratic Oath, for example, which in its modern form, reproduced here, is still administered in American medical schools, is in many respects very different from the original.

> I swear to fulfill, to the best of my ability and judgment, this covenant:
>
> I will respect the hard-won scientific gains of those physicians in whose steps I walk and gladly share such knowledge as is mine with those who are to follow.
>
> I will apply, for the benefit of the sick, all measures [that] are required, avoiding those twin traps of overtreatment and therapeutic nihilism.
>
> I will remember that there is art to medicine as well as science, and that warmth, sympathy, and understanding may outweigh the surgeon's knife or the chemist's drug.
>
> I will not be ashamed to say "I know not," nor will I fail to call in my colleagues when the skills of another are needed for a patient's recovery.
>
> I will respect the privacy of my patients, for their problems are not disclosed to me that the world may know. Most especially must I tread with care in matters of life and death. If it is given to me to save a life, all thanks. But it may also be within my power to take a life; this awesome responsibility must be faced with great humbleness and awareness of my own frailty. Above all, I must not play at God.
>
> I will remember that I do not treat a fever chart, a cancerous growth, but a sick human being, whose illness may affect the person's family and economic stability. My responsibility includes these related problems, if I am to care adequately for the sick.

I will prevent disease whenever I can, for prevention is preferable to cure.

I will remember that I remain a member of society, with special obligations to all my fellow human beings, those sound of mind and body as well as the infirm.

If I do not violate this oath, may I enjoy life and art, respected while I live and remembered with affection thereafter. May I always act so as to preserve the finest traditions of my calling and may I long experience the joy of healing those who seek my help.[3]

The original may have read:

1. (i.) I swear (ii.) by Apollo the Physician and by Asclepius and by Health and Panacea and by all the gods as well as goddesses, making them judges [witnesses], (iii.) to bring the following oath and written covenant to fulfillment, in accordance with my power and my judgment;

2. (i.) to regard him who has taught me this techne as equal to my parents, and (ii.) to share, in partnership, my livelihood with him and to give him a share when he is in need of necessities, and (iii.) to judge the offspring [coming] from him equal to [my] male siblings, and (iv.) to teach them this techne, should they desire to learn [it], without fee and written covenant, and to give a share both of rules and of lectures, and of all the rest of learning, to my sons and to the [sons] of him who has taught me and to the pupils who have both made a written contract and sworn by a medical convention but by no other.

3. (i.) And I will use regimens for the benefit of the ill in accordance with my ability and my judgment, but from [what is] to their harm or injustice I will keep [them].

4. (i.) And I will not give a drug that is deadly to anyone if asked [for it], (ii.) nor will I suggest the way to such a counsel. And likewise I will not give a woman a destructive pessary.

5. (i.) And in a pure and holy way (ii.) I will guard my life and my techne.

6. (i.) I will not cut, and certainly not those suffering from stone, but I will cede [this] to men [who are] practitioners of this activity.

7. (i.) Into as many houses as I may enter, I will go for the benefit of the ill, (ii.) while being far from all voluntary and destructive injustice, especially from sexual acts both upon women's bodies and upon men's, both of the free and of the slaves.

8. (i.) And about whatever I may see or hear in treatment, or even without treatment, in the life of human beings—things that should not ever be blurted out outside—I will remain silent, holding such things to be unutterable [sacred, not to be divulged], (i. a.) If I render this oath fulfilled, and if I do not blur and confound it [making it to no effect] (b.) may it be [granted] to me to enjoy the benefits both of life and of techne, (c.) being held in good repute among all human beings for time eternal. (ii. a.) If, however, I transgress and perjure myself, (b.) the opposite of these.[4]

The original oath's first substantive paragraph makes clear the expectation that healers were more or less apprentices in a family-like setting, probably with their occupation inherited from generation to generation. The original form resembled later guild oaths, particularly for apprentice "adoptees" into the "family." The modern version does not mention such deontological prohibitions as abortion, poisoning (assisted suicide?), or sex with one's patients nor does it set physicians apart from surgeons or, by implication, pharmacists. Scholars have cast doubt on whether Hippocrates actually wrote the version that wound up in his fragmented surviving documents, the degree to which the oath was actually taken or observed, and even the strict meaning of the wording. It seems clear, for example, that therapeutic abortions were widely accepted by physicians, that many "internists" nevertheless did some surgery, and so on. Furthermore, it is doubtful if the ancient world regarded life as beginning with conception. We should keep in mind that there has never been a "golden age" in which deontic codes of medical ethics were universally and equally adhered to—hardly a surprise when we think of today's realities.

If ethics constitute the high end of behavioral codes for professions, the lower end may be said to be related to outward signs of trustworthiness that are, however, closer to codes and conventions. Let us take as an example the white coat that many contemporary medical students put on in special school ceremonies. The symbolism carries on the millennia-old traditions of showing outward cleanliness and purity. But doctors wearing white coats are in fact a relatively recent phenomenon, not much more than a century old. The coats' degree of cleanliness has even been questioned recently by some American doctors who fear they may spread infection.[5] But at the turn of the twentieth century, they were an innovation imported from the scientific laboratory, where American medical students had first worn them, especially in the German universities they were attending. The white lab coat thus was introduced to symbolize and attest to its wearer's familiarity with laboratory sterility practices and, by extension, the application of scientific medicine to the patient. By contrast, physicians and especially surgeons, particularly in the United States, had made a professional badge of honor out of donning an old ordinary waistcoat stained and stiffened by previous patients' blood and bodily fluids. Surgeons often kept such soiled coats at the ready to exchange for their clean street clothes, which they would not think of dirtying. Despite the septic danger to the patient, the custom lasted far longer than the discovery of antiseptic procedures, if only because such early forms of antisepsis as a constant spray of carbolic acid irritated the surgeons' skin a bit. Thus it took a good half century for these procedures to become almost universal in North America—and the white coat replaced the black frock. Antisepsis (the killing of germs on hands and instruments, for example) was much easier to introduce than asepsis (the elimination of virtually all germs from the operating theater). Asepsis came to imply the wearing of additional professional clothing, notably surgical gowns, masks, gloves, and other relatively uncomfortable but effective measures. But one rarely sees doctors in scrubs outside the area (e.g., a hospital and nearby buildings) where they are required. And oddly, patient surveys reveal that they have more confidence in physicians wearing the white coat than those in scrubs or street clothes. The success of the medical profession in linking the white coat to professional competence is, interestingly, also indicated by a condition called "white coat syndrome." This accounts for some patients registering higher than normal blood pressure readings because of heightened anxiety when being treated by medical professionals!

Almost certainly the majority of American physicians during most of the nineteenth century were poorly trained, sometimes barely literate, and mostly helpless in the face of disease. Yet as we have seen, abilities to perform according to other social codes of conduct achieved success in elevating some physicians' social esteem and making them desirable consultants even when they could as yet offer little more than comfort and palliative care. We may recall that the very term "doctor" throughout most of the history of universities denoted familiarity with the classics more than therapeutic effectiveness, and the extra time and money required to get such a degree could be justified chiefly in terms of the higher social circles and fees to which it gave access. A clearer idea of how this worked may be cited in the case of German MD degree holders. As the profession of medicine became more and more based on scientific knowledge *and* certified by increasingly rigorous state licensing exams (beginning in the second half of the nineteenth century), the percentage of German medical students seeking the MD degree dropped even as the number of medical faculty graduates (and licensees) increased. Indeed, the unsuccessful battle of the German medical profession to force candidates for medical faculties to complete the full panoply of pre-university schooling in Latin and Greek demonstrated not the need of the classics for diagnosis so much as the need to brand the future young doctors as "cultivated" and worthy of social equality with other elite groups. The cachet of Latin tags (and perhaps a dueling scar on the face) told potential wealthy German clients that they were dealing with a *gentleman.* The newly medicalized workers getting basic care under Bismarck's medical insurance schemes might turn up at the office of mere licensed physicians (*Ärzte*), but the wealthier classes still generally preferred people with MDs. Once "anybody" could study and become licensed (and "anybody" usually included Jews, other minorities or immigrants, and women), symbolic cultural distinctions (to use the useful term of Pierre Bourdieu) became increasingly important as irrational signs of greater skill and success among members of the profession.

Therefore maintaining and sharpening the outward signs of a gentlemanly lifestyle became an increasingly important unwritten commandment—often, of course, observed in the breach—to dress well, maintain a respectable household (with servants) and family, use a carriage or motorcar, and so on.

All of this required money. Particularly in America during the course of the twentieth century, being a good and successful physician gradually came to be equated with being a prosperous gentleman. "For all the growth in medical education and licensing and the advancement of medical science, the basis on which Victorian medical men built their careers was not primarily that of expertise. Family, friends, connections and new variations on these traditional forms of social relationships and social evaluation were the crux of a man's ability to establish himself in medical practice."[6] In this they followed the example of British doctors in whom the better-off trusted as a gentleman likely to put the patients' well-being ahead of monetary gain like a tradesman. "If [the physician] spoke well, dressed well and behaved like a gentleman, he was judged to be a man worthy of trust. . . . And patients, ignorant, uncaring and without faith in the character of medical licenses, might finally select their medical man on the basis of his beard or his good looks."[7]

Chapter Thirteen

First, Do No Harm

The Introduction of Humanistic Values

A careful inspection of the ancient Hippocratic Oath or for that matter such fine variants on it as Ishaq bin Ali Rahawi's ninth-century *Conduct of a Physician*, the first Arabic book dedicated to medical ethics, reveals not only rules for the interaction of physician and patient, but also among fellow professionals. Rahawi advised not to criticize one's colleagues or other prominent members of the community, and even the Hippocratic Oath seems to set out limits between the internist and the surgeon. A good deal of the impetus for founding early medical societies both in Europe and America—based as they were originally on a sort of guild model—came not only from the need to harmonize and regulate the ethics of the members, but to imply that non-guild rivals were not as trustworthy.

Much of the evidence I have seen tracking the rise of medical professional organizations in modern Europe bears out the idea that they were more agencies of social control than patient-protection mechanisms. Professional ethics, in other words, focused mainly on unethical behavior by competitors. For members of the emerging unified medical profession in the nineteenth century, that is, for the university-trained and state-licensed physicians, ethics appeared principally to be a weapon against unfair competition from within this fraternity as well as a standard to apply (with public warnings) against the dubious or unlicensed, the quacks. (The German word for that—*Kurpfuscher*, a "cure-botcher"—makes the denunciatory intent quite vivid.) Under pressure from the organized medical profession, the definition of "quack" got shifted, though, from anyone who regularly passed off unhelpful or harmful treatments on patients to anybody practicing medicine without a license—a significant achievement of such professional organizations as the

Deutsche Gesellschaft zur Bekämpfung des Kurpfuschertums (German Society for Combating Quackery) founded in 1903 in Berlin. Within a few years of Hitler's seizure of power, one of the professionalizing projects of German doctors—especially those lured into supporting the Nazis—was reached with the Heilpraktikergesetz (Healing Practitioner Law) of 1939, ending the previous legal freedom of nonlicensed healers to offer their services (e.g., for practitioners of "alternative medicine").

The alliance between science and medical professional organizations came considerably later than the founding of most such organizations themselves. The American Medical Association (AMA), the British Medical Association (BMA), and their German equivalent, the Deutscher Ärtzevereinsbund (DÄV), as noted earlier, were all founded roughly in the third quarter of the nineteenth century (1847, 1856, and 1872, respectively). Although they were ostensibly devoted to the exchange of information leading to better medical practice, which they undoubtedly also promoted, there were other organizations of a more purely scientific orientation that predated them. One recent study perceptively suggested an explanation for the motivation to join such organizations before "scientific medicine" began to establish its therapeutic superiority over various competing sects. "To the degree that medical associations fostered medical men's belief in the primacy of their achieved status . . . they were performing an important psychological function. . . . As much as they might believe in the worthiness of their medical work, they shared with their lay patients and the rest of Victorian society a belief in the superior virtues of liberal learning and gentlemanliness and the inferiority of technical training and skill."[1]

What licensing boards, medical societies, and other professional bodies rarely did, however, was sanction or punish members for misconduct, incompetence, malpractice, and other specific deviations from general altruistic ethics. A couple of examples may suffice to underline this. The New York State Licensing Board received "230 complaints of unprofessional conduct and malpractice . . . between 1926 and 1939 [resulting] in only one disciplinary action and no suspension or revocation of license."[2] A 1960s study of 938 disciplinary actions by state licensing boards over five years resulted in only seven "actions" for gross malpractice.[3] Reliable national statistics are very hard to find, but random samples suggest that severe punishments remain the exception. The state of California, for example, placed only 135 cases on its disciplined physicians list for the years 2000–2013, but the vast majority involved temporary suspensions or even probation.[4] Civil suits for malpractice remain a practitioner's nightmare, but they are assuaged with insurance and, increasingly, demands on legislatures to pass laws limiting malpractice liability. The major defense for this apparent lack of teeth in licensing agencies lies in the need to assure the physician of discretion and autonomy. Obviously many cases involve so many unknowns and imponderables that second opinions and expert additional help are accepted as normal. The old maxim "operation successful; patient died" expresses the inability of even the most skilled and admired physician always to beat the grim reaper.

For more than a thousand years, the Mediterranean Basin was tri-cultural—Christian, Jewish, and Muslim—and ethical ideas blended. Despite their overall objectives of conquest and conversion, the Crusades brought humanistic values back to northern Europe. Although the Crusaders—originally feudal knights and retainers motivated by papal promises of indulgences as well as the hope for personal gain through looting and seizure of lands—shocked even contemporaries by their aggression, greed, quarrelsomeness, and impiety, they also reopened the Mediterranean to commerce and the exchange of ideas that flowed with it. Lasting from the end of the eleventh century into the thirteenth, the Crusades against the Islamic rulers of the Holy Land brought non-Byzantine Europe back into more regular contact with a cultural world considerably more advanced than their own. Other crusades such as the Spanish *reconquista* (finally ending with the taking of the Emirate of Grenada in 1492) had the gradual effect of absorbing and transmitting much Islamic and Jewish learning until its finish led to the persecution of Moors and Jews.

Whether or not the Hippocratic Oath was drafted by Hippocrates and his immediate followers, it can be taken as a model of the idealized essence of expectations that European and Middle Eastern society had for physicians and that physicians had for themselves and of each other. The degree to which the religiously heterogeneous societies of the Middle Ages and early modern period came to share a similar set of medical ethics argues that there was a certain universality to the ideas crystallized in the Hippocratic Oath.

By the sixteenth century, the relative stagnation of social and economic structures in the Middle East paralleled the rise in Europe of new forms of urbanism, early capitalist economics, the dissolution of localized feudal political systems, and an irrepressible movement toward religious and cultural diversity. Renaissance humanism, the Protestant Reformation, the Counter-Reformation, the rise of large fortunes and patronage of the arts and sciences, along with technological innovations such as Gutenberg's printing press and the ability to explore and colonize the New World, all had palpable long-range ramifications for the profession of medicine. Increased curiosity about the world, unprecedented attention to literacy and learning with the founding of new schools and universities, a heightened sense of the capacities and powers of individual humans, even new foods and newly recognized medicinal plants as well as new diseases and wounds of combat (thanks to gunpowder) called into question the relatively static medieval picture of the universe and man's place in it.

Without delving into a cultural history of the period, a few examples of these changes suffice to show how new conditions were being set for the profession of medicine. The Reformation commonly resulted in a shift of wealth and power from church to state with newly strengthened secular governments confiscating church property, dissolving religious orders, and taking over many of their previously dominant services, from care of the poor (and hospitals) to education and what might today be called the "information market." While such economic, social, and political changes did not have an immediate revolutionizing effect on the study or practice of medicine, they did foster new attitudes of respect for study, learning, and science.

These same upheavals brought chaos and destruction, as well—the Wars of Religion culminating in the Thirty Years' War wiped out large numbers of European civilians, not just armies, before the middle of the seventeenth century. The very idea that life was worth living, not simply surrendering as a curse of Adam with maximum guilt and deprivation to obtain eternal salvation, placed a new premium on prolonging healthy life without which much later medical effort would have seemed pointless. Still, the achievements of the European Renaissance, Reformation, and Scientific Revolution were more notable in art, literature, the physical sciences, and even practical areas such as navigation, banking, and government than in medicine. Already in the sixteenth century advances in optics, for example, enabled scientists to study the solar and star systems, but it took another century and more for the amateur Dutch scientist Leeuwenhoek to turn a telescope around into a microscope and to see blood cells and spermatozoa as well as microorganisms. Even then, such discoveries had few practical effects on medical diagnosis or treatment. It is easy to forget that discoveries celebrated in the early history of science coexisted with still dominant older beliefs today dismissed as superstitions. Noted astronomical discoveries did not dispel beliefs among learned men that illness had something to do with the position of the planets, for example. Acceptance of a Newtonian universe of mathematical elegance could cohabit with Newton's own persistent belief that gold could be made out of base metals.

So if medicine tended to lag behind the innovations of many new disciplines of science, the latter themselves took centuries to shake off many older ways of thinking. Some of the boldest advances were indeed made in the areas of moral and natural philosophy, and these were arguably as important for changing the ethics of medicine. A shift from mostly palliative care based on the speculations of ancient authorities to one based on observation, experimentation, and healing took place only gradually. It could not have taken place at all had the shift of broader values that started in the Renaissance not happened.

When the scientific method began to enter medical schools, it was preceded by a growing suspicion that the ethics of medicine should and could go beyond the rule, "first do no harm." Increasingly, the idea took hold that medicine could actually supply cures and even prevent the occurrence of disease. As obvious as this may appear to us today, it is important to recall that the effects of European humanism included a change in the ethical expectations of those standing by the sickbed—the physician and the priest. A human-centered medicine meant that the physician was there as more than a comforter and issuer of death certificates, leaving the traditionally more important role of saving the soul to the clergy. It meant increasingly a moral and professional obligation to improve the patient's health on earth.

Chapter Fourteen

The Physician as Gentle*man*

When we think of medical ethics today, we tend to focus on the obligation of the physician toward the individual patient, toward society, or toward defined groups. Indeed, one of the eight characteristics claimed by modern learned professions is altruism—a duty above and beyond that of other men and women to serve bravely and selflessly the needs of their fellow humans.

A prominent recent example of such altruism in action followed the disaster caused by Hurricane Katrina at Charity Hospital in New Orleans. Isolated by floodwaters and deprived of electrical power to run equipment and keep heat and humidity at tolerable levels, nurses kept ventilator-dependent patients alive using hand-operated bellows, although a physician and a nurse were accused of euthanizing patients who died after being given high doses of narcotics to keep them comfortable.[1] It was days before government rescue workers arrived by boat to evacuate critically ill patients. By then, the corpses of those who didn't make it reeked in the makeshift morgue. Yet neither the original ancient nor contemporary versions of the Hippocratic Oath require this kind of self-sacrificing dedication of medical professionals. Even more poignant examples may be cited in the cases of outbreaks of contagious diseases. Ebola is one of several highly contagious and lethal epidemic illnesses, in this case with no known cure. Heroic health care workers providing palliative care to its victims often fall prey to Ebola themselves. Can a profession reasonably require its members to treat patients under these circumstances, which put their own lives at great risk? The reactions of individual health care workers clearly cannot be mandated by codes or laws, and yet the tug of real altruistic, even heroic, behavior often surprises a cynical world.

Even in an everyday setting, medical professionals can quietly point to the often exhaustingly long shifts, depressing outcomes of life-and-death struggles, confrontations with ungrateful or hysterical relatives of the ill, chronic back trouble from too many years bent over the operating table, and many other aspects of working conditions not borne by other professionals. Interruptions even of leisure time by being on call, dashing off in the middle of the night to tend a patient, and donating one's time and skill for indigent patients are other examples of less dramatic sacrifices medical professionals often make in contrast to most other learned callings. The claim to altruism was also historically more sustainable when doctors and nurses were often poorly paid or, with respect to nursing, not paid at all. Before physicians became generally prosperous (as in twentieth-century America) and nursing a largely salaried occupation, their uncompensated service could rightly be claimed as reason for public esteem. To imagine this, one might refer to today's most visibly poorly compensated learned profession, teaching, which consistently turns up as highly regarded in public opinion surveys. Certainly the feeling that one is doing good despite the perception of insufficient financial compensation provides a motive for many forms of professional altruism.

Students of the learned professions have disagreed, though, about the relative importance of altruism as a defining characteristic of professionalism. Skeptics tend to regard altruism as more of a public relations gimmick in the struggle for monopolistic domination of the "market in services" than a realistically enforced code of conduct.[2] If a characteristic of a profession realistically cannot be expected from all of its members at all times, is it truly a useful measure? On the other hand, like most learned professions involving some kind of public service and trust, medicine clearly serves public needs and requires many sacrifices—from years of additional and complex education and practice to exposing oneself to danger—that can be and have been invoked to justify special social standing and privilege. The expectation of altruism, its nature and boundaries, and even its core definition are thus matters of ambiguity, and some students of professions would prefer to dismiss the term from any roster of professional characteristics.

As we have noted, though, the core of the doctors' oath for centuries has not involved a specific duty of self-sacrificing altruism but merely an ethic of potential service to others. Indeed, for many centuries "professional ethics" meant mainly responsibility toward one's fellow physicians.

Before the rise of modern medical professional organizations, most physicians were on their own or in direct competition. One German doctor likened the relationship of local physicians to one another as "spiders in their own webs" before the rise of professional ethical discipline rules and sanctioning boards. But it remains controversial how the almost simultaneous rise of increasingly inclusive professional organizations, with their self-promoting propaganda, licensing boards influenced by them (with the power to impose serious sanctions on ethical violators), and science-driven therapeutic efficacy interacted to buff up the reputation of doctors as "more ethical" than their unlicensed competitors (or even their licensed colleagues in nursing). Certainly by today's standards and hindsight, many of their practices and immunities to outside challenges seem a little ethically dubious and better designed to protect themselves than their patients. On the other hand, by pressing traditional practitioners of non-school or sectarian, irregular medicine to the wall, they may—as they claimed—have led to the overall improvement of therapeutic care. By that argument, modern professionalized physicians "did well by doing good."

Once established, professional rules of accreditation and licensing have nevertheless been misused at times, with the tacit or explicit support of the organized profession. Examples include the Nazis' revoking the medical licenses of Jewish doctors, then ending previous free-market legal freedoms for nonlicensed healers by the Healing Practitioner Law of 1939.

But the world did not have to wait for Nazi Germany to witness the application of racist and sexist principles aimed at excluding professional competitors. A recent self-review by the American Medical Association (AMA) admitted blatant prejudicial treatment of African American physicians. The consequences were far more serious than merely being unable to attend national conventions, as the study made explicit: "Medical societies were the crucibles in which the organized profession of medicine was formed. Within them, physicians met and developed relationships with professional colleagues and provided a forum to present papers and learn the latest techniques and treatments. After 1900, hospital admitting privileges became closely linked to medical society membership, as did relationships with state licensing and regulatory bodies. By the twentieth century, exclusion from these societies often meant professional isolation, erosion of professional skills, and limitations on sources of income."[3]

In the face of the failure of post–Civil War Reconstruction in the United States, the AMA effectively shut out African American doctors from its national conventions, and as late as the 1960s, while the landmark Civil Rights Act was being debated and made law (in 1964), the organization refused to invoke sanctions on mostly Southern local and state medical societies that continued to discriminate against African Americans. The latter had founded their own National Medical Association (NMA) in 1895—significantly enough, within a year of the U.S. Supreme Court decision *Plessy v. Ferguson*, which approved Jim Crow racial segregation as constitutionally legal.

Although women (themselves more likely than African Americans to belong to the educated and wealthier classes) struggled successfully to become MDs and—around World War I—members of the AMA in greater numbers than mostly poverty-stricken African Americans, they also constituted a tiny minority both of regular physicians and AMA members. Although the major organization of American professional physicians may have reflected rather than led broader public attitudes for more than a century, its own self-examination revealed one sad result after another. One was that African Americans comprised an even smaller percentage of American physicians and medical students in the early twenty-first century than they had a hundred years before (2.2 percent in 2006 versus 2.5 percent in 1910).

Although such reforms as those urged by the Flexner Report tended to close down separate, predominantly African American medical schools, as well as the few "cult" schools that had been open to women, at least Flexner had proposed medical coeducation at the scientific university faculties. Nevertheless, women had a hard time obtaining a voice in the AMA. They comprised less than 1 percent of the profession in 1870. By 1900 their share had risen to an estimated 2.5 percent of practicing physicians and 5 percent by about 1920, but the percentages did not increase significantly for another half century. In 1960 women still comprised less than 7 percent of practicing physicians.[4] Their numbers have increased dramatically over the past half century, thanks in large part to the 1972 American Higher Education Act (Title IX) banning discrimination by any institution receiving federal funding (almost all).

These latter figures, plus the fact that the United States was far ahead of Europe in the number of practicing women physicians (7,000 in 1900 versus around 350 in France and England combined)[5] and then saw those numbers stagnate for three quarters of a century, point to other explanations than the standard (and from today's viewpoint, ludicrous) excuses given by the mainstream community of (white, male) physicians for their dominance. As we have seen, licensing was a virtually ineffective method of limiting professional competition during most of the nineteenth century in the United States. Therefore, some other mechanisms of limiting the number of regular doctors had to be found. Once medical schools began to be serious scientific training institutions (with the opening of such schools as Texas and Johns Hopkins in the early 1890s) requiring many more years of school preparation, university study, and exposure to laboratory science, the competition of poorly trained quacks or "irregulars" could be denigrated with more safety—but only if the numbers of people admitted to the reformed medical schools could be kept under control. Quotas for racial and ethno-religious minorities (especially African Americans and Jews) were openly imposed. But what about quotas for female members of the dominant white, middle-, and upper-class families? Male-dominated medical school admissions boards generally got away with holding the women admissions down to around 5 percent overall (not that each school had that many).

After the AMA became interested in expanding postgraduate medical education from 1904 on, additional hurdles were added. The institutionalization of hospital internships or residencies after receipt of the MD began at

Hopkins and spread. By 1904 the AMA's Council on Medical Education estimated that half of all graduating MDs went on to do postgraduate hospital training; by 1913 the estimate was as high as 80 percent. By the onset of the Great Depression, many state licensing agencies (now back in force) required an internship for certification to practice, and it was very difficult to set up a successful medical practice without such training. Yet only a handful of American hospitals accepted women as interns—seven in the 1890s, forty out of 482 in 1921, 105 of 712 in 1941. And the total internships available from all those hospitals was a mere 185 in the 1930s (compared to more than 6,000 for males, even though there were not enough male graduates to fill them).[6] And the scarcity of internships for women reinforced the arguments of medical school admissions committees: even if we admitted women to the MD program, what good would it do when they cannot get licensed later, lacking internships? Finally, for those determined women who managed to get through the gauntlet before the 1970s, the practical restriction of most women doctors to the less lucrative specialties, for example, general practice, ob-gyn, pediatrics, psychiatry—resulted in their earning less than two-thirds what their male counterparts did (the latter dominating the more lucrative branches, starting with surgery).[7]

Since the beginning of World War II, there has never been a time in the United States when there were fewer residencies available than newly graduated MDs to fill them. "The advent of private, employer-based insurance during [the war] increased the demand for care at teaching hospitals and . . . resident manpower; the higher prestige of specialty . . . medicine decreased interest for classical general practice."[8] One result was not only falling resistance to inviting women and minorities into residencies, but also the need to recruit graduates of osteopathic schools as well as allopathic MDs from foreign medical universities.

Medical schools and hospitals did not, of course, wish to exclude women from giving medical care. They merely restricted the more elevated and rewarding role of physician to males while welcoming women as nurses. The gulf in authority, prestige, and income between the two groups remains institutionalized even today. Socially recruited from lower socioeconomic strata, nurses could safely be incorporated as the foot soldiers, as it were, with physicians as the officers in a professional army of health care workers. Although the lay and religious sisters of previous centuries remained important pillars of patient care, the school-trained modern nurse began to assert a new kind of professionalization after about 1890. In that year, there were already thirty nursing schools in the United States (including at University of Texas Medical Branch), graduating 470 nurses. By 1926 there were already 2,000 schools graduating nearly 18,000 nurses annually.[9]

Attempts to blur the rigid lines between physicians and other trained health care providers, from traditional nurses to other recently added subprofessionals, are part of a current debate. In the past, organized medicine in the United States has mounted opposition to allowing so-called physician extenders (nurse practitioners and physician assistants) to prescribe medications and perform therapeutic procedures. These are normally people with advanced degrees and training in medical care. They typically conduct physical exams, diagnose and treat illnesses, order and interpret laboratory diagnostic tests, prescribe medications, counsel on preventive health care, and assist in surgery, all under the (often cursory) supervision of physicians. As the need grows for primary care personnel (and predicted shortages of MDs loom in the field, especially in rural areas and inner cities), several states have amended regulations to allow at least nurse practitioners to practice autonomously. Nurse practitioners (NPs), for example, are usually registered nurses holding BA degrees followed by master's, state licensing, and sometimes board certification in a specialty. Physician assistants (PAs) typically have a four-year undergraduate degree (on a premed track) followed by two or three years of medical care training (sharing in some cases courses and clinical instruction with MD candidates) and are also state licensed. PAs do many of the things nurse practitioners do but under the supervision of a physician. Most are involved in primary and urgent care.

Responses to the seemingly endless spiral of rising costs for medical care and the search for more efficient ways of providing it have, however, brought about some reduction in physician resistance to turning over some forms of care to "extenders." One of the repeated arguments about redefining the role of nurses, for example, has stressed their role in preventive and holistic care of the patient, leaving treating the disease to the physicians. Extenders in turn can relieve physicians and even nurses of some of the relatively routine and technical sides of care (e.g., giving injections or making casts, fitting patient histories into computer-based algorithms or protocols). And everybody would like to have less time wasted on paperwork that could be spent on patient care.

So despite some continued tensions and conflicts, many MDs in the United States are increasingly willing to prescribe chiropractic, acupuncture, therapeutic massage, and herbal remedies to patients, and many insurance companies cover the expense of these treatments, especially if prescribed by a physician. The demonization of alternative medical care by the AMA during much of the twentieth century was finally ended by a series of legal actions by the Federal Trade Commission. But "regular" physicians have viewed this as enlightened self-interest. After all, in treating a patient for chronic back pain, monthly visits to a chiropractor and a massage therapist cost far less and generate infinitely less risk than spine surgery or even an extended regimen of muscle relaxants and opiate pain relievers and without the risk of complications or addiction.

Another ethical issue that happens to mesh with self-interest and monopoly on services revolves around advertising, or praising one's own medical success over that of rivals'. Combating false, misleading, or simply overblown claims has been a hallmark of most modern learned professions for obvious reasons. "Cures" advertised range from commercially available nostrums, snake oils, and fad diets to the recent growth of advertising by ambulance-chasing lawyers and large pharmaceutical companies urging TV viewers in direct-to-consumer (DTC) ads to "ask your doctor" about expensive (but potentially dangerous) new drugs for old conditions, skimming as quickly as possible over harmful effects. Although the United States and New Zealand, both after a wave of business ideology–driven deregulation, are the only countries to authorize DTC, other forms of "consumer empowerment" than those driven by pharmaceutical company greed will almost certainly emerge more strongly with the exponential explosion of the Internet and social networking.[10]

The magic potions and secret nostrums of charlatans have a history as long as that of medicine itself, to be sure. But the rapid transformation of transportation and communication starting in the nineteenth century with the railroad, telegraph, and cheap newspapers ushered in a new age for itinerant patent medicine salesmen, fly-by-night mail-order sources for useless (or sometimes worse) pills, and other remedies. The traveling medicine show—as much entertainment as enlightenment—was another popular device to sell snake oil and much else. A gullible public was offered (to cite just a few advertisements a century or less in the past) soaps that made women thinner; a hair tonic to get rid of dandruff, promote hair growth, and other benefits, except its active ingredient was cocaine; or pain relief from "violet ray ozone medical electricity." Not a few great fortunes were based on dubious or overblown nostrums whose main active ingredient was alcohol, an opiate, or some combination of simple and cheap chemicals marketed as a miraculous cure. Indeed, patent medicines were not patented at all but rather trademarked, so the common adage "accept no substitute" was meaningless chemically. The American advertising industry (perhaps the world's most active and insidious) actually began largely as an extension of the nostrum industry, offering free almanacs and other publications financed by patent medicine advertising.

The rise of a more sophisticated version of the advertising industry deserves a separate chapter (if not a whole book) regarding influences on health behaviors. Galveston-raised Albert Lasker (1880–1952) and his younger and much more cynical Vienna-born but New York–raised colleague Edward Bernays (1891–1995), who learned a lot from his Viennese uncle Sigmund Freud, perfected mass persuasion to shape the future choices of "the people," preferably without them being aware of it. While Lasker may be regarded as the father of modern American advertising, Bernays went one better and perfected the art of disseminating what had previously been called propaganda in the guise of objective news releases. He might be called the father of American public relations. Lasker, the son of German-Jewish immigrants to Texas (his father was a banker), started his training as a young newspaperman on the venerable *Galveston News* just as the University of Texas Medical Branch was having its first impact on that part of the country. His father urged him to move to Chicago and work in an early advertising agency, where his first success had some connection with medicine. It was an effective ad for a hearing aid device that was not particularly effective but sold much better after Lasker's ad. He soon bought out the Lord and Thomas agency where he worked and went on to increase vastly the sales of various products from soap to toothpaste. His most memorable contribution to health behaviors, however, consisted of convincing American women—who generally did not smoke—that a cigarette would keep them slim ("Reach for a Lucky instead of a sweet!").

Bernays made his own contribution to encouraging women to smoke. Rather than advising his tobacco client merely to pay for media advertising, he staged what would today be called a media event with a photo-op during the 1929 Easter Parade in New York. He hired a number of attractive and well-dressed models to impersonate socialites while strolling down Fifth Avenue and smoking in public as his own photographers to spread "news" of the event around the country. The image of sophisticated New York ladies flouting the previous taboos on women smoking (at least in public places) was astonishingly effective as a cynical exploitation of the women's emancipation movement. Bernays incidentally happened to share Lucky Strike cigarettes (dubbed "torches of freedom" for this event) as a client with Lasker. If Lasker and his wife Mary much later in life set up a foundation and the Lasker Awards for major contributions to medical science (since 1946), some of the motivation went back to recognition that smoking was a major threat to public health. Bernays, however, saw no reason to regret his shaping of "public relations," since he always believed the public was too fickle and irrational to make safe decisions without guidance from above. Although he also made some small voluntary contributions to anti-smoking campaigns after his retirement in the 1960s, the message of his 1928 classic handbook *Propaganda* continues to be a bible for the public relations field, if lacking the overt morality of scripture.

Ironically, the successes of American advertising in mobilizing public opinion (Bernays was a key player in George Creel's World War I Committee on Public Information) was not lost on European victims of America's postwar financial, technological, and commercial hegemony. Hitler's propaganda minister Goebbels was one such student. The weakness and disarray of Europe in the interwar years did not result in diminishment of European scientific and medical advances, but the United States had by this time emerged as a worthy and equal rival. The catastrophe of World War II continued the process of shifting wealth, power, and scientific, as well as medical, discovery from one side of the Atlantic to the other.

By the end of World War II, medicine clearly reigned in America as the queen of the professions, and the United States had replaced Germany, France, and the United Kingdom as having the world's most skilled, technologically advanced physicians. America is where aspiring young specialists came to train. (Of course, one reason was that many of Germany's top physicians, especially those who were Jews, had prudently relocated to the United States and elsewhere in the Americas during the Nazi regime, while the devastation of the war left France and Britain preoccupied with recovering their infrastructure and education systems.)

Chapter Fifteen

Balancing Individual and Public Benefit

Experimental Abuses

This chapter delves into the ethical consequences of the technological and scientific advances that marked the late nineteenth and early twentieth centuries. Values of decorum, deontology, and social responsibility clashed: what if, by sacrificing a few, medical science could save many?

The surge of an often naïve faith in science and technology—even in "progress" itself—created for the first time a set of attitudes favorable to a "science" of social engineering. One might call this version of paternalistic ethics "Big Brother bioethics." The new field of genetics appeared to unlock the possibility of "improving the race" by manipulating breeding. Genetic defects could be "weeded out" of the "valuable" races or nationalities by various means. An international eugenics movement fell on particularly fertile ground not just in Germany, but—somewhat willfully forgotten—also especially in the United States. If physicians made ethical decisions that we would today consider dubious at best, they often did so in the double confidence of what in Germany is called *Besserwisserei*, that is, based on their superior scientific training, as well as in the belief that experimenting with "less valuable" human subjects, despite the high risk of harming them, nevertheless could pay off for thousands of "more valuable" patients down the pike.

The Tuskegee syphilis experiments are only the most notorious example in the United States. The Nuremberg tribunal brought to light the cruel and often bizarre abuses perpetrated upon the inmates of Nazi concentration camps. The Tuskegee syphilis experiment was launched in 1932 to study the natural progression of syphilis in 600 poor male African American volunteers in the rural American south. It was initiated and monitored by the U.S. Public Health Service (USPHS) with the cooperation of the Tuskegee Institute in Alabama, a historically African American college founded by Booker T. Washington. The long-term study was finally shut down forty years later after a USPHS epidemiologist encouraged the *New York Times* to launch an exposé of the program's questionable ethics in 1972.[1] The study began innocently enough, and its findings were published in professional journals. At a time when there was not yet a completely reliable cure for syphilis, the volunteers, induced by various benefits such as meals, free medical care, and a free burial (to compensate for the pain of spinal taps needed for the experiment), were not clearly informed that they *had* syphilis. The ethical dilemma arose later when penicillin became a proven remedy for syphilis in the 1940s, but the test subjects were not treated with it, indeed, they were practically prevented from getting treatment. To have treated them would have naturally invalidated this unprecedentedly long-term study—the scientific reason for continuing it. But treatment, it was argued, could have saved the lives of many participants and prevented the infection of their wives and even infant children. Was this not, in Hippocrates' terms, "doing harm"?

In the 1970s public outcry resulted in federal laws and regulations (starting with the 1974 National Research Act) calling for institutional review boards (IRBs) to protect the volunteers in studies involving human subjects. The rules demanding telling the truth to subjects, not misguiding or misdirecting them, and informing them of their diagnosis came to be known as "informed consent."[2]

Before World War I, Darwinism, or more specifically social Darwinism, grossly distorting Darwin's evolutionary explanations into a justification of struggle and competition in and *between* human populations, was invoked to rationalize imperialism, racism, sexism, and even militarism. The new science of genetics appeared to unlock the possibility of "improving the race" by manipulating breeding. Genetic defects could be "weeded" out of the "valuable" races or nationalities by various means. This is not the place to describe the international eugenics movement in great detail. Suffice it to say that two countries developed it very strongly: Germany—no surprise in the light of what we know about its distortions by the Nazis—but also the United States. Of course racism, biological excuses for imperialism, and hypernationalist chauvinism that we so readily associate with Hitler found supporters in other lands that vaunted themselves as bastions of democracy. The American Jim Crow laws of the 1890s, the unprovoked takeover of much of the Spanish colonial empire in 1898, Teddy Roosevelt's Great White Fleet, and the 1917 abandonment of George Washington's long-respected advice to stay out of European conflicts were all milestones along this path.

Another memorable milestone was the Supreme Court decision favoring mandatory sterilization for the feeble-minded, summed up by Justice Oliver Wendell Holmes Jr. (whose father incidentally was a Harvard medical professor) in 1927's *Buck v. Bell* with the comment, "Three generations of imbeciles are enough." The eugenics movement was not, of course, entirely evil, and many of the genetically based theories we now denounce were not only fashionable among the well-educated but for many decades regarded as scientifically sound.

It should also be mentioned briefly here that the year 1917 not only brought the United States to a new level in its history, with some incidental consequences for medical ethics. That year also brought the Russian Revolution and subsequently the Red Scare, with the argument that the later USSR really cared about the health of the masses and had an undifferentiated, all-embracing form of medical ethics: the people owned the state, physicians were functionaries of the state, and the equal provision of health care was to be the top goal. Never mind that practice almost certainly never lived up to ideological claims and that wars, politically induced famines, shortages, and prison camps led to a massive population kill-off, if not technically genocide, under Stalin and even Lenin. The bugbear of Communism (reinforced by the increasingly apparent chasm between what Bolshevism promised and then grotesquely failed to deliver) helped defeat Progressive Era attempts to create a national health insurance system and, therewith, inevitably shape the course of medical ethics in Europe and the United States for many decades.

Situated somewhere between the hollow claims of the USSR to promote the health of all "comrades" (even as it terminated the lives of millions) and the reversion of the United States to a fee-for-service system, shutting out most of the poor from adequate care, Germany trod a third ethically dubious path under Hitler (1933–1945). The Bismarckian system of near-universal health insurance was maintained, fitness and healthy diet constituted a part of Nazi official policy, and the medical profession responded enthusiastically. But "Hitlercare" benefited only the "race" embraced by Nazi ideology, with its crude distortion of eugenics, and finally initiated a massive program of genocide in its last desperate years.

It was not, however, pure eugenics and many other Nazi distortions of medical ethics that led to the Nuremberg tribunal and, as a part of its many months of trials of Nazi leaders, the famous proceeding against two dozen Nazi doctors. The latter was conducted only by the U.S. military as the "subsequent trials" of twenty-three persons (of whom twenty were doctors) accused of inhumane Nazi human experimentation and mass murder in the name of euthanasia. The major American-only military court trial took place mostly in 1947, well after the Trial of the Major War Criminals before the International Military Tribunal (IMT) conducted by the four victorious Allied occupiers of Germany between November 1945 and October 1946.

The heart of the indictment accused the doctors and Nazi officials of performing medical experiments, without the subjects' consent, on prisoners of war and civilians of occupied countries; of committing murders, brutalities, cruelties, tortures, atrocities, and other inhuman acts. They were also accused of the mass murder of prisoners of war and civilians of occupied countries, particularly the aged, insane, incurably ill, and deformed by gassing, lethal injections, and other means in nursing homes, hospitals, and asylums during the Euthanasia Program and participating in the mass murder of concentration camp inmates.

The experiments carried out mostly on concentration camp inmates, including children, ranged over the following:

Josef Mengele's notorious experiments on about 3,000 twins in Auschwitz (of whom perhaps 200 survived)—but Mengele escaped to South America;

bone, muscle, and nerve transplantations (without anesthesia) among victims at the Ravensbrück concentration camp;

head injury experiments;

freezing experiments (to investigate ways to prevent and treat hypothermia);

exposing victims to conditions likely to afflict German troops in the field, from malaria to mustard gas, and even wounding and infecting them to test new medicines. Since it was implicitly understood that the concentration camp and Soviet prisoner-of-war victims were doomed to die anyway, the perpetrators rationalized that their suffering would serve some wider humanitarian purpose (or at least help the "master race").

This defense did not impress the American court, and seven of the twenty-three defendants were sentenced to death; another nine were given jail sentences. But seven were acquitted. This surprisingly mild outcome for the accused may have had something to do with their defense argument—that there were no binding international legal restrictions on medical experimentation.

One partial answer to that defense was a set of ten principles drawn up by the Nuremberg prosecutors (all Americans). These seem almost commonsensical to us almost sixty-five years later, but at the time they still were suggestions, not sanctioned by the world medical community—if there was such a thing:

1. The voluntary consent of the human subject is absolutely essential. *The experiment should . . .*
2. be such as to yield fruitful results for the good of society, unprocurable by other methods, . . .

3. be so designed and based on the results of animal experimentation and a knowledge of the natural history of the disease,
4. be so conducted as to avoid all unnecessary physical and mental suffering and injury,
5. not be conducted where there is a prior reason to believe that death or disabling injury will occur,
6. never exceed the degree of risk determined by the humanitarian importance of the problem to be solved,
7. make proper preparations and provide adequate facilities to protect the experimental subject against even remote possibilities of injury, disability, or death,
8. be conducted only by scientifically qualified persons,
9. leave . . . the human subject at liberty to bring the experiment to an end . . . if continuation seems to him to be impossible,
10. be terminated by the scientist in charge if he has probable cause to believe . . . that a continuation of the experiment is likely to result in injury, disability, or death to the experimental subject.

A subsequent world convention of physicians added the 1948 Geneva Declaration to update the Hippocratic Oath in the wake of Nuremberg. It agreed on a new oath:

> I solemnly pledge to consecrate my life to the service of humanity;
> I will give to my teachers the respect and gratitude which is their due;
> I will practice my profession with conscience and dignity;
> The health and life* of my patient will be my first consideration;
> I will respect the secrets which are confided in me;
> I will maintain by all means in my power, the honor and the noble traditions of the medical profession;
> My colleagues will be my brothers;
> I will not permit considerations of religion, nationality, race, party politics, or social standing to intervene between my duty and my patient;
> I will maintain the utmost respect for human life, from the time of its conception,* even under threat; I will not use my medical knowledge contrary to the laws of humanity;
> I make these promises solemnly, freely and upon my honor.

It is fair to add that the parts of the oath subsequent to a further congress in 2005, indicated by an asterisk, were struck out. This was a reaction to the legalization of abortion in most countries of the developed world. The "World Federation of Doctors Who Respect Human Life" (1974) complained, however, that neither the Hippocratic Oath nor the Geneva Declaration was being administered in most medical schools and that legalized abortion and euthanasia were being allowed under revised versions of the declaration.

Readers who have come this far will not be surprised that social and religious doctrines often intrude in a world allegedly informed by "science" nor that changing social perceptions of the environment and nonhuman species have entered the equation of medical ethics.

The Helsinki Declaration (1964) and subsequent revisions are a further attempt by the world medical community to suggest increasingly elaborate rules for adoption by states to govern experimental medicine (e.g., the 1981 U.S. Common Rule for government-funded research, as modified thereafter). The Helsinki Declaration is too long and detailed to include here but is readily available on the Internet. Currently there are twenty "basic principles" and five additional ones, adding provisions for treatment of animals and the environment, clinical trials, publication, and independent review boards (IRBs) among others.

The long-windedness and repetition of such results of international meetings may attest to the failure of the standards voted on to have reached the field in a planet populated by eight billion people. They also suggest the glacially slow process of world medicine trying to accommodate to reality, on one hand, and the impatience of more developed countries to hold the feet of less developed ones to the fire.

The habit of the so-called West vis-à-vis its allies and enemies does, however, go back to the Cold War. The U.S. government had no special reason to find the German medical system at fault in the 1940s when it dispatched specialists to make recommendations. The utility of a greatly exaggerated foreign threat (by the recent ally USSR or "communism") may help explain the failure of Allied, but especially American, attempts not only to try and punish the Nazi doctors, but to cleanse the German medical education system of the attitudes and preconditions held responsible for such tragic misconduct. Although the American occupation authorities collaborated with American physicians, teachers, and the American Medical Association in studying possible improvements, they came to virtually nothing practical. Cleansed of the most egregious Nazi collaborators, German medical education resumed much as before.[3] None of the most rudimentary reform demands enunciated by a visiting team of American physicians in 1945 was realized: "Complete denazification and reform with active American participation: complete denazification of the university; rigid selection of students; reorganization of the curriculum to introduce laboratory and bedside teaching in place of the present lecture system; establishment of a uniform, short, practical, final examination to replace the time-consuming *Staatsexamen*; the payment of adequate teaching salaries with the university retaining all student fees; provision of supplements to German libraries and laboratories from American sources, and sponsorship of each opened German medical school in the United States zone by some American medical school, which probably, if invited, would rotate some of its faculty members to the German school so that modern teaching methods could be established and maintained."[4]

Cold War politics increasingly suggested instead that we needed our former enemies. The hope that a thorough shape-up of the German medical profession would set an example for the rest of Europe and the world wound up being largely dashed. Furthermore, the U.S. medical establishment largely regarded the Geneva Declaration as solving a German problem, with no direct application to American practice. One does not have to be a cynic to hear undertones in the American professional world that medical ethics would take care of itself once the "infection" of Nazi ideology and its consequences were "burned out." The idea that the whole field of medical ethics—including in the United States—ought to be reexamined was far from mainstream thinking. Indeed, if there was any fear enunciated about German doctors after Hitler's defeat, it was not that they would continue to pervert basically sound ethical values, but that German doctors might massively emigrate to the United States and become competitors! Similarly, throughout much of the Cold War, attention to ethical principles was louder in criticizing foreign (Soviet, East European, Chinese, etc.) abuses, such as classification of political opponents as dangerous mental patients or the corrupt system of *blat* (bribes) and favors routinely required to obtain seriously effective medical treatment under socialized medicine from Prague to Vladivostok.[5] Meantime, ethically questionable experiments continued to be carried out in the United States, such as the Tuskegee syphilis study already mentioned, various human experiments involving exposure to radioactivity or dangerous psychotropic drugs (Pentagon, CIA, and pharmaceutical firms), experiments on unwitting prison inmates, testing of polio vaccine on institutionalized mentally retarded children, and many more.[6]

On the positive side, the awareness that medicine had a responsibility to society as a whole and not just to individual patients led to such advances in public health as clean drinking water, banning cigarette advertising on billboards and TV (including ads in which models dressed in white coats promoted smoking for weight control), and required vaccinations for children (still controversial among a small minority). Starting in the early 1880s with Germany's coverage of factory workers, one European country after another expanded toward universal access to health care. In the Soviet Union, as already mentioned, physicians were employees of the state, and the equal provision of health care was officially a top goal. In fact, however, the system was abused in numerous ways, such as by diagnosing critics of the state as victims of dangerous psychiatric disorders requiring institutionalization in psychiatric wards. So-called punitive medicine was not of course invented in Brezhnev's USSR (originated by the KGB) and has not ceased to exist around the world since the Russian Federation recognized it as a disguised form of extralegal punishment for a long list of now world-famous dissidents. The advance of treatment with psychiatric drugs and psychotherapy for legitimately diagnosed disorders finally produced enough alternatives to restraint and institutionalization that critics and reformers such as Franco Basaglia, Michel Foucault, and Thomas Szasz eventually succeeded in widespread deinstitutionalization of mental patients and the closing of state mental asylums, the cruelty and inefficacy of which were finally recognized.

At roughly the same time, however, the prison population in the United States began to climb alarmingly, multiplying from roughly a half million to two and a half million from the 1980s until around 2005. Longer sentences and higher rates of incarceration for nonviolent crimes (e.g., drug possession) are factors explaining the well-known fact that the United States now has locked up a greater percentage of its population than any country in the world. Inadequate facilities, diet, and other failings clearly promote ill health, but one of the most alarming trends is the vast increase in the mentally ill among prisoners. As Cook County sheriff Thomas Dart said, "Society was horrified to warehouse people in state hospitals [before the 1980s], but we have no problem with warehousing them in jails and prisons."[7] Experts do not agree that the medical and psychiatric treatment of as much as half the prison population constitutes an improvement over commitment to public mental institutions. This situation is naturally a frustrating challenge to the medical profession.

If such changes have released untold populations of people formerly "cared for" by the state, evolving views of social justice have also again questioned the fairness of allowing nearly 50 million Americans (2010) to go without health insurance. While some of these may be able to afford it but prefer to gamble with their continued good health and a small percentage refrain because of religious convictions, the vast majority have wound up in this position because they (1) earn too much to be eligible for Medicaid; (2) have not reached the eligibility age for Medicare; (3) are too poor (including a large number of "working poor"); (4) are unemployed, self-employed, or working for enterprises too small to be eligible for the kind of job-linked insurance common since the 1940s; or (5) have been ruled bad risks by the for-profit insurance industry. The Affordable Care Act (ACA or "Obamacare"), with all its flaws and compromises, was designed to extend such coverage to replace the patchwork of local, regional, or state hospital emergency room (ER) care. The ER is, of course, a horribly expensive alternative, burdening local taxpayers with the costs, and—given its general lack of preventive or primary care to head off later dire and chronic illnesses—a system both fiscally and morally questionable.

To be clear about the historical record, such charity ward treatments were regarded, at least until the middle of the twentieth century, as a useful component in the training of medical students and residents. In the wake of recent patient-rights movements, many disturbing past instances of using the illnesses or injuries of the socially marginal (without clear informed consent) have come to light. As at the beginning of this chapter, we can rephrase the question, "what if, by sacrificing a few, medical science could save many?" Sacrificing the long-term health of millions of the pauperized uninsured involved in the pre-ACA patchwork system—the many—cannot by any stretch of the imagination be justified further as advancing medical science. It might have saved "the few" from the painful prospect of paying higher taxes, but as Supreme Court Justice Oliver Wendell Holmes Jr. (son of a Harvard medical professor) noted, "taxes are the price we pay to live in a civil society."

Chapter Sixteen

Gods No More

The Rise of Patients' Rights

One outcome of the Nuremberg tribunal addressed the key defense argument that saved from the noose all but a few of the two dozen Nazi physicians facing capital charges—that there were no binding international legal restrictions on medical experimentation. The Geneva Declaration sought to update the Hippocratic Oath in the wake of Nuremberg, and other documents followed. But to an unprecedented degree, debates about medical ethics began to slip out of the control of the medical profession itself as powerful social movements beginning in the 1960s shaped a new and wider dialogue about human rights. Parallel to a worldwide rebellion against colonialism came the American civil rights movement, the anti-authoritarian student rebellions and antiwar movements, and a renewed struggle for women's rights. The overall climate of inclusion and redress of past social wrongs produced such results as the "Great Society" legislation in the United States. The Civil Rights Act (1964) and the Equal Opportunity in Education Act (1972) may seem at first glance to have little to do with medical ethics, but the underlying implications of recognizing the equality in principle of all citizens had profound indirect consequences. Because of Title IX, women found at last a chance to increase their percentage of American physicians from single digits to more than 30 percent by 2012.[1] The addition of old-age medical insurance (Medicare) and coverage for the indigent (Medicaid) in the mid-1960s created an entirely new market for medical services coupled with added state controls over their delivery. The women's rights movement, for example, emphasized the natural right of women to control their own reproductive systems. Issues such as the so-called right to die (more accurately, the right to refuse or forgo treatment) and abortion became contentious public issues. One result of such debates was an explicit concept of patients' rights, including informed consent and the right to refuse treatment. The paternalism that had marked medicine as a learned profession was dead, at least in the United States, the former British Empire, and Western Europe. If for no other reason, the discretion formerly typifying the doctor-patient relationship was now altered forever by the addition of a third party, private or government insurers expecting rigid adherence to written codes for treatment.

Physician autonomy, one of the eight earmarks of a profession, came under attack from other quarters. Revolutionary innovations like transplants and artificial organs, the rapid development and power of the pharmaceutical and insurance industries, the increasing influence of plaintiff's attorneys, and the distortion of research objectives by third parties rapidly undermined professional autonomy and individual ethical choices. When the National Institutes of Health declared the "war on cancer" and the Gates Foundation took up arms against malaria, the financial clout that they wielded often undermined the standards of scientific independence of biomedical research.

Other notable areas of heightened concern for the new field of bioethics include questions involving the right to die, for example, assisted suicide, or requests for euthanasia, for example, removing "hopeless" cases from artificial life support. One of the earliest of these controversial cases involved the New Jersey teenager Karen Ann Quinlan, whose parents requested termination of her artificial life support in the face of her likely permanent vegetative state. The hospital refused, and it took a court decision to disconnect her in 1976. Formal ethical boards in caregiving institutions and advance care directives were two of the results of that case, but they clearly did not end there. Public disputes over the right to die accompanied the later life of "Dr. Death" Jack Kevorkian even beyond his prison term and 2011 death.

Chapter Seventeen

Collisions of Cultures

As American physicians became more diverse so did their patients, and this raised new ethical questions. No sooner had complete patient confidentiality and informed consent been formally codified than situations similar to the following arose: Ms. G, a twenty-five-year-old married woman, is injured in a car accident. Her mother calls the hospital frantically, but the nurse on duty says that she is not allowed to reveal her condition. Ms. G has designated her husband as the person to be informed. The nurse, who has grown children herself, empathizes with Ms. G's mother, so she finds herself confronted with an ethical imperative (protection of a patient's confidentiality) that conflicts with another, more intuitive ethical value (compassion).

Many Americans can remember the time not so long ago when, if they heard that a friend or colleague was in the hospital, they could make a call and get the full story. The process was no more difficult than ordering a get-well bouquet sent to the room.

Or take the case of the R family, who emigrated to the United States from a country where, on the death or incapacitation of the father, the oldest son is considered the head of the family and responsible for making major decisions affecting the well-being of its members, as well as protecting them from suffering. His mother, Mrs. R, has been diagnosed with an aggressive form of pancreatic cancer. She's not a candidate for surgery, and her chances of surviving longer than six months are slim to none. Not only has she given written instructions that her son be informed of all matters regarding her health, she has also made clear, both verbally in discussions with her doctor and in writing, that she doesn't want to know. "Just tell him, and he'll talk to my other son and my daughters," Mrs. R has explained. "They'll decide together what to do."

Mrs. R's son wants to tell her that she's suffering from severe diabetes and will need to rest and follow her doctor's orders strictly. Maybe his sisters could arrange a special family get-together for her birthday next month, provided that wouldn't tire her too much. He's against informing her of the grave prognosis or even of the cancer diagnosis.

Once again, two conflicting ethical values face off: respect for cultural differences and informed consent. By insisting that Mrs. R be told the reality of her situation, the American medical profession is also insisting that the R family abandon their value, paternalistic though it may be, of sparing each other suffering and of designating someone to make serious medical decisions for a patient capable of doing so for herself.

And for a most recent example: in August 2013 the High Court of Justice in Northern Ireland authorized a blood transfusion for a young member of Jehovah's Witnesses over the opposition of his family and in recognition of his incapacity to make an informed decision. The court ruled that

> a young man with severe learning disabilities should be given a lifesaving transfusion of blood if that were to become necessary during extensive dental surgery, despite the fact that he and his mother belong to Jehovah's Witnesses, a faith which regards transfusion as sinful . . . [reflecting] warnings against consuming blood that occur in the New Testament book of Acts, and as well as in the books of Genesis and Leviticus in the Hebrew Scriptures. But transfusion for medical reasons did not exist in Biblical times; this is one of the many difficulties that arise when codes of ethics that were devised for life in the premodern desert are applied to the twenty-first century.[1]

One could go on to cite extensively other cases where cultural values and explicit professional and institutional ethical guidelines collide. To take a few random examples, we have already seen how concern for the human rights of patients used in medical experiments became acute in the wake of the Nuremberg trials. The search for new knowledge and cures can usually only conclude successfully with human trials (preceded by animal trials), and since the 1960s and 1970s these led increasingly to formalized oversight of experiments to guarantee patient/subject informed consent and, later, to ensure the humane treatment of laboratory animals.

The rapid and accelerating development of new technologies with medical applications or wider social issues brought on whole new areas of concern, for example, organ transplants (and donation), dialysis, life-sustaining respirators, birth control techniques, pregnancy surrogates, regulation of mood-altering, painkilling drugs (as well as alcohol, tobacco, and food components), and stem cell research and use. In addition to a host of ethical questions involving direct care of individual patients, there are those involving wider populations or the future of the human species itself. For example, broad public policies about euthanasia and assisted suicide will likely accompany the aging of populations in postindustrial societies, as will discussions about the imperative to limit or postpone medical procedures on demand. Who should make decisions about such matters as DNA manipulation, gene therapy, cryogenics, cloning, embryo preservation, or other broad consequences of innovations that could help or harm living organisms, not just patients? Who decides issues previously left largely to the doctor-patient relationship or practices or beliefs grounded in specific religious traditions such as the "beginning of life," the "right to die" or to refuse treatment, or even circumcision?

What is clear is that the field of biomedical ethics does not pretend to have all the answers to these questions, but most medical (and other) professionals agree they must be examined and not merely swept under the rug.

The pressure to resolve such conflicts gave rise in the late twentieth century to a new field of inquiry: biomedical ethics. In most cases prepared through academic postgraduate masters and doctoral programs either specifically in "bioethics" or more broadly in the medical humanities, bioethicists work in hospitals and teach in medical schools. Furthermore, today, all but a handful of America's medical schools require bioethics as part of the curriculum. Indeed, accreditation of medical schools by American accrediting agencies depends on their meeting a minimum standard of teaching biomedical ethics. But the minimum standard—for example, a lone professor offering courses and clinical consultations—may be inadequate for the constantly growing needs for education and advice in these areas. Furthermore, many of the larger degree-granting programs are financed by "soft" money, for example, from research grants and other nonsecure or impermanent sources.[2] Unlike endowed chairs and institutes, the contingent funding for such programs can be relatively easily slashed by administrative fiat.

It is indeed impossible to determine easily just how many such programs exist, since they bear different names, structures, and goals. According to various sources, though, there may have been as few as thirty postgraduate programs in American universities in 2011 or as many as nearly four dozen American centers for ethics involving medical ethics. A few were online and an additional few were in Canada or Europe (primarily the United Kingdom). Other programs focusing primarily on legal ethics may overlap with medical ethics, and some universities have begun offering undergraduate programs as well.[3] If one includes all North American institutions of higher learning (including undergraduate programs, centers devoted to philosophy, law, and other disciplines but overlapping with bioethics and medical humanities), the list might be closer to 120.[4] As scattered and thin as available information is, it does reinforce the impression that North America leads the world not just in the high technology and costs of medical care, but in concern about the moral, legal, social, religious, and humanistic underpinnings of current and future developments.

IV

The Future of Medicine as a Profession: From Hippocrates to Dr. House

Chapter Eighteen

Cures, at Last!

Major advances in biomedical science transformed the practice of medicine in the nineteenth and twentieth centuries, and the pace of innovation became ever more rapid. As each breakthrough—safe general anesthesia, penicillin, and antibiotics, kidney dialysis, chemotherapy, MRIs and PET scans—came on the scene, physicians had more tools with which to treat patients. Yet those subtle aspects of the art of medicine, as opposed to the science, shrank in apparent importance. As only one example, although medical schools teach students how to do physical examinations, at least at the undergraduate education level, complaints about such hands-on skills being poorly developed later and underused in a high-tech age have been common.[1]

This is not the place to examine in depth these discoveries, but a brief mention is warranted if only to recall the challenge to the medical profession to keep abreast of the latest techniques. We have already glanced at some of the major breakthroughs of the nineteenth century (e.g., Pasteur, Lister, Koch, and Virchow). The first decade of the twentieth century began with the discovery of different human blood types, Alzheimer's disease, electrocardiography, vitamins (with special consequences for rickets and scurvy), a first treatment for sleeping sickness (by Paul Ehrlich), the IUD, and safer surgical techniques.

The 1920s brought, in addition to the discovery of insulin to treat diabetes, vaccines against diphtheria, whooping cough, tuberculosis, and tetanus, rounded out by the discovery of penicillin and electroencephalography (EEG). The 1930s brought among other discoveries: a cure for streptococcus, a treatment for schizophrenia, a vaccine for yellow fever, and electroconvulsive therapy. The 1940s witnessed the first dialysis machine, chemotherapy, the defibrillator, acetaminophen, and the first cataract surgery involving an intraocular lens. In the 1950s came the first polio vaccine, cloning, the cardiopulmonary bypass pump, ultrasonography, the first kidney transplant, tetracycline, the pacemaker, and in vitro fertilization.

The especially fruitful 1960s brought cardiopulmonary resuscitation (CPR), oral contraceptives, hip replacements, beta blockers, the artificial heart, the first transplants of liver, lung, pancreas, and heart, vaccines against measles, mumps, and rubella, Valium, sophisticated drug delivery systems, and the cochlear implant. The even more fruitful 1970s witnessed cyclosporine, immunosuppressive drugs for transplant surgery, genetic modification, magnetic resonance imaging (MRI), CAT, and PET scanners, the insulin pump, laser eye surgery, liposuction, and antiviral drugs.

If the list of innovations seems at this point to become a little more arcane, those in the following thirty years become ever more complex, reflecting more often expensive collaborative and commercial research, complicated science, and highly specialized knowledge. Compared to Dr. Fleming's accidental discovery of penicillin in the late 1920s (as a result of his going away on vacation and coming home to find it growing in a dish!), many of the following require specialized training even to understand fully: extracorporeal shock wave lithotripsy (ESWL) for non-invasive treatment of kidney, gallbladder, and liver stones; hepatitis B and A vaccines; artificial skin; synthetic insulin; cloning of interferon; automated DNA sequencing; polymerase chain reactions (PCR) to produce large amounts of DNA sequence copies; a robot for surgery; DNA fingerprinting; capsule endoscopy; statins; tissue engineering (leading to regenerative medicine and the therapeutic use of stem cells); stents; laser cataract surgery; electroactive polymers with applications to artificial muscles; the mapping of the human genome; telesurgery; artificial liver; face transplants; human papilloma virus (HPV) vaccine, effective against various kinds of cancers; rotavirus vaccine against severe children's diarrhea; and the first laboratory-grown human kidneys and livers.

A standard response to the rapidly increasing complexity of fields of knowledge is, of course, the division of labor or, in the medical field as in many others, specialization. Although rarely cleanly separated before the twentieth century, we have noted what came to be called internal medicine, surgery, and pharmacology as original rough divisions in the field of medicine since ancient times. The nineteenth century worked up anatomy, physiology, and pathology as parts of medical science if not medical practice, and ob-gyn (obstetrics and gynecology), ophthalmology, laryngology, pediatrics, psychiatry/neurology, and radiology were developed as specialties before World War I. But the vast majority of licensed physicians in the United States and Western Europe remained general practitioners.

Recent surveys show that only about a third of practicing U.S. physicians were involved in internal medicine, family practice, pediatrics, or other fields that collectively would have been called general practice a century ago. All the rest of the 985,000 U.S. doctors in 2012 fell into about three dozen other specializations (the American Medical Association's 2010 Physician Masterfile breaks these down into many more). The specialties range from the largest (ob-gyn, anesthesiology, and psychiatry) to the least popular (neonatal-perinatal, geriatric and pediatric-internal medicine, as well as vascular surgery).[2]

In the United States prior to 1970, a young MD could still go into the practice of medicine after a further year of hospital internship and become a general or family practitioner. Since reforms beginning at that time, family medicine has been declared a specialty, requiring (as do all others) several additional years of postgraduate study (three to four in this case). The terminology is further confused by the recent use of the concept "primary care physician" (PCP) in the United States and some other Anglophone countries. A PCP by definition may have trained in the specialty of family or internal medicine, pediatrics, ob-gyn, and sometimes a few others (such as emergency care physicians or allergists). The decision about which broad specialties are included in a PCP practice are not only made by the doctors themselves, but also by such insurers as health maintenance organizations (HMOs) and massively influenced by such legislation and bureaucratic administration as exemplified by Medicare.

In effect, then, *all* American physicians licensed since the early 1970s are specialists, even those who would previously have considered themselves general practitioners. One could write an entire book just about the consequences of such specialization, but let us consider only one or two involving the impact on professionalization. The costs of all those extra years of preparation for practice now involved in residencies add to the vast cost of professional education. Even a family medicine specialist must reckon on three years of residency after already accumulating student loan debt: as already noted, the 2013 *median* loan balance for newly graduated MDs was $170,000 compared to $13,469 in 1978, or about $48,000 adjusted for inflation.[3] Although medical residents are paid a salary, it is barely enough to cover the living expenses of the MD and his or her spouse, let alone to provide a surplus to start paying back student loans, which in many cases go on piling up interest during the three to seven years of poorly paid residency. A resident's salary currently is about the equivalent of the median income in the United States, around $50,000. This is a bit less than the median starting income of an American law school graduate in general private practice after a total of seven years of higher education, compared to eleven or twelve minimum (and sixteen maximum) for a physician.

A further effect of the overall costs of becoming a practicing physician is the influence they have on the choice of specialties. As has been the case for a century or more, the more exotic specialties offer greater financial rewards than those associated with being a PCP. One imaginable result is a shortage of exactly the kinds of doctors needed by a population that is aging or that is more widely covered under improved national medical insurance. Yet the strong temptation among MDs choosing a specialty during their residency is to go for the more lucrative fields. Although the wider public and media often criticize such choices as motivated by greed, the rationality of the market is really in play. The more medical education costs, the more rational the choice to pursue the specialization path as a way of getting out of debt sooner. A legitimate fear among young MDs making such career choices—more or less for life, as is consistent with professionalization—is that if they choose wrong, they may be hounded by debt for decades. From the point of view of economic security alone, it is hard to explain why so many bright young people in North America and Europe still flock to medicine. An easy life and generous economic rewards are certainly not—or no longer—necessarily a prospect.

One other result of the trend toward specialization might be mentioned here, although many others could be. Membership in professional organizations and the power of them to influence regulation and attitudes about the profession has long been a measure of how well or badly the "professionalization project" is going. The size and complexity of a physician's obligations have promoted the growth of specialist organizations (just as it has in many other professional fields). Given a choice forced by lack of time and leisure, many physicians have come to devote their attention and support to medical professional subgroups whose activities most directly affect their daily practice. One result of this can be read from the statistics of the American Medical Association's (AMA's) membership. At one time regarded as the world's most successful professional lobby, and often because of its leadership's willingness to resort to quite unprofessional and distasteful tactics, the AMA has in recent decades witnessed a proportional decline in its "inclusiveness" for the profession. Although the exact current percentages are open to debate and according to definition, there is no doubt that the AMA recently counts only a minority (as little as 17 percent in 2012) of U.S. doctors, medical students, and residents among its members. While controversies over the direction of AMA policies undoubtedly play a role (many physicians dropped membership because of the organization's support of the Affordable Care Act), the trend in Europe also is toward the splitting up of the profession along lines of specialization, the nature of physicians' working and employment conditions, and similar factors.[4]

Because biomedical advances make headlines (and sound bites) and pharmaceutical companies are now permitted to advertise directly to the general public, today's patients are, in effect, being encouraged to diagnose and prescribe for themselves; this often amounts to demanding the latest, costliest remedy even when the older generic they have taken for years controls their symptoms just fine. Since the patient is normally not paying anything like the full cost of treatment, thanks to private and public medical insurance (or in the case of many of the uninsured and poor, to local tax-supported "free" programs), the pull of customer demand lies in the direction of "more is better." Unfortunately for most physicians, the cost containment (and profit incentive) concerns of such stakeholders as the insurers, taxpayers, and politicians create a push to limit or "ration" the quality and quantity of care. The combination of the old fee-for-service model of reward with caps, conditions, codes, and pre-approvals set by the insuring bodies not only limits physicians' incomes (and imposes a huge and exhausting burden of paperwork), but effectively limits patients' scope of decision making as well. In the ludicrously misleading advertising campaigns that have inevitably accompanied every attempt to reform American medical insurance, "choosing one's own doctor" has been one of the patient rights alleged to be threatened by universal insurance. A more serious threat is surely the foreclosure of the doctor's right to pick the best treatment without interference from a cost- or profit-obsessed corporate and bureaucratic complex or for that matter by the patient's often murky understanding of what is best for her based on TV advertising ("ask your doctor about . . .") or Internet surfing. The warnings of Arnold Relman, the editor of the *New England Journal of Medicine*, against a rising commercial "medical-industrial complex" three decades ago have proven all too chillingly prophetic.[5]

How will medicine and society cope if the present pace of breakthroughs continues? Are science, which made physicians more powerful professionals, and growing patient access to medical knowledge via the Internet now eroding their professional status and autonomy?

A recent work by the American cardiologist and geneticist Eric Topol may offer insight about the coming technological revolution in medical care.[6] Topol singles out several different technological developments that are likely to merge sooner or later to improve medical care and to put more control over it into the hands of individual patients. Cell phones, personal computers, the Internet, digital devices like advanced cell phones, genetic sequencing for individuals, and social networks will make the "creative destruction of medicine" inescapable, he argues. The patient of the future will be wired up and constantly monitored (although not with today's clumsy and obtrusive sensors) with physiological data being sent constantly and stored in the Cloud. Tiny sensors will monitor not only such vital signs as blood pressure, oxygen saturation, glucose, heart and breathing performance, but also metabolism, and sleep patterns or exercise, as well as deliver an EKG, anticipate a heart attack, and possibly release medications automatically. Topol harshly criticizes the medical profession for its foot-dragging and even opposition to this future utopia, explaining it as a justified fear that "consumers" of medical care rather than its providers will beat a path to the new mousetrap. One might imagine the motto of this new age to be "patient, heal thyself!"

Critics have justly pointed out that patients may not be as motivated as a techno-enthusiastic physician like Dr. Topol to invest the time and trouble required for all this self-monitoring and analysis. Nor is it clear what it will cost and who will want to pay whatever the price may be. Furthermore, the expense of buying and updating highly sophisticated equipment may be one of the forces nudging young emerging physicians—at least in North America—to go into highly demanding (and more lucrative) specialties rather than primary care. Some of Topol's "breakthroughs"—such as genetics research—have proven to be more difficult to apply to improving medical care than expected a decade or so ago.

Yet the substitution of machines and algorithms for the physician's judgment honed by years of education and experience is already happening. Walk-in clinics or urgent care centers relying heavily on non-physician clinicians (e.g., nurse practitioners and physician assistants) already deal with minor medical problems at a fraction of the cost of emergency room treatment.

Even when regular MDs are consulted, one can wonder whether they are motivated by pursuing the best interests of the patient ("client") since, under the traditional fee-for-service system, price is theoretically no object and the temptation to order unnecessary testing and treatments is strong. But how does the dynamic change if the physician is no longer an independent contractor (whether in a solo or group practice) in a sort of cottage industry but rather an employee (as in a managed care system, HMO, etc.) in a corporatized industry? In the relatively short span from 1983 to 1997 the percentage of American physicians in solo practice dropped from 40 to 26 percent, those in group practices from 35 to 31 percent, but those with employee status rose from 24 to 43 percent. Even more tellingly, the number of young physicians (with five or fewer years of practice) who were employees rose from 37 to 66 percent, mostly squeezing out the category of solo practitioners.[7]

At this juncture it may be useful to emphasize the difference between medical *science* and the medical *profession*. As we have seen, the latter had little overall effect on mortality before the end of the nineteenth century, although improvements in public hygiene and prevention brought about by medical discoveries certainly did. Throughout most of recorded history, pestilence, war, and famine kept human life spans short, and control of pandemics may have been a more important factor than direct physician care in extending average life expectancy around the beginning of the twentieth century. With expanded access to modern medical care in that century and longer life spans, chronic degenerative diseases like heart disease, stroke, and cancer became the big killers by 1960. It is presently unknown whether the next major (and unprecedented) challenge to both medical science and the profession—the increase in degenerative diseases associated with an aging population—can be met with not-yet-available diagnostic and treatment weapons: Can one sustain life indefinitely? And if not, at least keep the more or less terminally ill aged in palliative care? Finally, globalization has raised the risk of a comeback for old diseases like tuberculosis that have developed drug-resistant strains and of rapid global transmission of new ones. The medical profession reached its zenith of power and prestige precisely when patients largely survived because of what was uniquely allowed by law for the physician to prescribe or the surgeon to repair. But the individual licensed physician is no longer in control of all medical *care*, including, for example, that found in nursing homes or associated with environmental pollution or bioterrorism. No individual today could do what Virchow did for public hygiene in Berlin by insisting on public sewers or Pasteur in developing methods to defeat anthrax contamination.

Chapter Nineteen

The Conundrum of Insurance

Raising Income, Threatening Autonomy

The idea of national health insurance first developed in preindustrial Europe. Its "father" is commonly held to be Count Otto von Bismarck, the "Iron Chancellor" who guided the unification of Germany by 1870. In fact, however, Bismarck—a ferocious opponent of socialism—merely adapted on a national scale ideas already developed by German workers' organizations and cooperatives. The *Krankenkassen* (sickness funds) developed locally by these almost totally forgotten successes of the mid-nineteenth-century co-op or mutuality movement became the basis for Bismarck's attempts to woo the angry industrial working class back to loyalty to the Prussian/German Empire by providing medical (and later old-age and other) insurance protections. By World War I many European countries had seen the advantages of this system and had adopted some version of it. Its inclusiveness expanded during the period between World War I and World War II, after which it became in many variants the rule in European and many other countries since 1945.

Among industrialized nations, the United States was the odd man out in this trend, although Social Security legislation during the depths of the Depression in the 1930s did grudgingly offer some old-age pension rights, augmented in the 1960s by Medicare for the elderly and Medicaid for the incapacitated. Only with the Patient Protection and Affordable Care Act (PPACA), also known as "Obamacare," that became law in 2010 did an attempt to extend medical insurance to the remaining masses of patients previously uninsured come into effect. American attempts to limit burden sharing to the more affluent or work-able citizens no longer worked. Social Security old-age pensions had been politically acceptable from the 1930s on as a benefit co-paid by many American employers and their employees. As

American jobs began to disappear, the pool of uninsured but ill Americans threatened to overwhelm the antiquated and localized system of inadequate poor-care typified by city- or county-financed hospital emergency rooms (ERs). Primarily designed to provide fast, often lifesaving acute care to victims of accidents or other emergencies, ERs have always been required to treat anyone who showed up in need of immediate medical care. But increasingly, indigent patients unable to afford primary care allowed their conditions to progress until they became acute crises—until, for example, their uncontrolled diabetes resulted in kidney failure or an upper respiratory infection developed into pneumonia—then came to the ER for help, the manifold cost of which was borne by taxpayers.

The American medical profession has had a keen interest in insurance schemes, since they have a palpable impact on relations with patients and the conditions of physicians' work (as well as those of nurses and other caregivers). If the American Medical Association (AMA) may be taken as a bellwether, the initial reaction to European experiments was a mixture of ignorance, confusion, and fearful self-interest. The first serious suggestion of some kind of national American medical insurance was greeted initially, around World War I, with more interest than rejection. The Red Scare following the Bolshevik Revolution, however, quickly cemented a negative attitude toward national insurance by American doctors. (In Europe, by contrast, parties and interest groups of many stripes agreed it was a good idea and would, indeed, eliminate one of the competitive appeals of communism.)

The defeat of the AMA's long-standing opposition to the extension of Social Security (old-age coverage) to the medical needs of the elderly and disabled was sealed in the mid-1960s, and it soon became evident that Medicare/Medicaid insurance meant a substantial increase in physician incomes. Doctors, who during the Great Depression may have traded their services for a chicken or a few jars of homemade jam, now were assured payment at established rates, depending on the diagnosed condition. In many cases, fees could be negotiated with the insurance company if the physician practiced a rare subspecialty, was much in demand, or was located in a high-rent city. With the introduction of Medicare in 1965, all Americans aged sixty-five and older, plus many patients who were younger but disabled, were covered.

But as technology advanced, whatever became the gold standard of treatment grew increasingly expensive. According to some estimates, for example, the cost of having a baby delivered in a hospital has tripled since 1996 and now averages \$30,000.[1] Insurance companies responded to spiraling costs by taking tighter control. Procedures and hospitalizations had to be approved ahead of time. Charges for office visits were set so strictly that many physicians complained that they couldn't meet expenses. Whether this was an exaggeration or not (remembering that American physicians today still have the highest incomes in the world), many abandoned private practice for HMOs, large group practices, or on-staff positions with hospitals. Some of their motivation might include lifestyle choices, with physicians trading some autonomy for more predictable schedules and incomes, more time with their families, more equitably shared domestic responsibilities, reflecting also the increased number of women in medicine and even "pair-o-docs" physician couples. A few thousand physicians who opted to remain private opened boutique practices, in which patients paid a set amount per year, ranging as high as $5,000, for routine care and tests, plus prompt access to the doctor. Such access may include the doctor's personal cell phone number. Many boutique physicians make house calls. In return, the doctors are freed from much of the paperwork for insurance reimbursement (the patient's responsibility). Boutique care offers the affluent the kind of doctor-patient relationship enjoyed by many Americans with their family doctor in the 1950s. To be sure, these reborn "Dr. Welbys" operate for the most part on the level of primary care.

By the opening of the present century, American medicine had suffered substantial losses in one of the eight characteristics of a profession, autonomy. Would high social prestige and economic incentives be next?

Chapter Twenty

Expanding Access to the Physician's Role

The opening of the American medical profession to women and minorities, who had always participated but in far smaller proportions and unequal roles, changed its social status. This democratization is transforming, in more subtle ways, its values—or at least the ways it expresses them. No longer was medicine a white guys' club, with token women, African Americans, Hispanics, Asians, and, in somewhat larger numbers, Jews admitted on condition that they comport themselves like WASP men. Battlefield-style heroics came under question, and the idea that doctors themselves should lead healthy, balanced lives—both as examples to their patients and to promote sound judgment—arose. These ambiguities are well mirrored in popular cultural products such as TV's *House*.

Meanwhile, chiropractors, acupuncturists, midwives, and others who were denounced as quacks a few decades ago are acquiring many of the earmarks of professionals. States have established rigorous educational and licensing standards, more and more physicians feel comfortable referring their patients to them, and most health insurance plans cover treatment (recognizing that chiropractic adjustment, for example, costs a lot less than spinal surgery as a therapy for back pain and has a much lower risk of complications). Osteopaths (Doctors of Osteopathic Medicine) have achieved full status as physicians in the United States, although not always abroad, and are admitted to residency programs alongside MDs.

Other established healing sub-professions—among them occupational and physical therapy and nursing—are claiming full professional status. American organized medicine is currently engaged in a battle against demands for autonomy by nurse practitioners and physician assistants, who are insisting on the legal right to prescribe medications and conduct basic therapeutic procedures without the oversight of a physician. The American Medical Association (AMA) appears to be losing its rearguard battle for hegemony over medical practice by licensed MDs only.

Finally catching up to the rest of the developed world in extending medical insurance to the vast majority of its citizens, the United States will find a medical establishment understaffed for the new challenges, opponents argue. The "graying" of the general population is being accompanied by a similar phenomenon among doctors. Retirements are not being offset by new MDs sufficiently to guarantee treatment for the millions of newly insured Americans who can begin to afford to have a doctor. The result is a projected growing shortage: from nearly 14,000 too few in 2010 to 130,000 by 2025.[1] Doctors' incomes are sinking even as the cost of getting the education needed to become one is rising, leaving many facing almost insurmountable student debt.

Even for those who feel they can afford it, medical education is once again under attack just as it was by Flexner a century ago. Indeed, the centenary anniversary of the Flexner Report brought forth a new call for medical school reform.[2] One might wonder what prospective medical student would still want to send in her application after reading the 2010 evaluation of current medical schools by the editor of Britain's leading medical journal, *The Lancet*:

> Their questionable admissions practices, ossified curricula, out-of-date learning models, invalid assessment, lack of incentives to match health professional to public need, deficits in disease prevention, and the largely absent leadership to put social responsibility at the heart of their educational mission all point to a bankruptcy of vision by our overpaid academic leaders. Medical education is fundamentally conservative, indoctrinating new generations into the failed ways of the old. For too long we have hugged the shore of safe and acceptable.[3]

While somewhat less acerbic in their critique, a panel of expert medical school professors commissioned by the Carnegie Foundation for the Advancement of Teaching in the same year identified "the most overlooked aspect of professional preparation [as] the formation of a professional identity with a moral and ethical core of service and responsibility. . . . [T]he financial pressures on the clinical enterprise . . . are marginalizing teaching and learning."[4]

It is hard to disagree with their idealistic assessments about regrounding the medical profession in a sustainable ethical matrix. The cards may be stacked against such a hope, however: "Students become less empathic and less altruistic as they progress through medical education. . . . Students' empathic identification with their patients often conflicts with that of hospital team members, who can appear unempathic and distant."[5] Decoded, such analyses appear to boil down to the abrasive effect on professional morale by constant exposure to the unprofessional traits of highly developed, free-market economics—that is, indifferent at best, self-serving at worst. Freidson's first and second logics—remote, short-sighted, and greedy investors as well as remote, detached, and uninterested bureaucrats—make difficult or impossible the early formation of a professional ethos already in undergraduate medical schools.

And yet if we have noted any red thread running through the history of medicine during the last two millennia, it is that which relates the definition of "profession" to the social structure and needs of each age and place. The hand-wringing of American commentators all too often lacks (as is totally the case with legislators dealing with health issues) much acquaintance with foreign developments. If we look across the Atlantic, for example, we note that the type and nature of national health insurance coverage have more to do with professional ethics and behavior than formation in medical schools. "Formation" itself is a neo-American buzzword derived from French and, ultimately, German concepts of education: it is 200-year-old German *Bildung* refashioned to go beyond mere training to include the shaping of the individual personality (including its ethical dimensions). And we may recall at this point that *Bildung* was originally considered the sign of a gentleman. It was what elevated the commoner almost to the level of the aristocrat, justifying an elevated lifestyle and an appropriate income to achieve and reflect it.

While German medical schools—the medical faculties of universities—still today require the finishing certificates of secondary schools passing on humanistic and scientific knowledge equivalent at least to the sophomore level of American colleges, one can justifiably dispute their maintaining former high levels. But they presuppose the conclusion of *Bildung* before entering any university faculty, including medicine. Once past the university and subsequent residencies, German doctors tend to follow the group ethics of the type of doctor they are: insurance panel doctor (including almost all general practitioners), hospital employee, or other public service physician, and so forth. Professional organization tends to follow these career divisions, and the ethics of many medical societies are similar to those of industrial trade unions. In this respect, they are little different (at least in the Milton Friedman view) from the "old" AMA in its heyday before Medicare.

One cannot deny that Continental (e.g., French and German) physicians are, in contrast to their American colleagues, paid less—but then they do not have huge tuition loans to repay. There are many perennial complaints about the way western European (including British) medical insurance systems are run and the consequences for the medical profession as well as for patients. Yet there are very few outstanding examples of public complaint about a lack of professional ethics among European doctors. By this I do not mean anything remotely comparable to the excesses of Nazi or Soviet MDs under dictatorships. The question to ponder is rather: has the almost total inclusion of physicians in national universal health insurance systems produced ongoing public worry about the ethical approaches of European doctors in recent decades? The answer is clearly negative.

Indeed, the largely unfounded scare buzzwords of American opponents of universal medical insurance—for example, not being able to choose one's own doctor, rationed or denied treatments and tests, "death panels," and the like—are largely offset by the affordability of good health care for all, including the consequent boost in preventive care. The latter is one of the most significant factors in keeping total health care costs down (in comparison to the United States). Overall the medically insured public, at least in the original western members of the European Union and its associated countries, has not protested chronically about unethical or inadequate care. If anything, it has been the medical professional organizations that have stood up to what they regard as inadequate government policies regarding medical care of the public.

Chapter Twenty-One

What It All Means

Historians (at least professional historians) are not supposed to predict the future, and I make no claim to do so. But other social science fields do not always observe such constraints scrupulously. Throughout this book I have referred to some thinkers who have brought the tools of the humanities and social sciences to play. In the interest of full disclosure, I should mention my own intellectual descent from one of the founders of modern sociology and economics, Max Weber. My own teacher, Marion J. Levy Jr. (1918–2002), was both a student and challenger of Talcott Parsons (1902–1979), himself a student of (and to some degree a rebel against) Weber (1864–1920). It's useful to mention Weber here because one of his many despairs was the progression of bureaucracy and its overweening cultural force, the "rationalization" of modern life Weber feared would lead to an "iron cage" in which individual creativity would have little room to play.[1]

Weber did not concern himself much with modern professions as such, especially not with the medical community. He did distinguish in his writings between collectivities seeking to monopolize the market by exclusion (e.g., based on race or religion) and inclusion (based on education and training), the latter type being classified as a guild. Despite the translation of Weber's major work, *Economy and Society*, into English in 1968, many Anglophone sociologists have continued to think that Weber regarded such professional organizations as antiquated. This appears to be a misunderstanding of Weber, partly owing to not being able to read his work in the original German. Anglo-Saxon sociologists, in particular, have tended to build theories of professionalization exactly on the short-term, British and American individual-practitioner/fee-for-service model from about 1875 to 1950 and generalize it to other professions. Even when they were critical of the strenuous efforts of the American Medical Association (AMA) during this period to lead this kind of medical profession into a position of monopoly, many Anglophone sociologists (including Parsons and Freidson) could not imagine a modern medical profession as compatible with bureaucratization. Weber, on the contrary, gave many hints that he understood the relatively successful efforts of German learned professions to submit to limited bureaucratization in order to gain legally enforceable monopolistic privileges granted by the state. It may well be that Anglo-Saxon (professionalization) and Continental European (bureaucratization) paths wind up at the same goal.[2]

Even if he did not write much about them, Weber took notice of the signs of professionalization all about him (difficult for him to ignore as a professor in a German law faculty). He felt a great ambivalence about these signs. Today, almost a century after his death, one can see trends that validate his fears about coming developments in society. In particular, are the conditions of professionalization that sociologists have more or less agreed characterize modern developments still valid, and will they go on being so? In a broader context, many social scientists who are still inspired by Weber, especially in Europe today, tend to view the professions as bellwethers for a much larger group, the modern bourgeois class. They suspect that not only learned professions but the entire modern middle class may shrink or be seriously disenfranchised in Weber's "iron cage of rationality," fulfilling the worst-case prediction of Marx that it would eventually disappear altogether as society developed into two classes only, a small one of plutocrats and a vast one of proletarians. Is this something we need to worry about today?

One loud answer comes from neoliberal promoters of the unfettered free market, willfully misinterpreting the teachings of Adam Smith and, following their American guru Milton Friedman, radically denouncing learned professions not merely as inimical to the free market but actually just trade unions in fancy clothes. Friedman actually regarded the AMA as *the* most powerful labor union in the country—the very opposite of a compliment.[3] Although Friedman saw the need for some kind of advanced medical education and licensure, his solution included opening more medical schools and thereby increasing the supply of practitioners (including caregivers with lower levels of education)—ironically, suggesting something like the situation *before* the Flexner reform era. This oddly blinkered yearning for a return to a golden age of the free market glaringly ignored the absence of a highly informed "clientele" in an imaginary ideal "marketplace for services," a failing that has clearly not been overcome by the arrival of the so-called information age today.

One of the most distinguished sociologists of professions, including especially the medical profession, the late Eliot Freidson, dared to predict its future in his final book, *Professionalism, the Third Logic*. His analysis posits three "logics" of social organization: that of the market, that of bureaucracy, and that of the professions. To simplify Freidson's argument considerably, the purpose of the market under capitalism is to maximize profit.

Radical, run-amok capitalists naturally complain loudly about the second logic and its representatives in bureaucracy, especially state bureaucracy with its lust for regulating everything. When Max Weber expressed his fears about the "iron cage of rationality" he probably had in mind the one busily erected in his lifetime in Europe, led by Prussia. As a social scientist explicitly trying to repudiate Marx, however, he did not take as seriously the prediction that capitalism might someday take over the state or merge with it in a final stage of "state monopoly capitalism." Given the choice between untrammeled capitalism and a bureaucracy controlled by a constitutional monarchy, Weber—himself as a professor, a sort of royal civil servant—would have come down on the side of the latter. And although he did not write much about the learned professions of which he was a practitioner, one of his last and most famous statements spelled out the absolute need for brave and rigorous science and scholarship no matter how unpopular with bankers or bureaucrats—"*Wissenschaft als Beruf*," or science as a calling. Because the professions could not be created without the preexistence of academic freedom and the scientific spirit of universities, themselves part of the ethic of liberal middle-class values, Weber could well have agreed with the notion that they possess a "third logic" or at least special status exempting them from the primary requirement of producing profit at any cost or fitting quietly into a *dirigiste* hierarchy rigidly following elaborate Mandarin codes. Again one must ask, are these questions that only apply to wicked old Europe, to which Americans are immune according to the myth of "American exceptionalism"?

One of the ongoing debates I had during the last twenty years while working on the history of modern professions in Europe was largely with continental European colleagues who doubted the applicability of the Anglo-Saxon (American/British) model to European circumstances. You might call this a quarrel between the traditions of Parsons and Weber. And the central issue was: can one speak of the characteristics of modern Anglo-Saxon professions in a European context? The Anglo-Saxon tradition was based on a voluntaristic form of organization within a relatively free-market capitalist system; the European model was based on the premise of serious state interventionism. So the conventional wisdom went. Yet the Anglo-Saxon model depended on invoking guarantees by the state that, for a time, privileged the learned professions (especially medicine) to the point of their exclusive control of the market in their services. The Continental model similarly evolved into one where the representative professional organizations increasingly shaped public or state policy in the direction of monopoly over the market for professional services. One can argue that the events of the last forty or so years have shown a convergence in the two styles of professionalization.

Parsons, although often called a "functionalist" (he himself denied this), earned his PhD in 1927 at Heidelberg, analyzing Max Weber in his dissertation (and later introducing Weber's major conclusions in English). He also became close to Weber's recently deceased brother Alfred and his widow Marianne. As a founding member of the Harvard Sociology Department, Parsons had an immense influence on American and world sociological thought. He was convinced of the importance of learned professions and professionalization itself as a part of the modern social system.

He did not write much about the profession of medicine as such.[4] He did, however, insist that this learned profession, more than some others, was defined in part by its ethics. Such practices as advertising, bargaining about prices or undercutting competitors, refusing to deal with customers too poor to pay, and similar practices common to businessmen were properly denied to physicians. The fact that medical organizations rarely formally sanctioned egregious violations of accepted ethics appeared to Parsons to be the price paid for retaining a wide latitude of discretion and autonomy to the doctor, for that was the basis of trust between doctor and patient. Formalization of sanctions "always opens the door for the 'clever lawyer' whether he be a district attorney or merely the 'prosecutor' of the medical society's own Committee on Ethics."[5]

There are of course many wider developments that must be kept in mind, such as the simple facts that technological, economic, demographic, and even cultural developments have altered the roles of many learned professions more in my own lifetime than in the preceding two millennia or more. To cite merely one example, the number of physicians has soared (as have lawyers and some other professions), since fewer and fewer people in advanced societies today can escape inclusion in the medical treatment system, just as fewer and fewer major business and personal activities can be transacted without legal advice. While this means there will always be a need for lots of health care professionals and lawyers, it also produces asymmetries and conflicts within the old professions.

Put another way, the German or American doctor at the time of Flexner's report was more likely to live in a small community or town, interact with the local educated and power elite on equal footing, treat primarily the middle and upper classes of society, meet patients in their home or a home-like dispensary (not infrequently in his residence), enjoy respect bordering on awe, and earn mostly an income corresponding to the dignity of middle-class professionals. Urbanization, specialization, hospitalization, universal medical insurance, the rise of Big Pharma with its drive to bypass the profession in pursuit of greater profit, and the sheer complexity and rapidity of change have altered all of that. Likewise, the cultural, one might say anthropological, setting of politics—an arena in which members of the professions and representatives of government met—has changed radically. Can the local medical societies that were the backbone of the once-powerful AMA, for example, compete today for attention of legislators who depend, for the continuation of their roles as "professional" politicians, on the heavy funding that large corporations can muster? (We might recall that this trend was already becoming apparent before World War II, when Will Rogers referred to "the best Congress money can buy.")

One nightmare scenario for the future harkens back to the experience of professions under such fusions of state power and single-party dictatorships as Nazi Germany and Stalinist Russia. Although Freidson quibbles with what I and other historians have dubbed "deprofessionalization," one cannot deny that these regimes crushed or co-opted autonomous professional organizations, despite early promises to respect them, and arbitrarily changed the conditions of professional life almost at whim. The Nazis, for example, pleased many "Aryan" doctors by eliminating competitors who were female, Jewish, liberal, socialist, and so forth, but since their real aim was the violent conquest of Europe, they ultimately violated some of their own ideological stances after 1939, for example, by watering down medical education and licensure and even overturning their sacred promises to keep women banished to the distaff world of *Kinder, Küche, Kirche* when there were suddenly not enough males left to feed both the battlefields and the much-impaired medical home front. Stalin famously imposed the "barefoot scientist" Trofim Lysenko (1898–1976) on Soviet biological and medical scientists because of his mad contention that environmentally acquired characteristics of organisms—for example, by surviving Communist Party apparatchiks—could be passed on to their offspring. Had Stalin not died in 1953, he probably would have carried out a purge of Russian doctors who were "plotting against the Soviet leaders" perhaps as a prelude to rounding up all Jews and shipping them to camps.

Freidson is probably correct in saying that this kind of nightmare scenario is unlikely to overtake the professions in modern industrial (or is it now postmodern, postindustrial?) societies: history does not repeat itself exactly. Yet one can salvage a certain amount of gloom by reflecting on the fact that one thing Mussolini's fascism, Hitler's Nazism, and Stalinism shared was a deep ideological suspicion of individualism and uncontrolled free spaces of autonomous thought and action—precisely the scientific skepticism and liberal, even humanistic, respect for dissent and questioning associated with most modern professions. Mussolini, Hitler, and Stalin were incidentally all in their own way failed and rejected professionals (journalist, artist, and priest, respectively) unlikely to retain much affection for the realm of seasoned, independent, and learned autonomy of the professions. But are the chief executive officers (CEOs) of huge corporations—including but not limited to some of the more egregiously ill behaved and sanction laden as BP, Halliburton, Microsoft, and AT&T—likely to view the special and privileged status of the professions with the concern, say, of Carnegie and Rockefeller, who between them reshaped the modern American medical profession? Even with the most benign of intentions, foundations established by the beneficiaries of the wealth generated by megacorporations run the risk of warping the rules of scientific investigation. We may recall the fact that the Gates Foundation has devoted so much research funding to eliminating malaria worldwide that it has made virtually all researchers in the field dependent on it for funding, thus potentially undermining the very possibility of completely honest peer review.[6] When national and even international corporations have a stronger vested interest in running hospitals, nursing homes, joint practices, the provision of medicines and instruments, as well as insurance reimbursements, with the primary goal of maximizing profit, do local physicians have, I would ask, a better chance of remaining autonomous than they did when communities owned the hospitals or many smaller pharmaceutical companies had strong reasons to cultivate research professors of medicine?

Sweeping generalizations based on various future scenarios could take up the rest of this chapter. More profitable, I think, would be a return to our initial list of characteristics or attributes shared by modern learned professions. Let us look at each of them, first, to put them in a weighted balance both in the past and hypothetical futures. Then, second, we may want to make some comparisons with other professions, and, last, with comparable situations in other advanced countries. It will not be up to us to judge how shifting values of these attributes will affect professional standing in the future, but rather to the members of the professions themselves. And if we use the past as a guide, the representatives of the learned professions—not just the AMA or its foreign counterparts—will ring alarm bells much more loudly than anybody else, so a grain or two of salt should be kept handy.

Let us recall the eight characteristics of modern professions: (1) highly specialized and advanced education; (2) a special code of personal conduct—"ethics"; (3) a spirit of altruism and public service; (4) rigorous tests of competence, such as examinations and licensing; (5) high social prestige and corresponding economic incentives; (6) occupational career patterns or "ladders"; (7) a drive to monopolize the market of services; and (8) autonomy. Three of them are still quite intact. At no other time and place in history have physicians been required to have so much educational preparation (1) or undergo such rigorous testing (4)—not just at the start but throughout their careers, and the possibility of multiple, hierarchical career patterns (6) may well be on the way to reshaping American medicine. The spirit of altruism and public service (3) that professions almost universally claim as a major justification for their special and elevated status continues to be under attack. Dr. Welby may not have been replaced by Dr. Frankenstein as a pop culture representative of the medical profession, but he may have been replaced by

Dr. House. Brilliant and obsessive, House almost always saved the patient, but he seemed to be driven more by arrogance and oxycodone than by altruism and public service, and he wreaked havoc with hospital budgets.

Reverting to the more or less intact characteristics, we can claim that never before in history has so much educational preparation, testing of qualifications, and complexity of careers characterized the medical profession. But the *quality* of education, the *standards* for evaluating it, and the possibility of multiple and hierarchic career patterns may be well on the way to reshaping the medical profession. Few med school professors or students need to be persuaded, for example, that medical education has become lopsidedly technological, science based but perhaps less infused with scientific curiosity and far less designed to promote those humanistic values called for by Sir William Osler. Furthermore, while Flexner saw the firm placement of medical education in the matrix of science-oriented universities, the future of those institutions appears less and less certain, as Ellen Schrecker and many others keep reminding us.[7] With the rapid development of cybernetics, it is not unthinkable that machines may take over many of the functions now provided by human health care professionals or that advancing technology will require that many physicians are trained to be more like computer programmers than wielders of stethoscopes and seasoned judgment. National health care systems that press for routinized, even partly automated treatment—and this includes pressure from insurance carriers and hospital administrators to adopt best practices—in the name of efficiency and reduced costs *might* produce a multifaceted profession, much as is emerging in American universities under the influence of big-business models. If 70 percent of the teachers in American universities and colleges now are part-time or "contingent" faculty, often lacking benefits, job security, and the time and reward structure to pursue the continuing education that a life of scholarly research entails, despite comparable graduate educational credentials to their tenured peers, can one not imagine similar splits in other professions between elites and underclasses with more of a vocational than a professional outlook?

The future for characteristics 2, 3, 5, and 8 is even more problematic. It is dubious if medical care professionals will continue to enjoy as much individual autonomy (8) as in the past, perhaps partly because their conditions of work—including medical ethics (2)—are now increasingly imposed from outside the profession. When the "spiders in their webs" of nineteenth-century practice gave way to national medical societies and codes of ethics, as I have noted, it was largely to regulate competition within and outside the profession, using rules set by the profession. A century later, in Europe as well as in North America and worldwide, we witness rules of conduct being imposed from outside the profession, whether by the "first logic" of the capitalist market or the "second logic" of the legislators and bureaucrats, national, regional, and local.

The spirit of altruism and public service (3) that professions almost universally claim as a major justification for their special and elevated status continues to be under withering attack. A widespread social ethic that proclaims "greed is good" reflects a corrosive cynicism about any higher motive for human effort. Is it not disturbing, for example, that a recent survey of more than 5,000 faculty at twenty-six nationally representative U.S. medical schools showed more than half of the respondents believe "the administration is only interested in me for the revenue I generate" and that their institution does not value teaching? Almost a third believe "the culture of my institution discourages altruism."[8]

We have already mentioned the questions raised about the altruism of TV's fictional Dr. House. One must further wonder if the orchestrated (and up to now mostly American) media attack on educated elites (including the negative aspects of Dr. House) could be better represented than by the Australian owner of the Fox television network and many other world media, Rupert Murdoch. This mogul started as a sort of professional himself—a journalist—then succeeded over more ethical rivals by using sex and scandal to raise circulation and profits. His stated aim is ultimately to decide who gets elected president of the United States. It might be well to recommend here an almost prophetic but not much read novel by D. H. Lawrence from his time in Australia, *Kangaroo*. Then as now, Australians have often bemoaned the "tall poppy syndrome" in the national culture, that tendency to resent the excellence and talent that used to drive so many excellent and talented Australians into voluntary exile. As a cynical media weapon for channeling public anger away from manipulative multibillionaires like Murdoch, ripping the halo from the noble physician or nurse is a tricky but promising gambit.

While the Murdochs of the global megacorporations plot their next acquisition and merger, they thunder at the right of anybody else to strive for a monopoly. For now, the state-sanctioned exclusive privilege of the medical profession to supply the most complex care is still holding firm. But imagine a future in which the TV ads for pharmaceuticals no longer contain the words "ask your doctor," but merely urge one to go to the local *farmacia*, as one can do in less developed countries? And what of the argument that many routine acts of patient care could be—and often, in fact, are—carried out by nurses or other health care personnel—"physician extenders"? Isn't having a physician sign off on these exams and procedures just a scam to guarantee his high income?

Indeed, looking ahead to the fate of the high social prestige and corresponding economic incentives (5) of the medical profession, can even today's standards, which have in some ways slipped a bit compared to a generation ago, be maintained? Here a comparison with Europe is especially apt. If the American medical profession does in fact lose ground as the best-compensated one in the world, it may still cling to high social prestige. After all, there has never been a cohort of European physicians as wealthy as their American colleagues. Yet, of all the subjects one can study in German universities today, the only one that has had to limit enrollment (against German traditions of free access to higher education) is medicine. The best and brightest want to be doctors, even though the economic rewards are little better than other learned professions and a good deal less than in the business world. It must be admitted that the social value of a "Dr." after the "Herr" or "Frau" generally remains greater in Germany and Europe than in the United States. This may be, among other reasons, because the mystique of higher education has been deflated by American willingness to hand out tertiary educational certificates to practically anybody who can walk and breathe. But the trend in Europe is ominous in this regard. As the late brilliant historian Tony Judt pointed out in his memoirs, forcing elite British universities to accept masses of secondary graduates in no way qualified for the experience is a way of discouraging excellence, not fighting "elitism." This, from a committed socialist. What made the kind of special expertise exemplified by university-trained professionals so socially valuable—like a beautiful work of art—was its rarity.

Finally we come to autonomy (8). The concept has many facets of course. Oddly it has come to be also a sort of shorthand for patients' rights, but let us not quarrel with those. What a professional must have, existentially, is the education, experience, resources, freedom, and maybe even character or decorum to exercise good judgment. The asymmetry between professional and client is also an essential part of the professional relationship. Otherwise, if you are feeling ill in some hypothetical American future, you could Google your symptoms and wander down to the next Mexican-style *farmacia*, but who would certify that the Wikipedia article was right, or that you were, or that the *farmacista* was? *Doctor* is, after all, the Latin word for teacher (*medicus* was a physician), implying a greater degree of information and wisdom than the student, patient, or "client."

But not only vis-à-vis the client, also in the face of third parties to the relationship, professional autonomy is essential. Even as the personal, individual autonomy of the physician or nurse may be eroded by the demands of state and private insurers, employee status in privately or publicly owned care facilities, and so on, there may be new forms of *collective* autonomy that supplement the traditional type of the family general practitioner in her single-practice office. In Germany, for example, many physicians are now employees, but they have their own organization, the Marburger Bund, more like a labor union than a medical society. It has been an effective force in negotiating working conditions and remuneration for physicians, even though the notion of "unionized doctors" flies in the face of Anglo-Saxon–model countries. It might be hard for U.S. doctors to imagine the 2006 strike by the Marburger Bund or the fact that an Organization for Economic Cooperation and Development (OECD) study showed German physicians earning 15 percent less than their counterparts in the United Kingdom and 40 percent less than U.S. doctors.[9] But what was unthinkable in the past may become likely in the future.

Many of the wonder drugs and powerful diagnostic and therapeutic devices that have greatly amplified physicians' ability to cure are produced, and in many cases invented, by large corporations (either directly, in corporate labs, or indirectly, through "privatizing" discoveries in university laboratories). These companies claim legitimacy by alleging a "fiduciary responsibility" to their shareholders to maximize profits. Government agencies, often responding to political pressure, determine the diseases for which research will be publicly funded, establish educational standards and licensing requirements, and control reimbursement for Medicare, Medicaid, and whatever systems of expanded coverage will emerge in the coming years. This puts increasing bureaucratic pressure on medicine. Although Freidson doubts that American medicine will ever experience the true "deprofessionalization" suffered by physicians under Hitler or Stalin, the era of the seasoned, independent, and learned autonomy of this country's physicians has likely passed.

Indeed, looking ahead to the fate of the high social prestige and corresponding economic incentives (5) of the American medical profession, these seem to have reached their peak a few decades ago. In this country, medicine will likely be well respected and well rewarded among all occupations and even among the learned professions. We will always hold in high regard the skilled practitioners who help us maintain our lives and our health and those of the people we love. Anything else we possess—money, property, diversions, even opportunity—can be replaced or done without. But, as insurance and pharmaceutical companies on one hand and government regulators on the other put increasing pressure on physicians and on medicine as a whole, the American medical profession may find itself increasingly dependent on, and thus ceding power and place to, MBAs or the legal profession. Medicine may remain the queen of the professions, but law may become the king.

What one can learn from researching the long history of medical professionalization is that change was and shall remain the common theme. In a mere two millennia, a blink of the eye compared to the much longer history of human civilization, medicine has changed from the realm of shamans and metaphysical explanations of illness into the science-based and above all therapeutically effective profession we know and properly reward today.

Concurrently, the rise to prominence of all learned professions, of endlessly seeking better solutions to human problems, has been accompanied and often has been helped by the rise of the modern state and the capitalist system of market interchange—by the first and second logics, to use Freidson's terms. Just as the preeminence of the German medical system and its scientific background could not have been achieved without the staunch support of the German federal states, its adaptations in America could not have been accomplished without the massive financial support and leverage of foundations whose wealth derived from the most terrible exemplars of cutthroat capitalism of the Carnegie and Rockefeller varieties. At least these titans of oil and steel had the wisdom to call upon trusted advisors like Abraham Flexner to work out the details of philanthropy.

Will the global megacorporations of the future, whose CEOs wield a sense of stewardship over the massive wealth generated for faceless stockholders from giant pension funds to the Chinese and Saudi governments, be able to do the same? The faint hope of liberals that powerful (and, one must add, democratic) governments might be able to constrain and regulate these forces in the name of the public good may be undercut by the virtual salability of public offices as well as the decline of trust in a professional and autonomous civil service and judiciary. A public that can be bought and seduced by television ads and spin may not be the best guarantor of the third logic, and it may be the logic of Galveston's Albert Lasker and his cynical New York colleague Edward Bernays, who learned a lot from his Viennese uncle Sigmund Freud, the logic of mass persuasion and advertising, that shapes the future choices of the people. Perhaps this was the "iron cage of rationalization" that Max Weber feared, that Talcott Parsons bravely opposed with a dream of the independent and mediating role of the professions, and that even Freidson seems to think may leave a special little side-cell for physicians.

Social historians must also stress that not all phenomena of the recent and coming changes in the professions—often a perceived decline from some previous golden age—are bad. As the witty and provocative Oxford historian A. J. P. Taylor once remarked, "The decline of academic civilization began when professors had to help with the washing up." The inability to hire cheap domestic labor was a first sign of the integration of women into the previously almost all-male provinces of professional life. It may be politically incorrect to suggest this, but the fact that half the human population has been allowed and encouraged to enter the professions, at differing rates, to be sure, has altered forever their exclusivity. It has also driven down the price of professional labor. The trend toward or beyond female-to-male ratios among physicians already evident in the United States will likely be the immediate future trend in many European countries. "Women make up 54 percent of physicians below the age of 35 in Britain, 58 percent in France and almost 64 percent in Spain, according to the latest figures from the Organization for Economic Cooperation and Development, which tracks the trend in more than 30 countries."[10] By 2017, according to some estimates, the majority of physicians in Britain will be women.

Indeed, in the opinion of Dr. Bernard Ribeiro, recent past president of the English Royal College of Surgeons, "Medicine has moved from being a vocation, which is sad. . . . Smart kids coming out of school are looking at medicine as any other job—what are the prospects and the terms of remuneration." This despite the overall lower incomes of women physicians compared to their male colleagues in Britain's National Health Service ($24,000 in 2009), according to the British Medical Association.[11] The likely future predominance of women in the medical profession does not mean, of course, that it will stop being a "vocation," but the shape of the profession may be altered by the tendency of women physicians to gravitate to activities and specializations that allow for more calculability in one's personal life (involving such issues as parenting, time management, etc.) or might require less physical strength (e.g., cosmetic rather than orthopedic surgery). Many observers, particularly in Europe where heavy educational debt is less of a motivating factor, note also a trend especially among women doctors toward altering one of the definitions of learned professions regarding full-time and lifelong dedication to its practice. Those who worry about the declining power of organized learned professions to shape the structure of care for the public's needs may also quietly point to the low state of influence by a largely feminized medical profession in the old Soviet Union and its satellites. Yet that may be confusing consequences with causes: although the USSR paid lip service to women's equality, it in fact gave priority of resources to many other causes from militarism to grandiose if disastrous industrial projects over public health. And as far as the rapid increase of women as a proportion of new physicians is concerned, that has been very recent in more developed societies.

Even many historians have been slow to take notice of this major recent shift. A history of one of the medical schools used as a benchmark in this book, the University of Texas Medical Branch (UTMB), years in the making and intended to mark the centennial of UTMB in 1993, made almost no mention of the ratio of male to female students over the years.[12] Nobody could write a history like that again. The inclusion of ethnic minorities, especially in Britain and the United States, is a similar sign of "de-exclusivity" without "deprofessionalization." True, most of the contingent faculty at American higher education institutions mentioned before are women, and there is an issue of social equity, preventing them from achieving the same kind of professional status and career ladder that their mostly male colleagues would have had thirty years ago. On the other hand, the worldwide reliance on medical professionals has had an undoubted impact on the quality of life everywhere. One might call this the "altruism benefit" of worldwide professionalization.

This work began with questions asked to history about the ethical values of the first famous ancient medical treatment center in the Greek colony of

Pergamon. Nobody left unhealed, as the letters over the vanished entrance door had promised—at least not through that portal. But many, perhaps, exited dead out the unobtrusive back door to the pits hundreds of feet below the cliff's side. And all who entered there could afford to pay. As far as we know, there were no refunds for failed therapies or bad diagnoses.

Those who picked up the bodies at the bottom of the cliff, like many who worked in the Pergamon center, were slaves, and nobody then expected special treatment for them. Indeed, a social system that tolerated slavery and the expectation of radically different treatment for slaves and masters defined much of the professional behavior of medical practitioners until very recently. "Gentlemen" and their families might prefer to pay for the attentions of "learned" doctors; hoi polloi could, for a price, get their wounds and maladies treated by assortments of wise persons, herbalists, or drug mixers.

The profession of medicine as we now know it was created primarily by the acceptance of modern science into the *definition* of "doctor" (and later "nurse") through the revolution in modern university medical training. That revolution was carried out largely over the heads—and sometimes against the will—of masses of medical practitioners threatened by it. Yet throughout disagreements about the way forward, all sides maintained that professional ethics must be upheld.

Much of the history of professional organizations and their efforts to maintain professional ethics, as this book has tried to show, really concerned sheltering one group of practitioners from another or gaining an advantage over them, no matter how well the arguments were founded. (There were in fact *many* quacks, even though the charge of "quackery" could be abused for market advantage.)

Recent social studies have called into question, as this book has reflected, the claim to altruism that has long been a basis for learned professions claiming a higher and more privileged status than other groups of skilled people from plumbers to barbers. The claim has a certain basis in the need to rely upon the skills of learned professionals, not only physicians but also lawyers, priests, teachers—whose judgment and moral reliability should surpass that of a mere tradesman, who can be taken to court for being dishonest. Learned professions imply a level of discretionary trust beyond refraining from botching a job or not showing up when promised to do the work. One can understand the viewpoint of one distinguished retired American doctor summing up "the transformation of the physician during the second half of the twentieth century from shaman to skilled labor."[13]

Thus there remains a question about the "ethics" of the learned professions. Will they simply disappear as technological beeps replace the personal and experienced touch of the medical professional? Will "greed is good" become the ethical leitmotif of medicine as it has for the financial and large parts of the legal and political "elite"? If real-time conferences on iPhones among various specialists replace the face-to-face conferences about difficult cases, who will sue whom for results that go wrong? Whom will the ambulance-chasing lawyers sue? Multibillion-dollar hegemonial international communications companies whose systems went down during an important conference call among doctors from various specialized disciplines for important minutes or hours? Would things work better if the hugely overburdened if nominally autonomous American court system, which has much responsibility for setting the rules for dreaded medical tort suits, gave way to an administrative bureaucracy (as in many European countries) when Americans tend to mistrust the latter even more than the courts?

There is, of course, no expected ethical response from those companies: they have convinced (or bought off) the world that they are merely following alleged "market rules." These, according to them (but not Adam Smith, whom they habitually misquote), cross no ethical boundaries.

But a medical profession without ethical boundaries—one that operates on the same market principles as laid down by, say, Milton Friedman—does not really require humans to operate it. It would be a fantasy world in which machines, not humans, make life-and-death decisions. Information technology dispenses with responsibility (except perhaps the kind lawyers and courts can fight over for financial allocations).

Ethics cannot really be introduced for the first time in medical school or later: much of a sense of right and wrong is already there from childhood upbringing or should be. Yet it is all too easy to neglect or discourage the development of ethics in the context of professionalization. Medicine in particular frequently raises issues of competing goods. For example, when dealing with a diagnosis of terminal cancer, which trumps which: patient autonomy or shielding the patient from the harsh reality that treatment can do nothing?

Those who actively advocated the introduction of modern laboratory science as well as scientific skepticism into medical training (such as Sir William Osler) also noted and warned against a certain "Germanic" clinical distancing from humanity that could lead to arrogance and moral indifference toward patients. In its most exaggerated form, this attitude could lead to the kinds of crimes against humanity defined by the Nuremberg trials. Other skeptics have cast the claims of the medical profession to a special kind of altruism—and attempts to inculcate such ethical values through training—as a fig leaf to justify a drive for monopoly over services, high incomes, and other perks. Yet other analysts point to the continually expanding role of agents outside the profession who claim a right to regulate the best practices formerly left to physicians' autonomous ethical decisions. Legislators, regulators, courts, trial lawyers, and the media, among other "stakeholders," increasingly gainsay or challenge the ethical standards that the (also increasingly fragmented) medical profession struggles to reshape in the face of rapidly changing factors such as technology. Altogether, arguments that the teaching of medical ethics should occupy a larger part of all medical education must compete with claims that there is not enough time available even for the ever-multiplying "basics." And they must overcome defeatism in the face of powerful external agents—including insurers and ignorant bureaucrats—ready to override ethical decisions.

In conclusion, then, while recent trends in the characteristics that have made learned professions viable and prosperous are troubling, there is also room for cautious hope. Among the eight characteristics of modern professions, highly specialized and advanced education (1) and rigorous tests of competence (4) can confidently be expected. These could, however, become so expensive and demanding that they may discourage people who otherwise feel a "calling." Likewise, occupational career patterns or ladders (6) may continue, but likely in a direction of disaggregation of the profession, for example, into "foot soldiers" of primary care versus "stars" in more exotic specializations. One can expect special codes of personal conduct or ethics (2) and a spirit of altruism and public service (3) to continue, but they could be made less meaningful by the lip service and spin so characteristic of public discourse today. Most problematic and even unlikely for the future profession are high social prestige and corresponding economic incentives (5), monopolizing the market in services (7), and autonomy (8).

Still, anybody who naively projects current trends forward and describes the result as "the future" is likely to be wrong. That is why historians warn each other not to engage in futurology. Too many expectations have been dashed in the past by unforeseen events and almost overnight have brought down empires and systems that once seemed eternal. It may be that the characteristic of professional ethics (and its necessary frame of operation, autonomy) among health care workers over the millennia may persist while all the currently rising forces undermining them prove to be passing phenomena. One hopeful sign has been the persistence, since ancient times and across cultures, of attempts to subject the profession of medicine to ethical standards. Indeed, that special code of personal conduct has arguably been the characteristic of learned professions most consistently shared during most of the times and civilizations mentioned in this book. Cynics may argue, since "prestige" can also be associated with its show business cousin "prestidigitation," that such codes have always been a part of the physician's professional bag of tricks to impress a gullible laity. Yet throughout history men and women have earned that prestige by selfless and (not seldom fatal) devotion to their patients. Only a society that itself respects ethical behavior will have a right to expect physicians of the future to maintain their own high standards as well.

Notes

INTRODUCTION

1. For an informative introduction to this notion of professionalism, see David T. Stern, ed., *Measuring Medical Professionalism* (New York: Oxford University Press, 2006).

2. For further discussion, see Charles E. McClelland, *The German Experience of Professionalization: Modern Learned Professions and Their Organizations from the Early Nineteenth Century to the Hitler Era* (Cambridge: Cambridge University Press, 1991), 14.

3. Magali S. Larson, *The Rise of Professionalism* (Berkeley: University of California Press, 1977), 50.

4. For a good, readable history of medicine (albeit with scant references to professionalization), see Roy Porter, *The Greatest Benefit to Mankind: A Medical History of Humanity* (New York: W. W. Norton, 1997).

1. SWEARING BY APOLLO

1. Edmund D. Pellegrino and Alice A. Pellegrino, "Humanism and Ethics in Roman Medicine: Translation and Commentary on a Text of Scribonius Largus," *Literature and Medicine* 7 (1988): 34.

2. For a much more nuanced description of the rowdy disagreements during the heyday of ancient Greek philosophical discourse—long before the narrowing and partial ossification of these teachings after the collapse of the Western Roman Empire, see Geoffrey E. R. Lloyd, *The Revolutions of Wisdom: Studies in the Claims and Practice of Ancient Greek Science* (Berkeley: University of California Press, 1987), esp. 158–71.

3. See full text in chapter 12 and in Ludwig Edelstein, *From the Hippocratic Oath: Text, Translation, and Interpretation* (Baltimore: Johns Hopkins University Press, 1943).

4. For an example of a contemporary oath, see Dr. Louis Lasagna's in chapter 12.

5. Erwin H. Ackerknecht, "Zur Geschichte der medizinischen Ethik," *Praxis* 17 (1964): 579.

2. THE LEVANT

1. The Oath of Maimonides is often offered as an alternative to the Hippocratic Oath in American medical school ceremonies, including the University of Texas Medical Branch. It is shorter, more general, more humanistic, and in many ways a more modern-sounding oath to a monotheistic god. For a translation of the oath, see S. Y. Tan, et al., "Moses Maimonides (1135–1204): Rabbi, Philosopher, Physician," *Singapore Medical Journal* 43 (2002): 553.

2. For a classic exploration of such number symbolism, see Gerhart B. Ladner, *God, Cosmos, and Humankind: The World of Early Christian Symbolism* (Berkeley: University of California Press, 1995), 115–31.

3. Robert Fossier, *The Axe and the Oath: Ordinary Life in the Middle Ages* (Princeton, NJ: Princeton University Press, 2010), 12.

3. PHYSICIANS, BARBERS, AND "OLD WIVES"

1. Ronald L. Numbers and Darrel W. Amundsen, eds., *Caring and Curing: Health and Medicine in the Western Religious Traditions* (Baltimore: Johns Hopkins University Press, 1998), 85.

2. Edward J. Kealey, *Medieval Medicus: A Social History of Anglo-Norman Medicine* (Baltimore: Johns Hopkins University Press, 1981), table 1, 31–33.

4. HOSPITALS OR HOSPICES?

1. The word "quarantine" comes from the forty (*quaranta*) days Venetian authorities required people arriving on ships suspected of carrying plague to stay aboard until danger of contamination was determined to be passed.

2. For the development of hospital buildings by the American army and navy, see Adam Smith, et al., *Military Hospitals Historic Context* (Washington, DC: Department of Defense, 2008), 138.

3. Richard A. Gabriel and Karen S. Metz, *A History of Military Medicine*, 2 vols. (New York: Greenwood Press, 1992), vol. II, *From the Renaissance through Modern Times*, 151, 154, 156, 160, 203.

4. See, for example, Michel Foucault, *The Birth of the Clinic: An Archaeology of Medical Perception* (London: Tavistock, 1973).

5. Sioban Nelson, *Say Little, Do Much: Nurses, Nuns, and Hospitals in the Nineteenth Century* (Philadelphia: University of Pennsylvania Press, 2001), 151–64; also Ronald L. Numbers and Darrel W. Amundsen, eds., *Caring and Curing: Health and Medicine in the Western Religious Traditions* (Baltimore: Johns Hopkins University Press, 1998), 135.

6. See, as an example, Dr. James Currier's *The Effects of Water, Cold and Warm, as a Remedy in Fever and Other Diseases* (1797).

5. GIFTS FROM THE SISTER SCIENCES

1. Nicholas Jardine, "The Places of Astronomy in Early-Modern Culture," *Journal for the History of Astronomy* 29 (1998): 49–62.

2. *De Motu Cordis* [An Anatomical Study of the Motion of the Heart and of the Blood in Animals], first Latin ed. (Frankfurt, 1628).

3. Norman Howard-Jones, "Robert Koch and the Cholera *vibrio*: A Centenary," *British Medical Journal* 288 (1984): 390–91. Also see Howard Brody, et al., *Cholera, Chloroform, and the Science of Medicine: A Life of John Snow* (Oxford: Oxford University Press, 2003).

4. Thomas S. Kuhn, *The Structure of Scientific Revolutions* (Chicago: University of Chicago Press, 1962).

5. Louis Pasteur, "Discours prononcé à Douai, le 7 décembre 1854, à l'occasion de l'installation solennelle de la Faculté des lettres de Douai et de la Faculté des sciences de Lille" [Speech delivered at Douai on 7 December 1854, on the occasion of his formal inauguration to the Faculty of Letters of Douai and the Faculty of Sciences of Lille], in *Oeuvres de Pasteur*, ed. René Vallery-Radot (Paris: Masson, 1939), VII, 131.

6. Claude Bernard, *Introduction à l'étude de la médecine expérimentale* [*An Introduction to the Study of Experimental Medicine*] (Paris, 1865), trans. Henry Copley Greene (New York: Macmillan, 1927) is still used today.

6. ACOLYTES AND APPRENTICES

1. For a recent study about the various sources of revived medical knowledge related to the Crusades, see Piers D. Mitchell, *Medicine in the Crusades: Warfare, Wounds and the Medieval Surgeon* (Cambridge: Cambridge University Press, 2004), 205–12.

7. STARTING WITH SALERNO

1. Ronald L. Numbers and Darrel W. Amundsen, eds., *Caring and Curing: Health and Medicine in the Western Religious Traditions* (Baltimore: Johns Hopkins University Press, 1998), 93.

2. Nancy G. Siraisi, *Medieval and Early Renaissance Medicine* (Chicago: University of Chicago Press, 1990), 43–44.

3. Siraisi, *Medieval and Early Renaissance Medicine*, 17–18.

4. Siraisi, *Medieval and Early Renaissance Medicine* , 31, 57.

5. As cited in Götz von Selle, *Die Georg-August-Universität zu Göttingen, 1737–1937* (Göttingen: Vandenhoek und Ruprecht, 1937), 27.

6. Edward Gibbon, *The Autobiographies of Edward Gibbon* (London: Murray, 1897), 124, 224. The original edition dated from 1799.

7. Johann Heinrich Campe, "Über Universitäten," in *Allgemeine Revision des gesamten Schul- und Erziehungswesens*, 16 vols. (Hamburg: Campe, 1785–92), XVI, 154.

8. FROM SACRILEGE TO SCIENCE

1. Jacques Brunschwig, G. E. R. Lloyd, and Pierre Pellegrin, *Greek Thought: A Guide to Classical Knowledge* (Cambridge, MA: Belknap Press, 2000), 422–23.

2. David H. Freedman, "20 Things You Didn't Know about Autopsies," *Discovery* 9 (2012): 72.

3. Nancy G. Siraisi, *Medieval and Early Renaissance Medicine* (Chicago: University of Chicago Press, 1990), 89.

4. Charles E. McClelland, *The German Experience of Professionalization* (Cambridge: Cambridge University Press, 1991), 81.

5. Ellen S. More, *Restoring the Balance: Women Physicians and the Profession of Medicine, 1850–1995* (Cambridge, MA: Harvard University Press, 1999), 118.

9. THREE PATHS LEADING TO MODERN MEDICAL EDUCATION

1. Mary Roth Walsh, *Doctors Wanted, No Women Need Apply: Sexual Barriers in the Medical Profession, 1835–1975* (New Haven, CT: Yale University Press, 1977), 76–81.
2. No prizes were awarded 1915–1918 and 1921.
3. Robert N. Proctor (*The Nazi War on Cancer* [Princeton, NJ: Princeton University Press, 1999]) correctly points out that many Nazi medical policies continued earlier initiatives favoring effective public health, at least for the "master race." Hitler's own aversion to smoking, alcohol, and meat, the Nazi promotion of exercise and fitness, and serious medical-scientific contributions should not be dismissed, either. Nazi ideology was after all an amalgam of both popular and cranky notions. In the final analysis, though, the *uses* to which it put science, including medical science, contradicted the most fundamental principles of openness to discovery and humanistic purpose in medicine.

10. MONEY TALKS

1. William Frederick Norwood, *Medical Education in the United States before the Civil War* (New York, Arno Press, 1971), 32.
2. Kenneth M. Ludmerer, *Learning to Heal: The Development of American Medical Education* (New York: Basic Books, 1985), 15.
3. James N. Angell, *The President's Report to the Board of Regents: For the Year Ending June 30, 1875* (Ann Arbor, MI: University of Michigan, 1875), 9–10.
4. Charles W. Eliot, *Annual Reports of the President and Treasurer of Harvard College: 1878–79* (Cambridge, MA: Wilson and Son, 1880), 33.
5. Thomas Henry Huxley, "The State and the Medical Profession," *Nineteenth Century* 15 (1884): 230–31.
6. For a careful analysis of the RCP in relation to its changing functions as a professional organization, see Jeffrey L. Berlant, *Profession and Monopoly: A Study of Medicine in the United States and Great Britain* (Berkeley: University of California Press, 1975), 130–65.
7. Roger Boxill, *Shaw and the Doctors* (New York: Basic Books, 1969), 97.
8. George Bernard Shaw, *The Doctor's Dilemma: A Tragedy* (Baltimore: Penguin Books, 1974).
9. Richard Gordon, *The Alarming History of Medicine* (New York: St. Martin's Press, 1993).
10. Berlant, *Profession and Monopoly* , 168.
11. Congressional Research Service, "U.S. Health Care Spending: Comparison with Other OECD Countries" (Washington: U.S. Government Printing Office, 2007), table 2, "Average Compensation in Certain Health Professions."
12. Berlant, *Profession and Monopoly*, 112.
13. Molière, *Le Malade Imaginaire* (1673), act 3, scene 3.
14. Berlant, *Professions and Monopoly*, 234–35.
15. House Bill 173, 27th Texas Legislature, 1901.
16. The term "medical ethics" itself was coined by British Dr. Thomas Percival (1740–1804), whose book *Medical Ethics, or a Code of Institutes and Precepts, Adapted to the Professional Conduct of Physicians and Surgeons* (Manchester: S. Russell, 1803) has been called the first modern work on the subject and was taken over wholesale by the early AMA. It has also been criticized for being more concerned about deference to other members of the physicians' guild than patients' interests. For a critique see Berlant, *Profession and Monopoly*, 75–78.
17. Sir William Osler, "Books and Men, #210," in *Aequanimitas: With Other Addresses to Medical Students* (Philadelphia: Blakiston, 1932).
18. Maria Malatesta, *Professional Men, Professional Women* (London: Sage, 2011), 134.

19. www.gatesfoundation.org/Who-We-Are/General-Information/Financials/2011-Annual-Snapshot-of-Grants-Paid.

11. HIGH TECH, LOW TOUCH?

1. Carl F. Ameringer, *The Health Care Revolution: From Medical Monopoly to Market Competition* (Berkeley: University of California Press, 2008), 22–23.

2. Ameringer, *The Health Care Revolution*, 22–23.

3. Eliot Freidson, *Profession of Medicine: A Study of the Sociology of Applied Knowledge* (New York: Dodd, Mead, 1973), 384.

4. Glenn Sonnedecker, ed., *Kremers and Urdang's History of Pharmacy* (Philadelphia: Lippincott, 1976), 282.

5. Jeffrey Berlant, *Profession and Monopoly: A Study of Medicine in the United States and Great Britain* (Berkeley: University of California Press, 1975) , 106.

6. Elton Rayack, *Professional Power and American Medicine: The Economics of the American Medical Association* (Cleveland, OH: World, 1967), 164–65.

7. Berlant, *Profession and Monopoly*, 109.

8. "Report of the Coordinating Committee," *JAMA* 140 (1949): 697.

9. Paul Starr, *The Social Transformation of American Medicine* (New York: Basic Books, 1982), 285. Also see a wry and prognostically acute contemporary source, Bernard Devoto, "Doctors on the Boardwalk," *Harper's* 195 (1947): 215–24.

10. *Time*, April 17, 1950. Robeson's campaigning for Henry Wallace in the 1948 presidential race combined with his activism against racism and colonialism reaped him many shameful examples of the smears and denials of civil rights typical not only of the McCarthy era generally but of many U.S. government agencies, particularly the FBI. See Peter Conrad, *The Sociology of Health and Illness*, 8th ed. (New York: Worth, 2009), 306.

11. Roger Collier, "American Medical Association Membership Woes Continue," *CMAJ* 183 (2011): E713–E714.

12. One recent sociological study nevertheless claimed that data fail to support the belief among physicians and others that the growth of managed care has substantially reduced the duration of office visits. David Mechanic, et al., "Are Patients' Office Visits with Physicians Getting Shorter?" *NEJM* 344 (2001): 198–204.

13. John B. McKinlay and Lisa Marceau, "The End of the Golden Age of Doctoring," in *The Sociology of Health and Illness: Critical Perspectives*, ed. Peter Conrad, 8th ed. (New York: Worth, 2009), table 18.1, 230.

14. James Youngclaus and Julie A. Fresne, "Physician Education Debt and the Cost to Attend Medical School 2012 Update" (Washington, DC: Association of American Medical Colleges, 2013), 1. Also worth reading are the subsequent Youngclaus et al. article, "Can Medical Students Afford to Choose Primary Care?" *Academic Medicine* 88 (2013): 16–25, and a reply by a young doctor, ibid., 555.

15. Molly Cooke, et al. *Educating Physicians: A Call for Reform of Medical School and Residency* (San Francisco: Jossey-Bass, 2010), 173, 254.

16. Cooke et al., *Educating Physicians*, table 5.2, 175. Academic medical centers often include, in addition to a medical school, faculty practice plan and hospital, programs in allied health sciences, pharmacy, dentistry, graduate studies, public health, and so on.

17. Cooke et al., *Educating Physicians*, 16.

12. A SACRED TRUST

1. Wolfgang P. Müller, *The Criminalization of Abortion in the West: Its Origins in Medieval Law* (Ithaca: Cornell University Press, 2012).

2. Albert R. Jonsen, *A Short History of Medical Ethics* (New York: Oxford University Press, 2000), 54–55.

3. This contemporary version by Dr. Louis Lasagna of Tufts University, 1964.

4. Translation by Heinrich von Staden, "'In a Pure and Holy Way': Personal and Professional Conduct in the Hippocratic Oath," *Journal of the History of Medicine and Allied Sciences* 51 (1996): 406–8. In the older translation by Ludwig Edelstein, *The Hippocratic Oath: Text, Translation, and Interpretation* (Baltimore: Johns Hopkins Press, 1943), *techne* is rendered as "art," regimens as "dietetic measures," and pessary as "abortive remedy." For an interesting survey of what is left out or added by contemporary North American medical schools, see R. D. Orr, et al., "Use of the Hippocratic Oath: A Review of Twentieth-Century Practice and a Content Analysis of Oaths Administered in Medical Schools in the U.S. and Canada in 1993," The Journal of Clinical Ethics 8 (1997): 377–88.

5. Derek Wong, K. Nye, and Pat Hollis, "Microbial Flora on Doctors' White Coats," *BMJ* 303 (1991): 1602–4.

6. M. Jeanne Peterson, "Kinship, Status and Social Mobility in the Mid-Victorian Medical Professions," (PhD dissertation, University of California Berkeley, 1972), 153.

7. M. Jeanne Peterson, *Medical Profession in Mid-Victorian London* (Berkeley: University of California Press, 1978), 130.

13. FIRST, DO NO HARM

1. M. Jeanne Peterson, *The Medical Profession in Mid-Victorian London* (Berkeley: University of California Press, 1978), 135.

2. Berlant, *Profession and Monopoly: A Study of Medicine in the United States and Great Britain* (Berkeley: University of California Press, 1975), 79.

3. Robert C. Derbyshire, *Medical Licensure and Discipline in the United States* (Baltimore: Johns Hopkins University Press, 1969), 77.

4. www.dir.ca.gov/dwc/medicalunit/DisciplineList.html.

14. THE PHYSICIAN AS GENTLE*MAN*

1. Bradford H. Gray and Kathy Hebert, *After Katrina: Hospitals in Hurricane Katrina; Challenges Facing Custodial Institutions in a Disaster* (Washington, DC: Urban Institute, 2006), 5–8.

2. Magali S. Larson, *The Rise of Professionalism* (Berkeley: University of California Press, 1977), 50.

3. *JAMA* 300 (2008): 307.

4. Ellen S. More, *Restoring the Balance: Women Physicians and the Profession of Medicine, 1850–1995* (Cambridge, MA: Harvard University Press, 1999), table 4.2, 98.

5. Mary Roth Walsh, *Doctors Wanted, No Women Need Apply: Sexual Barriers in the Medical Profession, 1835–1975* (New Haven, CT: Yale University Press, 1977), xvi.

6. Walsh, *Doctors Wanted*, 219– 24.

7. Walsh, *Doctors Wanted*, 258.

8. Molly Cooke, et al., *Educating Physicians: A Call for Reform of Medical School and Residency* (San Francisco: Jossey-Bass, 2010) , 15.

9. Walsh, *Doctors Wanted*, 246.

10. Eric Topol, *The Creative Destruction of Medicine: How the Digital Revolution Will Create Better Health Care* (New York: Basic, 2012), 36.

15. BALANCING INDIVIDUAL AND PUBLIC BENEFIT

1. Jean Heller, "Syphilis Victims in U.S. Study Went Untreated for 40 Years," *New York Times*, July 26, 1972. Also see Fred Gray, *The Tuskegee Syphilis Study: The Real Story and Beyond* (Montgomery: New South Books, 1998). For a brief summary and chronology of the experiment, see "U.S. Public Health Service Syphilis Study at Tuskegee," www.cdc.gov/tuskegee/timeline.htm.

2. "The importance of consent to therapy (v. research) was stressed as early as 1914 in *Schloendorff v. Society of New York Hospital*. The actual wording informed consent entered the legal lexicon with *Salgo v. Leland Stanford University* in 1957," Dr. Howard Brody to author, January 2014.

3. Charles E. McClelland, "American Reform Efforts: German Professional Education after World War II," in *Mutual Influence on Education: Germany and the United States in the Twentieth Century*, ed. Jürgen Heideking, Mark Depaepe, and Jurgen Herbst, *Paedagogica Historica* 33 (1997): 265–75.

4. Wilbur C. Davison, "The German University Medical Schools during the Occupation," *JAMA* 129 (1945): 1225. The author had been dean of Duke University School of Medicine since its founding in 1927.

5. For an excellent analysis of the problems facing physicians shifting from a state-run to a more free market system in the post–Velvet Revolution era in the former Soviet bloc, see Lily M. Hoffman, "The Institutional Careers of Medicine and Urban Planning in the Communist and Postcommunist Czech Republic," in *Professions in Modern Eastern Europe/Professionen im modernen Osteuropa*, edited by Charles McClelland et al. (Berlin: Duncker & Humblot, 1995), 189–212.

6. For a partial list of American medical ethics cases since World War II, see http://en.wikipedia.org/wiki/List_of_medical_ethics_cases.

7. Gary Fields and Erica E. Phillips, "The New Asylums: Jails Swell with Mentally Ill," *Wall Street Journal*, September 25, 2013.

16. GODS NO MORE

1. Association of American Medical Colleges, *2012 Physician Specialty Data Book* (Washington, DC: AAMC, 2012), figure 1, 171.

17. COLLISIONS OF CULTURES

1. "A matter of life or death," *Economist*, August 28, 2013. The text of judgment is available at www.courtsni.gov.uk/en-GB/Judicial%20Decisions/PublishedByYear/Documents/2013/[2013]%20NIFam%208/j_j_MOR8964Final.htm.

2. For an illuminating brief survey of American bioethics developments, see Albert R. Jonsen, "The Discourses on Bioethics in the United States," in *The Cambridge World History of Medical Ethics*, ed. Robert Baker and Laurence B. McCullough (Cambridge: Cambridge University Press, 2009), 477–85.

3. See, for example, the following Web sites: www.thehastingscenter.org/BioethicsWire/BioethicsGraduatePrograms/Default.aspx; www.gradschools.com/search-programs/bioethics; and www.vanderbilt.edu/CenterforEthics/othercenters.html#medical

4. For a recent list compiled by the *American Journal for Bioethics*, see www.bioethics.net/bioethics-resources/centers-departments-institutions. For a further discus-

sion, see also G. C. Persad, "The Current State of Medical School Education in Bioethics, Health Law, and Health Economics," *Journal of Law and Medical Ethics* 36 (2008): 89–94.

18. CURES, AT LAST!

1. Jill Max, "The Lost Art of the Physical Exam," *Yale Medicine*, 43 (2009): 30–35.
2. AAMC, *2012 Physician Specialty Data Book*, figure 3, 9; American Medical Association, *Physician Characteristics and Distribution in the U.S., 2012* (Chicago: American Medical Association, 2012), table 3.1, 67.
3. James Youngclaus and Julie A. Fresne, *Physician Education Debt and the Cost to Attend Medical School 2012 Update* (Washington, DC: Association of American Medical Colleges, 2013), 1.
4. Jeffrey Berlant, *Profession and Monopoly: A Study of Medicine in the United States and Great Britain* (Berkeley: University of California Press, 1975), 60; " but only about 17 percent of the 1.2 million doctors and medical students in the U.S. are members of the AMA," (www.medpagetoday.com/MeetingCoverage/AMA/33320).
5. Arnold S. Relman, "The New Medical-Industrial Complex," *NEJM* 303 (1980): 963–70.
6. Eric Topol, *Creative Destruction of Medicine: How the Digital Revolution Will Create Better Health Care* (New York: Basic, 2012).
7. John B. McKinlay and Lisa Marceau, "The End of the Golden Age of Doctoring," in *The Sociology of Health and Illness: Critical Perspectives*, 8th ed., ed. Peter Conrad (New York: Worth, 2009), 219–21 and figures 18-4 and 8-5.

19. THE CONUNDRUM OF INSURANCE

1. "Britain's Baby Bargain," *USA Today*, July 24, 2013.

20. EXPANDING ACCESS TO THE PHYSICIAN'S ROLE

1. www.aamc.org/download/153160/data/physician_shortages_to_worsen_without_increases_in_residency_tr.pdf
2. Molly Cooke et al., *Educating Physicians: A Call for Reform of Medical School and Residency* (San Francisco: Jossey-Bass, 2010) gives a good contrast between the Flexner reform proposals and those deemed necessary today. The primary need now, according to this work, is to recenter medical education on teaching and learning rather than the current overemphasis on clinical care of revenue-producing patients. See esp. 3, 13–14, and 16.
3. Richard Horton, "Offline: If I Were a Rich Man," *The Lancet* 376 (2010): 1972.
4. Cooke, *Educating Physicians*, ix, 7.
5. Cooke, *Educating Physicians*, 99. See also 26, 41, and 60.

21. WHAT IT ALL MEANS

1. It is an interesting sidelight that Max Weber's only visit to the United States, to attend the St. Louis World Exposition in 1904, took place because of an invitation by Hugo

Münsterberg, who readers may recall was Abraham Flexner's most cherished professor at Harvard.

2. See Jeffrey Berlant, *Profession and Monopoly: A Study of Medicine in the United States and Great Britain* (Berkeley: University of California Press, 1975), 48–49, 308; George Ritzer, "Professionalization, Bureaucratization and Rationalization: The Views of Max Weber," *Social Forces*, 53 (1975): 627–34. For an analysis of the German variants, see McClelland, *German Experience of Professionalization* (Cambridge: Cambridge University Press, 1991), esp. 6–11.

3. Milton Friedman, *Capitalism and Freedom* (Chicago: University of Chicago Press, 1962), 150.

4. See Talcott Parsons, *The Social System* (Glencoe, IL: Free Press, 1951); "The Professions and Social Structure," in *Essays on Sociological Theory* (London: Free Press, 1954), 34–49; and "Social Change and Medical Organization in the United States," *Annals of the American Academy of Political and Social Science*, 246 (March 1963): 21–33.

5. Parsons, *The Social System*, 471.

6. "The Side-Effects of Doing Good," *Economist*, February 21, 2008.

7. Ellen Schrecker, *The Lost Soul of Higher Education: Corporatization, the Assault on Academic Freedom, and the End of the American University* (New York: New Press, 2010).

8. Linda Polili, et al., "The Culture of Academic Medicine: Faculty Perceptions of the Lack of Alignment between Individual and Institutional Values," *Journal of General Internal Medicine*, 24 (2009): 1289–95.

9. www.dw-world.de/dw/article/0,,1942544,00.html.

10. Doreen Carvajal, "The Changing Face of Medical Care," *New York Times*, March 7, 2011.

11. Carvajal, "The Changing Face of Medical Care."

12. Chester R. Burns, *Saving Lives, Training Caregivers, Making Discoveries: A Centennial History of the University of Texas Medical Branch at Galveston* (Austin: Texas State Historical Association, 2003).

13. J. Joseph Marr, "Fall from Grace," *The Pharos* (Winter 2014): 8.

Bibliography

American Medical Association. *Physician Characteristics and Distribution in the U.S., 2012.* Chicago: American Medical Association, 2012.

Ameringer, Carl F. *The Health Care Revolution: From Medical Monopoly to Market Competition.* Berkeley: University of California Press, 2008.

Angell, James N. *The President's Report to the Board of Regents: For the Year Ending June 30, 1875.* Ann Arbor: University of Michigan, 1875.

Association of American Medical Colleges. *2012 Physician Specialty Data Book.* Washington, DC: AAMC, 2012.

Auerbach, Jerold S. *Unequal Justice: Lawyers and Social Change in Modern America.* New York: Oxford University Press, 1976.

Baker, Robert, and Laurence B. McCullough, eds. *The Cambridge World History of Medical Ethics.* Cambridge: Cambridge University Press, 2009.

Barzansky, Barbara M., and Norman Gevitz. *Beyond Flexner: Medical Education in the Twentieth Century.* New York: Greenwood Press, 1992.

Berlant, Jeffrey. *Profession and Monopoly: A Study of Medicine in the United States and Great Britain.* Berkeley: University of California Press, 1975.

Bernard, Claude. *Introduction à l'étude de la médecine expérimentale.* Paris, 1865. Translated by Henry Copley Greene as *An Introduction to the Study of Experimental Medicine* (New York: Macmillan, 1927).

Bonner, Thomas N. *American Doctors and German Universities: A Chapter in International Intellectual Relations, 1870–1914* (Lincoln: University of Nebraska Press, 1963).

———. *Becoming a Physician: Medical Education in Britain, France, Germany, and the United States, 1750–1945.* New York: Oxford University Press, 1995.

———. *Iconoclast: Abraham Flexner and a Life in Learning.* Baltimore: Johns Hopkins University Press, 2002.

Boxill, Roger. *Shaw and the Doctors.* New York: Basic Books, 1969.

Brody, Howard. *The Future of Bioethics.* Oxford: Oxford University Press, 2009.

———. *The Golden Calf: Economism and American Policy.* Charleston, SC: CreateSpace, 2011.

Brody, Howard, et al., *Cholera, Chloroform, and the Science of Medicine: A Life of John Snow.* Oxford: Oxford University Press, 2003.

Brown, E. Richard. *Rockefeller Medicine Men: Medicine and Capitalism in America.* Berkeley: University of California Press, 1979.

Brunschwig, Jacques, G. E. R. Lloyd, and Pierre Pellegrin. *Greek Thought: A Guide to Classical Knowledge.* Cambridge, MA: Belknap Press, 2000.

Burns, Chester R. *Saving Lives, Training Caregivers, Making Discoveries: A Centennial History of the University of Texas Medical Branch at Galveston.* Austin: Texas State Historical Association, 2003.

Congressional Research Service. *U.S. Health Care Spending: Comparison with Other OECD Countries*. Washington, DC: U.S. Government Printing Office, 2007.

Conrad, Peter. *The Sociology of Health and Illness*. 8th ed. New York: Worth, 2009.

Cooke, Molly, *Educating Physicians: A Call for Reform of Medical School and Residency.* San Francisco: Jossey-Bass, 2010.

Cruikshank, Jeffrey L., and Arthur W. Schultz. *The Man Who Sold America: The Amazing (but True!) Story of Albert D. Lasker and the Creation of the Advertising Century.* Boston: Harvard Business Review Press, 2010.

Cunningham, Andrew, and Perry Williams, eds. *The Laboratory Revolution in Medicine.* Cambridge: Cambridge University Press, 1992.

Cushing, Harvey. *The Life of Sir William Osler*. 2 vols. Oxford: Clarendon Press, 1925.

Derbyshire, Robert C. *Medical Licensure and Discipline in the United States.* Baltimore: Johns Hopkins University Press, 1969.

Eliot, Charles W. *Annual Reports of the President and Treasurer of Harvard College: 1878–79.* Cambridge, MA: Wilson and Son, 1880.

Flexner, Abraham. *Medical Education: A Comparative Study.* New York: Macmillan, 1925.

———. *Medical Education in the United States and Canada* [The Flexner Report]. New York: Carnegie Foundation for the Advancement of Teaching, 1910.

Fossier, Robert. *The Axe and the Oath: Ordinary Life in the Middle Ages.* Princeton, NJ: Princeton University Press, 2010.

Foucault, Michel. *The Birth of the Clinic: An Archaeology of Medical Perception.* London: Tavistock, 1973.

Freedman, David H. "20 Things You Didn't Know about Autopsies." *Discovery* 9 (2012): 72.

Friedman, Milton. *Capitalism and Freedom.* Chicago: University of Chicago Press, 1962.

Freidson, Eliot. *Profession of Medicine: A Study of the Sociology of Applied Knowledge.* New York: Dodd, Mead, 1973.

———. *Professionalism, the Third Logic: On the Practice of Knowledge.* Chicago: University of Chicago Press, 2001.

Gabriel, Richard A., and Karen S. Metz. *A History of Military Medicine*. 2 vols. New York: Greenwood Press, 1992.

Ginsberg, Benjamin. *The Fall of the Faculty*. New York: Oxford University Press, 2011.

Gordon, Richard. *The Alarming History of Medicine.* New York: St. Martin's Press, 1993.

Gray, Bradford H., and Kathy Hebert. *After Katrina: Hospitals in Hurricane Katrina; Challenges Facing Custodial Institutions in a Disaster.* Washington, DC: Urban Institute, 2006.

Harvey, A. McGehee. *A Model of Its Kind: A Centenary History of Medicine at Johns Hopkins*. 2 vols. Baltimore: Johns Hopkins University Press, 1989.

Hoffman, Lily M. "The Institutional Careers of Medicine and Urban Planning in the Communist and Postcommunist Czech Republic." In *Professions in Modern Eastern Europe* [Professionen im modernen Osteuropa], edited by Charles McClelland, et al., 189–212. Berlin: Duncker & Humblot, 1995.

Howell, Joel D. *Technology in the Hospital: Transforming Patient Care in the Early Twentieth Century.* Baltimore: Johns Hopkins University Press, 1996.

Johnson, William R. *Schooled Lawyers: A Study in the Clash of Professional Cultures.* New York: New York University Press, 1978.

Jonsen, Albert R. *A Short History of Medical Ethics*. New York: Oxford University Press, 2000.

Kealey, Edward J. *Medieval Medicus: A Social History of Anglo-Norman Medicine.* Baltimore: Johns Hopkins University Press, 1981.

Ketch, Joseph F. *The Formation of the American Medical Profession: The Role of Institutions, 1780–1860.* New Haven, CT: Yale University Press, 1968.

Kuhn, Thomas S. *The Structure of Scientific Revolutions.* Chicago: University of Chicago Press, 1962.

Ladner, Gerhart B. *God, Cosmos, and Humankind: The World of Early Christian Symbolism.* Berkeley: University of California Press, 1995.
Larson, Frances. *An Infinity of Things: How Sir Henry Wellcome Collected the World.* Oxford: Oxford University Press, 2009.
Larson, Magali S. *The Rise of Professionalism.* Berkeley: University of California Press, 1977.
Le Fanu, James. *The Rise and Fall of Modern Medicine.* New York: Carroll & Graf, 2000.
Lloyd, Geoffrey E. R. *The Revolutions of Wisdom: Studies in the Claims and Practice of Ancient Greek Science.* Berkeley: University of California Press, 1987.
Ludmerer, Kenneth M. *Learning to Heal: The Development of American Medical Education.* New York: Basic Books, 1985.
Malatesta, Maria. *Professional Men, Professional Women.* London: Sage, 2011.
Max, Jill. "The Lost Art of the Physical Exam." *Yale Medicine* 43 (2009): 30–35.
McClelland, Charles E. "American Reform Efforts: German Professional Education after World War II." In *Mutual Influence on Education: Germany and the United States in the Twentieth Century*, edited by Jürgen Heideking, Mark Depaepe, and Jurgen Herbst. *Paedagogica Historica* 33 (1997): 265–75.
———. *The German Experience of Professionalization.* Cambridge: Cambridge University Press, 1991.
McClelland, Charles E., et al. *Professions in Modern Eastern Europe* [Professionen im modernen Osteuropa]. Berlin: Duncker & Humblot, 1995.
McKinlay, John B., and Lisa Marceau. "The End of the Golden Age of Doctoring." In *The Sociology of Health and Illness: Critical Perspectives*, edited by Peter Conrad. 8th ed. New York: Worth, 2009.
Mitchell, Piers D. *Medicine in the Crusades: Warfare, Wounds and the Medieval Surgeon.* Cambridge: Cambridge University Press, 2004.
More, Ellen S. *Restoring the Balance: Women Physicians and the Profession of Medicine, 1850–1995.* Cambridge, MA: Harvard University Press, 1999.
Nelson, Sioban. *Say Little, Do Much: Nurses, Nuns, and Hospitals in the Nineteenth Century.* Philadelphia: University of Pennsylvania Press, 2001.
Norwood, William Frederick. *Medical Education in the United States before the Civil War.* New York: Arno Press, 1971.
Numbers, Ronald L., and Darrel W. Amundsen, eds. *Caring and Curing: Health and Medicine in the Western Religious Traditions.* Baltimore: Johns Hopkins University Press, 1998.
Orr, R. D., et al., "Use of the Hippocratic Oath: A Review of Twentieth-Century Practice and a Content Analysis of Oaths Administered in Medical Schools in the U.S. and Canada in 1993." *The Journal of Clinical Ethics* 8 (1997): 377–88.
Osler, Sir William. *Aequanimitas: With Other Addresses to Medical Students.* 3rd ed. Philadelphia: Blakiston, 1932.
Parsons, Talcott. "The Professions and Social Structure." Chap. 2 in *Essays on Sociological Theory*, 24–49. Glencoe, IL: Free Press, 1954.
———. "Social Change and Medical Organization in the United States." *Annals of the American Academy of Political and Social Science* 246 (1963): 21–33.
———. *The Social System.* London: Free Press, 1951.
Percival, Thomas. *Medical Ethics, or a Code of Institutes and Precepts, Adapted to the Professional Conduct of Physicians and Surgeons.* (Manchester: S. Russell, 1803).
Peterson, M. Jeanne. *The Medical Profession in Mid-Victorian London.* Berkeley: University of California Press, 1978.
Polili, Linda, et al., "The Culture of Academic Medicine: Faculty Perceptions of the Lack of Alignment between Individual and Institutional Values." *Journal of General Internal Medicine* 24 (2009): 1289–95.
Porter, Roy. *The Greatest Benefit to Mankind: A Medical History of Humanity.* New York: W. W. Norton, 1997.
Proctor, Robert N. *The Nazi War on Cancer.* Princeton, NJ: Princeton University Press, 1999.
Rayack, Elton. *Professional Power and American Medicine: The Economics of the American Medical Association.* Cleveland, OH: World, 1967.

Ritzer, George. "Professionalization, Bureaucratization and Rationalization: The Views of Max Weber." *Social Forces* 53 (1975): 627–34.
Rodwin, Marc A. *Conflicts of Interest and the Future of Medicine: The United States, France, and Japan.* Oxford: Oxford University Press, 2011.
Rothman, David J. *Strangers at the Bedside: A History of How Law and Bioethics Transformed Medical Decision Making.* New York: Aldine de Gruyter, 2003.
Rothstein, William G. *American Medical Schools and the Practice of Medicine: A History.* New York: Oxford University Press, 1987.
Schrecker, Ellen. *The Lost Soul of Higher Education: Corporatization, the Assault on Academic Freedom, and the End of the American University.* New York: New Press, 2010.
Schudson, Michael. "The Flexner Report and the Reed Report: Notes on the History of Professional Education in the United States." *Social Science Quarterly* 55 (1974): 347–61.
Schuster, Jack H., and Martin J. Finkelstein. *The American Faculty: The Restructuring of Academic Work and Careers.* Baltimore: Johns Hopkins University Press, 2008.
Shaw, George Bernard. *The Doctor's Dilemma: A Tragedy.* Baltimore: Penguin Books, 1974.
Siraisi, Nancy G. *Medieval and Early Renaissance Medicine.* Chicago: University of Chicago Press, 1990.
Smith, Adam, et al., *Military Hospitals Historic Context.* Washington, DC: Department of Defense, 2008.
Sonnedecker, Glenn, ed. *Kremers and Urdang's History of Pharmacy.* Philadelphia: Lippincott, 1976.
Starr, Paul. *The Social Transformation of American Medicine.* New York: Basic Books, 1982.
Stern, David T., ed. *Measuring Medical Professionalism.* New York: Oxford University Press, 2006.
Tan, S. Y., et al., "Moses Maimonides (1135–1204): Rabbi, Philosopher, Physician." *Singapore Medical Journal* 43 (2002): 553.
Thorndike, Lynn. *A History of Magic and Experimental Science.* 8 vols. New York: Columbia University Press, 1923–1958.
Topol, Eric. *The Creative Destruction of Medicine: How the Digital Revolution Will Create Better Health Care.* New York: Basic, 2012.
Tuchman, Arleen. *Science, Medicine, and the State in Germany: The Case of Baden, 1815–1871.* New York: Oxford University Press, 1993.
Walsh, Mary Roth. *Doctors Wanted, No Women Need Apply: Sexual Barriers in the Medical Profession, 1835–1975.* New Haven, CT: Yale University Press, 1977.
Warner, John H., and Janet A. Tighe. *Major Problems in the History of American Medicine and Public Health: Documents and Essays.* Boston: Houghton Mifflin, 2001.
Wheatley, Steven C. *The Politics of Philanthropy: Abraham Flexner and Medical Education.* Madison: University of Wisconsin Press, 1988.
Winau, Rolf. *Medizin in Berlin.* Berlin: de Gruyter, 1987.
Youngclaus, James, and Julie A. Fresne. *Physician Education Debt and the Cost to Attend Medical School 2012 Update.* Washington, DC: Association of American Medical Colleges, 2013.
Youngclaus, James, et al., "Can Medical Students Afford to Choose Primary Care?" *Academic Medicine* 88 (2013): 16–25.

Index

www.ingramcontent.com/pod-product-compliance
Ingram Content Group UK Ltd.
Pitfield, Milton Keynes, MK11 3LW, UK
UKHW012039150926
475560UK00001B/93

9 781442 226302